TECHNICAL ANALYSIS FOR THE TRADING PROFESSIONAL

Other Books in the Irwin Trader's Edge Series

The Options Edge by William Gallacher   (0-07-038296-4)
The Art of the Trade by R. E. McMaster   (0-07-045542-2)

TECHNICAL ANALYSIS FOR THE TRADING PROFESSIONAL

CONSTANCE BROWN

McGraw-Hill

New York   San Francisco   Washington, D.C.   Auckland   Bogotá
Caracas   Lisbon   London   Madrid   Mexico City   Milan
Montreal   New Delhi   San Juan   Singapore
Sydney   Tokyo   Toronto

Library of Congress Cataloging-in-Publication Data

Brown, Constance M.
    Technical analysis for the trading professional / by Constance
Brown.
        p.   cm.
    ISBN 0-07-012062-5
    1. Speculation.   2. Investment analysis.   3. Stocks—Charts,
diagrams, etc.   I. Title.
HG6041.B74   1999
332.64'5—dc21   98-31377
                                                          CIP

McGraw-Hill

A Division of The McGraw·Hill Companies

    3 4 5 6 7 8 9 0   DOC/DOC   9 0 4 3 2 1 0 9

ISBN 0-07-012062-5

The sponsoring editor for this book was Stephen Isaacs, the editing supervisor was John M. Morriss, and the production supervisor was Suzanne W. B. Rapcavage. It was set in Times Roman per the IPROF design specs by Kim Sheran and Michelle Zito of the Hightstown McGraw-Hill Desktop Publishing Unit.

Printed and bound by R. R. Donnelley & Sons Company.

McGraw-Hill books are available at special quantity discounts to use as premiums and sales promotions, or for use in corporate training programs. For more information, please write to the Director of Special Sales, McGraw-Hill, 11 West 19th Street, New York, NY 10011. Or contact your local bookstore.

 This book is printed on recycled, acid-free paper containing a minimum of 50% recycled de-inked fiber.

CONTENTS

Oscillators, contrary to popular belief, can be used to define market trend. A discussion focusing on RSI and Stochastics reveals how specific indicator ranges can confirm larger trends and identify an upcoming trend reversal.

The concept of multiple market cycles and the determination of cycle dominance for a specific trading time horizon are fully discussed. An explanation is offered why symmetrical and Fibonacci cycles fail. Methods for handling the weaknesses inherent in both cycle methods are discussed.

The correct method for determining the time period for an oscillator is discussed. Recommendations are given as to when to change initial oscillator setups and the methods for making these adjustments. This chapter also reveals how institutional traders can benefit from inexperienced technical traders.

Trend lines of greatest significance may not originate from major price highs and lows. Visual exercises help demonstrate geometric proportions that extend beyond traditional charting techniques. The market timing of high-risk trend changes can be identified by projecting trend lines forward from specific chart signals.

Chapter 5

Signals from Moving Averages Are Frequently Absent in Real-Time Charts   65

Time-sequenced charts show that trading signals from moving averages and indicators that incorporate averages may not be present in real-time market analysis. Knowing how these indicators change their screen positions when the current bar is displaced with new data will allow traders to adjust to real-time conditions and miss fewer signals.

PART TWO

CALCULATING MARKET PRICE OBJECTIVES   83

Chapter 6

Adjusting Traditional Fibonacci Projections for Higher-Probability Targets   85

Weaknesses exist in the industry's standard use of Fibonacci relationships. The industry in general determines 0.382, 0.500, and 0.618 retracement levels from distinct price highs and lows and also projects: 618, equality, and 1.618 market swings from the same pivot levels. This chapter reveals methods for more accurate price projection to accommodate the normal expansion and contraction cycles present in all markets. In addition, it demonstrates why price spikes or key reversals should not be used to determine Fibonacci retracement targets.

Chapter 7

Price Projections by Reverse-Engineering Indicators   107

The concept of reverse-engineering an indicator to forecast price objectives is discussed using Microsoft's *Excel* software. This chapter includes a detailed, step-by-step picture illustration of how to export data from Omega Research's *TradeStation* to Microsoft's *Excel* software for advanced custom analysis.

Chapter 8

Price Objectives Derived from Positive and Negative Reversals in RSI   121

RSI can be used to calculate price objectives from specific indicator patterns called *Positive and Negative Reversals*. Signal probability and price objectives can be dramatically improved by measuring the amplitude of the oscillator. The price projection method and filtering technique are fully explained and illustrated.

Chapter 9

Calculating Price and Time Objectives from a Gann Wheel   143

A detailed foundation for Gann analysis and how to use a Gann Wheel to calculate both time and price objectives are illustrated. This discussion reveals why most students of W. D. Gann abandon this methodology in frustration after much effort and expense.

Chapter 10

Using Oscillators with the Elliott Wave Principle   161

A market move that requires several days to develop is used to walk readers through a real-time, step-by-step progression to show how to apply the Elliott Wave Principle. As the market unfolds through a time-sequenced event, all the rules, guidelines, and patterns are discussed to show how they are used to predict future market action.

The prior chapters are also applied to clarify how the different techniques are combined. Wave counts in hindsight versus developing wave scenarios unfolding in real-time to predict future market movement require different skills. The differences are discussed, and common misunderstandings in the industry are identified.

The chapter concludes with an in-depth look at an analytic method used to develop long-horizon wave interpretations for the S&P 500. The method can be used for any Global Equity Index.

The potential long-term market forecasts for T-Bonds and the DJIA are offered.

PART THREE

NEW METHODS FOR IMPROVING INDICATOR TIMING AND FILTERING PREMATURE SIGNALS   237

Chapter 11

Volatility Bands on Oscillators   239

A volatility band formula is discussed that has a different character than Bollinger Bands. The chapter also discusses the importance of establishing independent variables for upper and lower bands because markets do not decline in the same manner as they advance.

Chapter 12

The Composite Index   251

The Composite Index is a custom formula that forms bullish or bearish divergence with RSI to identify RSI signal failures before they occur. The Composite Index becomes an inseparable companion to RSI as has been demonstrated throughout the book. In this chapter it is combined with Japanese Candlesticks to show how Eastern charting techniques might apply this formula. Using Volume as a signal confirmation is examined.

Chapter 13

Evaluating the Comparative Strengths and Weaknesses of Common Indicators 263

This chapter discusses the strengths and weaknesses of common indicators in order to isolate desired characteristics for developing a custom formula. Personal biases contribute to the effectiveness of an indicator's signal. Depth perception is discussed to clarify how we evaluate charts graphically in a two-dimensional environment. Depth perception needs to be understood as it will affect our judgment of chart signals and will dictate how indicators should be plotted to accommodate personal strengths and weaknesses.

Chapter 14

The Derivative Oscillator 289

An original formula to resolve trading problems associated with time-consuming complex market corrections or reentry problems when markets are in strong trends. The testing of a new indicator and considerations that should be made prior to using a new formula in real-time markets are described. This particular formula displays an unusual characteristic of forming equal and opposite peaks and troughs that minimize traditional signal lag.

APPENDIXES

Written by a brilliant trader for only those seasoned traders who are willing to work at their analysis of the markets in a disciplined way, this book contains the most advanced methodology I've ever seen!

Connie Brown's credentials come in the form of nine years on the front line as a research analyst and fund trader. She is, herself, a disciplined professional, who has grown to the point where she is a force to reckon with in the financial markets. At the same time, she publishes a daily bulletin on the Dow, the S&P, and Bonds. This is faxed to some of the world's most sophisticated, large traders. Her predictions as to price objectives and trend of the market are unequaled anywhere in the industry.

There are fourteen separate chapters in this book, each a separate subject. Six of these subjects have been written on before, and these chapters serve as improvements on old indicators. There are, also, fifteen major breakthroughs in technical analysis! Seven of these breakthroughs are new—never-before-revealed material! Eight more dissect, change, and improve old concepts.

In her discussion of Stochastics and of RSI as oscillators, she introduces the concept that oscillators do not necessarily fluctuate between 0 and 100 and that all signals do not fall within the traditional default overbought and oversold bands. The oscillator may actually travel within a larger or a narrower range that can be pinpointed with precision. To correct what the writer perceives as a flaw in commercial software packages, she suggests the use of an upper resistance band and a lower support band within this range to help identify signals that might otherwise have been missed. She also introduces the concept that this effective signaling band may travel up and down within the range, and that it may expand or contract. She suggests that the trader should adjust this effective signaling range to compensate for the idiosyncrasies of strongly trending bull and bear markets, and even suggests some better parameters! This alone would change the way we look at oscillators—and, consequently, our entry timing.

Connie also utilizes RSI as a price predictor by applying Andrew Cardwell's Positive and Negative Reversal Signals and by using historical price levels at the extremes where signals have occurred in the past to forecast similar prices when signals will occur in the future. To my knowledge, this use for oscillators has never before been published. It is a new and valuable concept!

But this inventive young trader does not stop there. She goes on to discuss the application of moving averages over oscillators, third-generation indicators created by applying oscillators on oscillators, and filtering indicators with variants of different lengths. She introduces the Derivative Oscillator, its correct use and caveats, and the Composite Index she created to accompany RSI.

In a theme she returns to frequently, she kids the "Stochastics Default Club"— both the uneducated public that accepts the default values in software and tries to use them to trade without a clue as to why and the educated but lazy trader who knows better but does it anyway. She remedies this deficit by giving a great deal of attention to procedures for determining and inputting the proper data to construct responsive, customized indicators. She makes a passionate case for keeping a flexible state of mind and adjusting indicators to changes in the markets.

To the subject of cycles, Connie introduces the concept of "growth and decay," which leads to asymmetrical cycles, and the application of a weighted factor to them, versus Fibonacci cycles. She explains the use of charts with differing time cycles to perfect cycle timing.

Approaching the subject of market price objectives, this writer naturally turns to the Elliott Wave, her starting point in the industry. For some, the Elliott Wave is frustrating in the extreme because the wave count appears to change when a larger cycle begins. Understanding their frustration, Connie agrees that some people are "wave-deaf"; just as a tone-deaf person cannot hear the music, they cannot perceive the beauty of the composition because they are caught up in counting the beats and analyzing the notations. She stresses that it is necessary to understand the structure, but more important to keep a sense of proportionality to the analysis.

Then, she teaches the three simple rules that form the basis of Elliott Wave analysis, takes the reader through an "easy to take" explanation of flats and zigzags, and analyzes a number of charts real-time "to the T," showing as she goes how she integrates oscillators, Fibonacci ratios, and Gann into her analysis. She is a proponent of a hypothesis I've long espoused: Stochastics can prove Elliott Wave—and help clarify an indistinct wave count!

Connie also discusses Fibonacci methodology in depth. The chapter on Fibonacci measurement truly upgrades this old friend. She rightly points out that markets may gap past a price objective and that the trader has to remove the differential of the gap in order to properly calculate the correct price objective of the affected retracement. In her discussion of the use of multiple Fibonacci swing objectives, Connie's projections are plotted from numerous pivot levels. She has found that these levels tend to cluster into tight support and resistance levels, which are useful in and of themselves.

I was particularly impressed with the discussion and the upgrades. This chapter has been badly needed. The discussion on spikes and internal Fibonacci guidance is to be especially appreciated by the reader. The explanation of the Fibonacci price projection method—and specifically the use of multiple Fibonacci swing projections—is worth the price of the whole book!

Before tackling the subject of trend lines as price predictors, the writer challenges us to solve a puzzle, the Nine Squares. The task is to connect the squares with four lines, without removing the pencil from the page. To come up with the correct answer, the reader is required to work outside the mindset established by the puzzle. So, too, the writer asks us to suspend our preconceptions that trend lines must be established from absolute highs and lows. Because she believes spikes at tops and bottoms are caused by aberrations in the market, she prefers less conventional approaches, such as ignoring spikes or using intermediate highs or lows. She discusses the intersection of trend lines as a timing tool—a subject that has needed clarification for years! Then, she demonstrates a very unconventional use of trend lines to "reverse engineer" a triangle that can be bisected into two right triangles by a line extended into the future that will point to a final bottom. She goes on to introduce an entirely new approach to trend lines—the intersection of trend lines from divergent highs on an oscillator with the long-term trend line. The results are astounding! This is "eyeball training" from which a good chartist can profit!

The Nine Squares connected by four unconventional trend lines in the formation of a pyramid is an excellent lead-in to the subject of Gann. Because his methods seemed enigmatic, it has been suggested that Gann used astrology to arrive at his predictions, and his work has been obscured by the veil of occultism. Connie has correctly perceived that this is not the case and has done an exceptional job of returning his use of an astronomical clock, the third oldest calculator known to humankind, from the occult to the realm of science and simple mathematics!

In doing this, she correctly arrives at the conclusion that Fibonacci and Gann took two routes to arrive at much the same place. This has led her to another valuable concept: that, just as areas of confluence in time or price within different charts with the same indicator should be respected, confluence in areas of time or price between the different methods she uses should be treated with even greater respect.

However, while she explains how Gann's time and price wheels can be used to locate dates of changes in trend and price objectives, she is holding back on some of the specific information needed for a non-Mensa trader such as myself to actually use Gann to make money in the markets. Connie, I challenge you to prove to us it can be done—in the next book, of course!

—-**George C. Lane**
Watseka, Illinois
September 29, 1998

ACKNOWLEDGMENTS

There are four mentors whom I still turn to today for guidance. They first taught me their techniques for predicting the markets: Dave Allman, Elliott Wave; Andrew Cardwell, Relative Strength Index (RSI); Joe DiNapoli, Fibonacci; and George Lane, momentum and volume. Through the hours and years of study, these individual methods eventually merged into something unique that became my livelihood. When individuals give you the wisdom of experience, it is insufficient to just say thank you. Perhaps in some small way this book will show the respect and gratitude I have for the time they invested in me.

All four further contributed to the technical editing and review of this book. Dave Allman reviewed the Elliott Wave chapter, Joe DiNapoli the Fibonacci chapter, and Andrew Cardwell reviewed his method of using RSI for price projections. George Lane took on the formidable task of reading the entire book when it was the first manuscript. Manning Stoller reviewed the chapter on Volatility Bands. The confidence I had to keep plugging away on the keyboard night after night for three months was largely due to their encouragement. A book is a massive undertaking, and its author needs both emotional and technical support.

There are quote vendors and chart services who also made contributions. *TradeStation* and *PowerEditor* are registered trademarks of Omega Research, Inc. The data feed for my *TradeStation* is provided by FutureSource Information Systems, Inc. Nearly all the charts in this book represent these products.

The Gann Square of 52 chart displaying the S&P 500 Index in Figure 9–5 was prepared by Peter Pich using *GannTrader 3.0*, from the Gannsoft Publishing Company, e-mail address gann @plix.com.

The Moody's Aaa Bond data displayed in Figure 10–38 was prepared by Grant Noble, Topline Investment Graphics [(303) 440–0157].

Excel and *Windows 95/98* are registered trademarks of Microsoft Corporation.

Finally, the chart preparation: I had to deliver camera-ready charts to McGraw-Hill. Know that each chart in the book was carefully supervised by Sam, my faithful Beagle, and my two cats Ashley and Muffin. By the way, if you have cats that also monitor your work on a computer, pay special attention to the message: "Do you want to save these changes?" If you leave the keyboard unattended briefly, you may find your four-legged editors have made changes on your behalf.

Constance Brown

DISCLAIMER

It should not be assumed that the methods, techniques, or indicators presented in this book will be profitable or that they will not result in losses. Past results are not necessarily indicative of future results. Examples in this book are for educational purposes only. This is not a solicitation of any order to buy or sell.

The NFA requires us to state that "HYPOTHETICAL OR SIMULATED PERFORMANCE RESULTS HAVE CERTAIN INHERENT LIMITATIONS. UNLIKE AN ACTUAL PERFORMANCE RECORD, SIMULATED RESULTS DO NOT REPRESENT ACTUAL TRADING. ALSO, SINCE THE TRADES HAVE NOT ACTUALLY BEEN EXECUTED, THE RESULTS MAY HAVE UNDER- OR OVER COMPENSATED FOR THE IMPACT, IF ANY, OF CERTAIN MARKET FACTORS, SUCH AS LACK OF LIQUIDITY. SIMULATED TRADING PROGRAMS IN GENERAL ARE ALSO SUBJECT TO THE FACT THAT THEY ARE DESIGNED WITH THE BENEFIT OF HINDSIGHT. NO REPRESENTATION IS BEING MADE THAT ANY ACCOUNT WILL OR IS LIKELY TO ACHIEVE PROFITS OR LOSSES SIMILAR TO THOSE SHOWN."

TECHNICAL ANALYSIS FOR THE TRADING PROFESSIONAL

PART ONE

Dispelling Some Common Beliefs about Indicators

CHAPTER 1

Oscillators Do Not Travel between 0 and 100

"Why does it appear that conventional technical indicators are failing us as we approach the twenty-first century? What has changed?"

These two questions far exceed any other asked of me by professional traders before a lecture or seminar. The implications are that the technical studies that brought a trader prior success have changed. Traders employed by major institutions throughout Europe, Asia, and the United States seem puzzled by this same phenomenon. The traders affected utilize both Eastern and Western technical analysis. The problem is clearly widespread and undiscriminating. Have the indicators failed, or have the markets changed making older methods obsolete? The changing character of our markets along with our common indicators are only symptoms. The cause affecting both is technology.

Technology alone has changed the speed and pace of technical analysis. Skills of judgment and interpretation mark the line in the sand that separates the retail trader from the professional. The small investor is now armed with rapid access to the markets through the Internet, real-time plug-n-play software for trading and analysis, and they have access to instant news from CNN and CNBC. The retail segment is learning to turn off the endless media chatter in favor of making trading decisions based on their own independent technical tools. This growing independent mass of inexperienced technical traders is actually adding to the problem of increasing market volatility. In reality this new breed of technologically armed traders within the market is not independent at all.

How did this group become so tightly linked together when they were working independently with their own technical tools? All quote vendors use the same default variables within their analysis software. Professional systems and retail software products alike all use the exact same defaults. Think about that statement for a moment. Every quote system shipped to a new location anywhere in the world with charting capabilities starts off with the exact same setup periods and formulas. The less experienced trader rarely changes these default variables as they are overwhelmed with the long list of indicators available to them by the click of a mouse button. It is all too easy to set up a chart and then read a quick description in a manual that proclaims, "Sell your Stochastics when it rolls over and crosses the 80 line with divergence, and buy when you roll back up through the 20 line." In mass, the one-lot trader and novice technical trader grab the phone to enter their order from the same signal. To make things worse, the access is instantaneous.

I do not fear what the professional trader might do. Nor do I have strong views about market realities such as S&P programs that are triggered when the spread between the S&P Cash and Futures market becomes out of line. Programs are measurable, generally predictable, and also a known entity in the market. The problem is not the professional but the growing mass of novice technical traders that operates as one large institutional wildcard. The professional trader that fails to move forward beyond this group is unknowingly operating within this new technically armed and dangerous mass. The impact of this new breed of mass psychology is indicator failure and capital erosion. *This group cannot only be avoided but also used to the professional's advantage.* The time has come to change conventional thinking about technical indicators.

The nineties have brought dramatic changes to the way technicians and traders apply their tools. At the same time the need for technical analysis has grown because it is becoming increasingly more difficult to manage the global volume of fundamental factors and cross-market ramifications. More people are discovering the value of charting techniques. But to evolve beyond the foundations of technical analysis, we must change the way we utilize technical studies.

Traders still working under the premise that there are two groups of technical indicators—indicators for trending markets like moving averages and then indicators for nontrending markets such as the oscillators MACD, Relative Strength Index (RSI), and Stochastics—are now outdated. The books that segregated indicators into two primary groups are not wrong. Do not lose sight of the fact that the original works provided us with the foundation upon which our industry is growing today. The important distinction is that early books on technical analysis will eventually be viewed as classics, but traders that fail to evolve beyond these original concepts face a far less pleasant fate: extinction.

A good place to begin to dispel some of the common beliefs about our technical indicators is with oscillators. The mainstream believe that oscillators generally travel between a scale of zero and 100. Generally 20 and below is viewed as oversold, and 80 or above is an overbought market. Wrong.

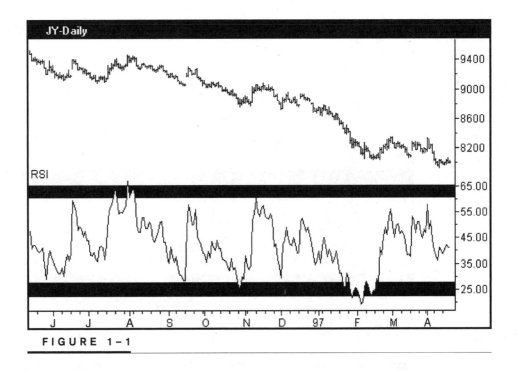

FIGURE 1-1

In Figure 1–1 the standard default period of 14 is used for the Relative Strength Index with a daily bar chart of Yen futures. The Yen is falling in a bear market within this time horizon. The graph showing the RSI indicator has an upper black band marking a range of resistance from 60 to 65. A lower band marks 23 to 28 to highlight a support zone for the indicator. Study the indicator tops closely. At no time is the Yen strong enough to push the RSI oscillator successfully through the 65 level. (Spot traders need to keep in mind that this is a futures chart, which will be inverted from the spot market.) Each time the indicator tests the range from 55 to 65, the Yen renews its former downtrend and establishes new lows against the dollar. The oscillator then declines to a support zone within a range of 20 to 30. There will be many more examples to reinforce this concept. The general rule to follow for a bear market is that RSI will oscillate within a range of 20 to 30 at the low end of the scale up to an upper resistance zone of 55 to 65. This is true regardless of market or time horizon.

In a bull market the RSI will shift and begin to oscillate within a range marked by a support zone of 40 to 50 toward an upper resistance zone of 80 to 90. Figure 1–2 shows the same Yen futures market but over a weekly time horizon when the Yen is in a bull market or the dollar is weak. Each time the Yen declines, the oscillator falls to a support zone near 40 to 50. The 40 level is never broken. The strong Yen rallies push the oscillator into the 80s. Even minor advances that

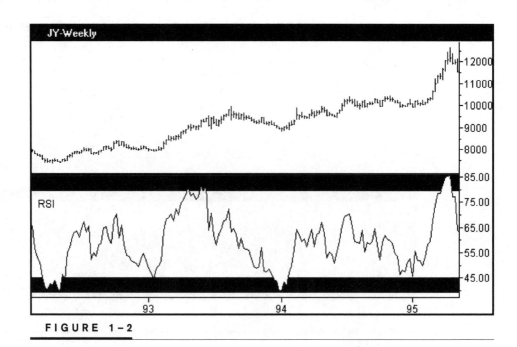

F I G U R E   1 – 2

lead to more complex consolidations allow the RSI to decline only as far back as the 40 to 50 zone.

Do these RSI ranges defining bull and bear markets apply to other oscillators? Yes, when the period used for the indicator has been correctly defined. We'll cover how to find the correct period in the next chapter, and we will readdress the issue of buy and sell ranges as other oscillators are discussed. As an example, in Chapter 14 a price projection method is described for the Stochastics Oscillator that gives the trader permission to buy a market when the Stochastics indicator falls from an extreme high down toward the 75 area. Yes, buy, as the signal will warn the trader that the market could target an additional move *equal* to the rally that preceded the minor pullback that allowed the indicator to decline from its extreme high over 80. This is only one example of instances when it would be incorrect to sell just because the Stochastics indicator has crossed the 80 range. Conversely a trader would have permission from Stochastics to sell the market when the oscillator moves back up to the 25 zone as the market would then target a new price low *equal* to the decline that preceded the minor rebound from the oversold condition. Examples for this price projection method from Stochastics will be offered in their right context in Chapter 14, but the point to make at this time is that oscillators can be used to forecast market trends, which is contrary to popular belief today.

Let's build upon the introduction of the range rules for RSI by moving on to Figure 1–3 showing a weekly Dow Jones Industrial Average chart. The chart shows

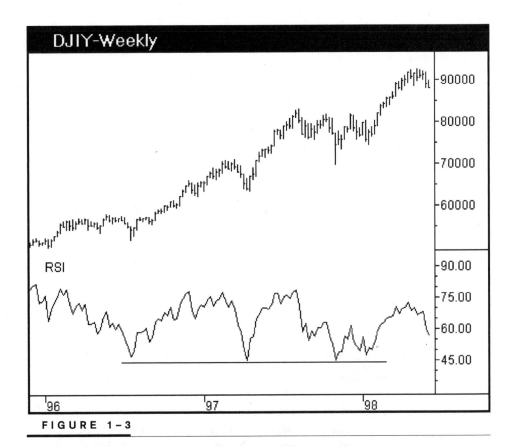

FIGURE 1-3

clearly that the market corrections in 1996 and 1997 all pressed the RSI down to the lower support zone defined for a trending bull market. The indicator holds the 40 to 50 support zone and signals correctly that the market will rally toward new highs. The oscillator moves to the upper range for a bull market in each follow-up advance and then finds resistance at the 75 level or higher. Asian, European, and North American equity indices will all display this characteristic of predetermined range rules that help to define a market's trend. A dramatic example can be seen in Figure 1-4, which charts Hong Kong's Hang Seng Equity Index in both a daily and monthly time horizon. This market entered a sharp decline in 1997 when the Asian currencies had to contend with a weakening Yen. The Hong Kong dollar peg and concerns about the strength of the fixed Chinese renminbi triggered a chain reaction that was ultimately felt throughout the Asian stock markets. The Asian woes contributed to the global equity correction that unfolded in late October 1997 in Europe and North America. The daily chart in Figure 1-4 shows the decline in the Hang Seng Index from March to June of 1998. The range rules warn that the decline is incomplete as of June 3, 1998, when this chart

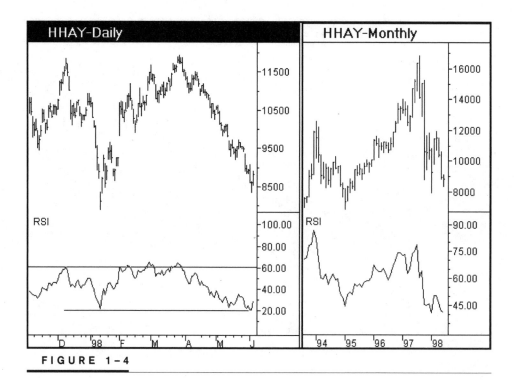

FIGURE 1-4

was captured for this book. The RSI oscillator fails to exceed the 55 to 65 resistance level throughout the advance in February and March. A market that can press the RSI only to the 55 to 65 zone is indicating a topping formation within a bear market.

The monthly chart shows a brighter picture as the severe decline is within the context of a larger bull market. The RSI in the monthly chart has fallen only to the 40 to 50 support zone. It can be said about the Hang Seng that the daily chart in Figure 1-4 warns that a price bottom is not in place as of June 3, 1998, and a sharp freefall in the daily time horizon could occur, but in the context of the monthly chart such a capitulation spike down could then form a key bottom as the 45 zone is being tested a second time now and a third test seems required.

How can you tell when the trend is about to change? The bear market illustrated in the daily Hang Seng chart allows the RSI oscillator to travel between 20 and 65, consistent with the range rules for a bear market. When the market's trend is about to reverse, so too will the oscillator ranges. In the case of the Hang Seng daily chart, the oscillator will develop the following RSI pattern when it is ready to trigger a transition from a bear market to a bull market (not presently shown in the current chart data offered in Figure 1-4). After an RSI failure at the upper boundary for a bear market, 55 to 65, the market will then decline. The first indication of a trend reversal will come when the market moves the RSI only to the lower support zone reserved for a bull market between 40 to 50. That is why this market does not have a bottom in place within this chart. When a bottom is forming, the RSI will not break 40. True, sharp secondary declines that fail to make a new price low can produce a similar indicator formation. Elliott wave traders would call such a decline a "deep second wave down" or a "fifth wave failure," depending on the internal structure of the decline, but in both the market would fail to establish a new price low.

Regardless of a new price low or only a double bottom, the market decline will move the RSI to the support zone near 40 only if it is ready to reverse its former trend. An actual price projection method will be discussed in Chapter 10, so let's not stray from this discussion about trend reversals at this time. An RSI indicator that declines to 39 or 38 will still fit this transition phase, so use some common sense. Use the market's past history to define more accurately the range that will be tested in the transition. If the support range for this market was 37 to 45 in prior bull market trends, use that as your guide. The market that is making a transition will clearly find support for the first time at this prior zone. The rally that follows will likely be insufficient to press the RSI through the upper resistance range defined for a bear market. The failed attempt to exceed 65 will be met with another price decline that moves the RSI oscillator back to support within the 40 to 50 range once again. Should the market produce an RSI oscillator decline that successfully holds the 40 to 50 support zone a second time, it should be interpreted as a clear warning to a sleeping bear–biased trader that conditions are changing. The market is attempting to reverse and will eventually produce a price rally from this oscillator position that is strong enough to press the RSI into the upper resistance range reserved for a bull market—75 to 85 and higher. It is not necessary for a market to test the new lower boundary more than once before successfully breaking out into the higher range, but it is a common occurrence to see double bottoms develop, especially in longer-horizon charts such as weekly, monthly, and quarterly time intervals. The reverse would be true for a market preparing a transition from a trending bull market to a bear market. It is so important to know how to interpret an approaching trend reversal that we will go through this transition step by step with the next chart.

Our discussion about trend reversals using the RSI indicator will now focus on one of the largest markets in the world: Deutsche Marks per U.S. Dollar (DMK/$). The weekly DMK/$ chart in Figure 1–5 covers a five-year time interval that includes a trend reversal from a bear market for the dollar prior to April 1995 to the bull market that follows into 1998. The levels at 40 and 80 are marked with a double line that denotes the approximate range the RSI will travel within a trending bull market. The 30 and 65 levels have solid single lines that mark where the RSI will travel within a bear market. The discussion that follows addresses each of the oscillator pivot levels that are numbered on the RSI in Figure 1–5:

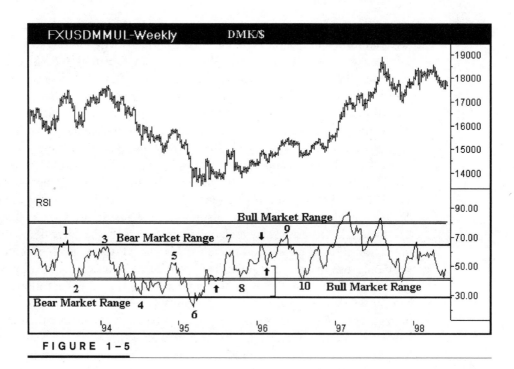

FIGURE 1-5

Point 1. The RSI pivot at point 1 has occurred near the upper resistance zone reserved for a trending bear market. The dollar declines and moves the oscillator down to point 2.

Point 2. The market finds support allowing the RSI to form a double bottom near the 40 level. The ability of the RSI to stay above 40 should warn us that the dollar has sufficient strength to attempt a new high and that the prior trend remains in force. At this point we would not know that a trend reversal was developing unless the support zone at point 2 were broken. The dollar proceeds to rally and makes a marginal new high relative to the high that occurred when the RSI topped at point 1.

Point 3. As the dollar squeaks past the prior high, the RSI forms a bearish divergence pattern. Point 3 in the oscillator is lower than point 1 though the dollar closes at higher levels. While the less experienced technical trader will likely catch the divergence between price and the oscillator suggesting that another minor correction could develop in the dollar, the trader with more experienced judgment should see that point 3 is an oscillator peak that occurs within the 55 to 65 resistance zone denoting a bear market. This is of far greater value and significance. The dollar then begins to weaken, or it might be more favorably stated that the Deutsche Mark becomes stronger, as the RSI oscillator declines to the 40 level. The RSI tests the 40 level three times before it is finally broken and declines to the 30 level, which is normal support for this indicator in a bear market.

Point 4. The dollar attempts a rebound from point 4 in Figure 1-5, and the oscillator becomes trapped between the 30 and 40 levels as a market consolidation occurs. The market actually forms a bearish contracting triangle over this same period of time, and the fact that the RSI was unable to break above the lower boundary used for a bull market is extremely bearish. A downward resolution could have been favored, and the chart shows that the dollar makes a new low as the RSI forms a second test of the 30 level just beyond the pivot low that was labeled point 4. If you do not see the small contracting triangle in the price data, not to worry at this time, as we will be introducing other tools and indicators that will be far more obvious. Just focus on the oscillator ranges.

Point 5. The dollar then rebounds, allowing the RSI to form an M pattern well below the upper resistance zone defining a bear market. This particular indicator pivot at point 5 is occurring at an extremely interesting level. Some readers will see it with just the naked eye. Measure the distance between the two single black lines that denote a bear market oscillator range. The pivot high in the RSI at point 5 is a 0.618 Fibonacci retracement of the zone. Don't measure the oscillator high at point 3 and then take the oscillator low at point 4 to determine the Fibonacci relationship as we would with price data; instead, use the range itself. The oscillator is also forming a very bearish M pattern at the peak that is forming at a precise Fibonacci retracement level within the bear market range. The chart is signaling to traders to sell dollars for Deutsche Marks immediately.

What do traders use to easily calculate the Fibonacci ratios on a paper chart? Call an engineering or drafting supply store, and ask to purchase a tool called a *Proportional Divider.* These tools are constructed from one of two materials, stainless steel or aluminum. Do not buy the stainless-steel variety as they are excessively heavy. You will also want to buy a divider that is at least 8 inches in length. There are several financial firms selling a $7^1/_2$-inch divider that is too small for use with most computer screens or for charts printed on a full page. Most art supply stores will be clueless if you ask to buy a Proportional Divider as this is an engineering tool. One brand that is particularly easy to handle is made by a German company called Alvin—at least "Alvin" is the name stamped on the instrument being distributed in the United States. Mine shows its age as it is stamped "Alvin—West Germany." The exact same tool is also called a *Precision Ratio Compass* (PRC) by many in the financial industry. But many traders that try to purchase a PRC from their local engineering or drafting supply store will find that the store does not know what they are talking about. Just call it a "Proportional Divider" to avoid the headache. How to use it in a very fast summary: Set the grid line on the moveable prongs to 10 on the scale called *circles.* Tighten the screw, which also serves to keep the two prongs of the tool together. Some models will have a grid line labeled "GS" which stands for "Golden Section," which is the same ratio as a divider with a "10" grid line. Both the 10 and GS line will be just off center relative to the length of the tool. To use it, measure the distance by opening the two sharp points on the ends of the long side. Then flip the divider over without changing the measured ratio. The points on the opposite side will mark an exact .618 ratio of the original measurement within 0.1 mm. To use the tool for calculating other Fibonacci relationships, please refer to one of the many books already published on the subject. Just one last note about a divider: *Don't drop it— very painful.*

Point 6. Back to the DMK/$ chart and the oscillator low at point 6 in Figure 1-5. Nothing very notable at point 6 except that it is an extreme low that occurs below the bear market support zone. The market will allow the support level at 30 to be tested after a minor rebound whenever the market has fallen through this zone and become extremely oversold. The tight back-and-fill chop that forms in the market after this oscillator squeezes the RSI back over the 30 level and subtly tests the 30 zone before the dollar begins to rebound. Focus on the oscillator movement exactly halfway between points 6 and 7. The dollar has a small rally and immediately pulls back. The RSI tries to hold support on the lower range defining a bull market at the 40 level.

Point 7. Point 7 is an oscillator high under the resistance zone for a bear market. The M pattern in the indicator is also significant. The dollar fails and moves the RSI down to point 8.

Point 8. The oscillator is clearly at the support zone reserved for a bull market. This is actually the second time the market has tried to develop support at this zone, but the first attempt was subtle as it developed between points 6 and 7. If you miss this transitional signal that the dollar is developing a major trend reversal, move along the chart to point 9.

Point 9. The dollar rallies and the RSI breaks above the bear market resistance line. The breakout is only briefly maintained, and a decline unfolds in the dollar from point 9.

Point 10. Now the bull trend is in force with confirmation. Point 10 shows the RSI once again holding the support zone for a market correction within a trending bull market. The dollar remains in an uptrend, and the RSI travels between the 40 and 90 levels.

There is one subtlety that can be pointed out now without risk of breaking the discussion about the trend transition that develops from points 8 to 10. Between points 8 and 9 there is an oscillator peak in the middle of these points that develops exactly at the 60 level. Follow the oscillator down from this pivot high marked with an arrow. The oscillator low that follows the peak at the 60 level occurs exactly at a 0.382 retracement of the bear market range. Use your Proportional Divider to see that the distance from the RSI pivot low relative to the support zone for a bear market is an exact 0.618 measurement. Because we know that the space under the RSI pivot to the support zone is exactly 0.618, we know without further measurement that the oscillator has found support at the 0.382 retracement level from the 60 level. Lost on this point? It will be discussed again at a later time in greater detail. The important points to grasp from Figure 1–5 are the trend reversal signals. As the chapters build concepts, you will begin to focus on different levels of detail within the same indicator. We have only begun to discuss technical indicators, and I suspect many might already be surprised at the depth of information available to us. Let's keep digging deeper.

About now the stock trader may be feeling somewhat left out of the examples discussed so far. All that has been defined to this point will apply to individual stock charts. Figure 1–6 shows the weekly chart for Caterpillar. The stock is clearly in a bull market, and the oscillator lows show that each correction in this stock was within the context of a trending bull market. The RSI is traveling between 40 and 70+, denoting a bull market. The oscillator highs directly below line 2 are developing under the 60 level. This could be a warning that would have to be watched closely for a transition into a bear market if a pullback breaks below the 40 level from this danger zone. Individual stocks will abide by the range guidelines

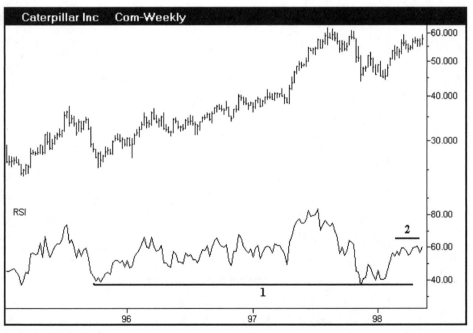

F I G U R E   1 – 6

described at length in the prior figures. However, it should be asked if synthetic indices can be expected to follow these same ranges when they themselves are never actually traded?

Figure 1–7 shows a monthly chart for the S&P sector Beverages (Soft Drinks). Regardless of the Sector evaluated, the range rules will apply. The Sector consolidates in 1988 and 1994, but the RSI declines only to the support zone within the 40 to 50 range. There is ample warning in 1988 that a major rally will follow. You might be thinking that this particular sector is itself more like a stock as it is heavily weighted toward Coca-Cola stock. Regardless of the S&P sector's compositional weighting of stocks, these trend ranges will still occur.

So let's test this premise in a tougher market environment. We will create a synthetic market by developing a bar chart of relative performance between two markets. In Figure 1–8 we have a monthly bar chart created by dividing the S&P Sector for Electric Companies by the Cash S&P Index. The data are in a downtrend, which is interpreted as a severe underperformance for this sector relative to the S&P 500 Index. Had the data shown an uptrend, the chart would have implied that the sector was outperforming the S&P 500 Index. The RSI at points 2, 3, and 4 show characteristic pivots for a trending bear market. The critical support zone

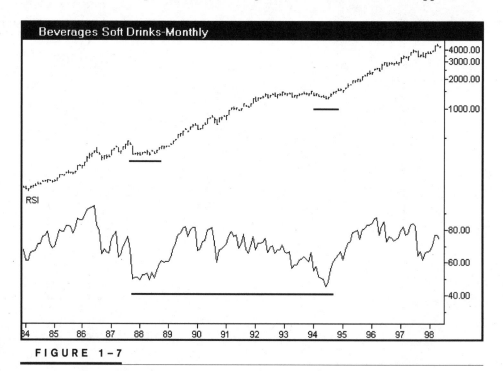

FIGURE 1-7

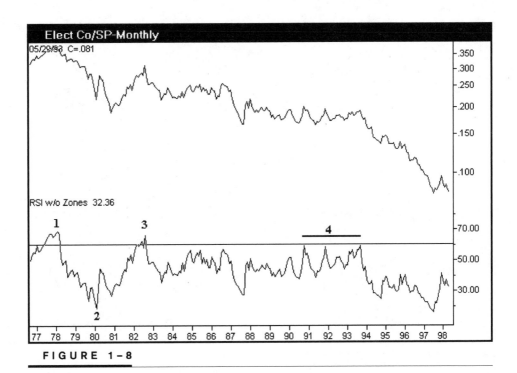

FIGURE 1-8

at 45 to 55 is continually broken as the sector underperforms the Cash S&P 500 and displays all the characteristics discussed previously for a bear market.

About now you might be seeing that the range rules clearly apply to various financial markets, but you can rightfully ask now if similar formations will occur within various time horizons. In Figure 1–9a is the weekly chart for the stock Novell. For comparison, Figure 1–9b offers the daily chart for the U.S. Treasury 30-Year Yields. U.S. rates have been falling in a market action that is similar in appearance to Novell. Clearly there is no relationship between these two charts, and none is implied except that both markets are presently in bear markets. While the markets are different and the time horizons displayed vary, the ranges that the RSI oscillator is traveling is the same for both markets. While the boundaries may be very slightly different as bond rates use 25 to 35 as their RSI support zone, when the stock establishes 30 to 35 as the support zone, the guidelines first introduced at the start of this chapter remain in effect. The resistance zone at 55 to 65 marks trouble for both markets.

The market action we have not discussed to this point is a sideways or range bound consolidation. The monthly chart for Bethlehem Steel covers a period of 15 years in Figure 1–10. Over this period of time Bethlehem Steel has been range bound in a listless drift. It has been tradable, however. The oscillator peaks

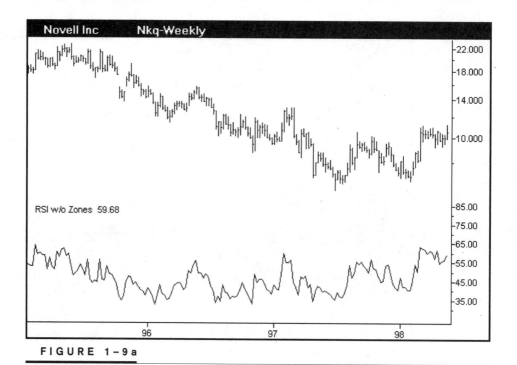

F I G U R E   1 – 9 a

are all at the 55 to 65 resistance zone, and the key oscillator lows are displaying the characteristic support zone for a bear market. The transition from this extremely long consolidation will be no different than what was discussed in detail for DMK/$.

Has there been a nagging question in your mind as the series of charts for various markets and time horizons has been discussed? "What period is being used for RSI in all these charts? Are we seeing different time periods in order to fit the oscillator to the example to create an ideal range?" No. Every chart regardless of market or time horizon has displayed an RSI with a 14-period interval. Every single one of them. Now, let me ask you, "What would be wrong with using these range rules to establish the correct time period?" Nothing, except you will later discover that the RSI has a specific price projection capability that is best applied to a 14-period RSI. For this reason all of these charts are using the same interval within the RSI formula.

We can conclude this chapter on an upbeat note with Figure 1–11. The weekly Du Pont stock is the image to keep in mind for an ideal bull market. The 75 to 85 range has marked the tops while the 40 to 50 support zone has marked all the pull-backs within the developing bull market. The chart also shows an immediate buy

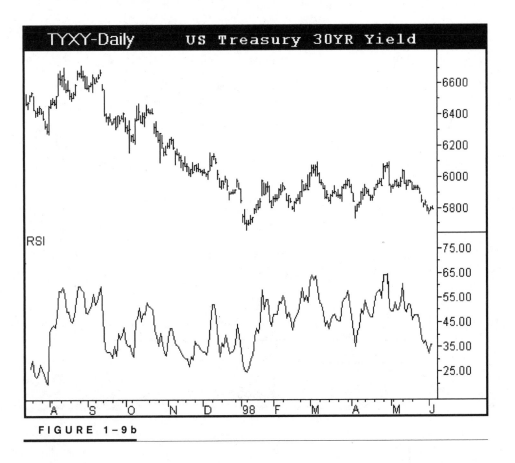

FIGURE 1-9b

signal at the time of this screen capture. A new price high is indicated as long as the 55 to 65 level is exceeded and the 40 level is not broken. However, a rally will then lead to a pattern of great risk as we will see when we discuss wave interpretations much later in this book. Indicators require us to develop a choreographed balance of different methods. We still have much to explore together.

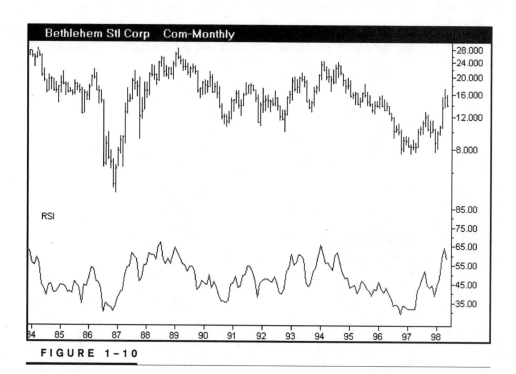

FIGURE 1-10

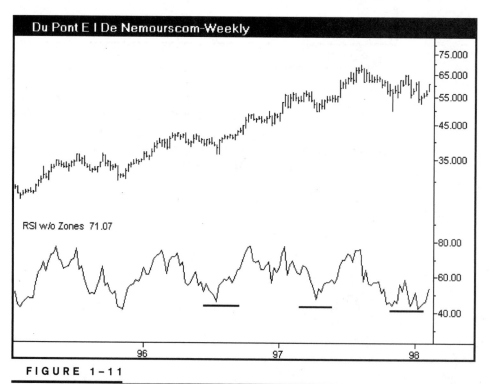

FIGURE 1-11

CHAPTER 2

Dominant Trading Cycles Are Not Time Symmetrical

While the analyst will swear by the accuracy and predictive value of a predetermined symmetrical cycle bottom, the trader will more commonly experience several emotional deaths as his or her positions are squeezed out of the market by a minor displacement in the analyst's predicted cycle low. Assuredly, as soon as the "perfect" period is defined for a cycle, it will on the next swing down be the one that the market ignores all together or be sufficiently early or late to cause bottom-line damage to our accounts. The individual who is a diehard cycle enthusiast does not make his or her livelihood from trading the market but from predicting it, and that is an entirely different discipline. The cycles an analyst frequently identifies are symmetrical based on past market performance. However, the trader must make a living based on real-time decisions within a market that is a living entity that abides by the growth and decay laws found in nature. A growth-decay cycle means expansion and contraction attributes and the difference between the analyst's and trader's worlds is the element of "time."

In Figure 2–1 is one of the most cyclically symmetrical markets in the world today: the monthly chart of the Japanese Nikkei Index. A 52- and 89-period cycle on the chart argues the case well that cycles are measurable, predictable, and for some markets exceptionally accurate. These two independent cycles also project extreme problems again for the Japanese market around the end of 2005 and the first quarter of 2006 when these two cycles bottom in a close juxtaposition. We know that cycles have a cumulative effect and multiple cycle lows that bottom in a close proximity of time will exacerbate the market decline into those projected market lows.

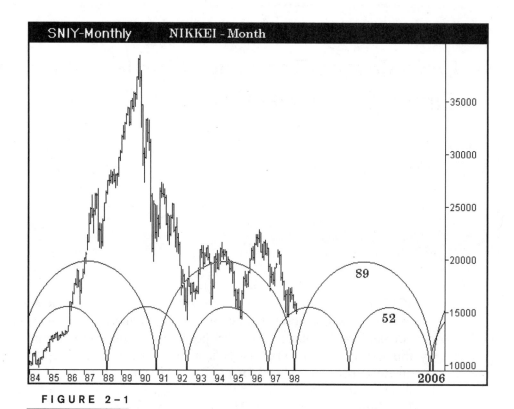

FIGURE 2–1

While the monthly Nikkei Index displays the same 52-period cycle in Figures 2-1 and 2-2, the 89-period cycle has been replaced by an 85-period cycle in Figure 2-2. Both the 89- and 85-period cycles are anchored from lows just out of view to the left of the chart, which makes more recent market lows the third cycle bottoms for these cycle periods. The 85-period cycle accurately warned that a decline would unfold into January 1998. The 89-period cycle accurately warns of the decline unfolding now in June 1998. The trader who used the 85-period cycle was not wrong but would likely be confounded by this June decline if he or she thought that the Nikkei had established a bottom six months earlier. The 89-period cycle in conjunction with the 52-period warns that early 2006 will be a major problem for this market. By shifting the preference from the 89-period to that of an 85-period cycle, the forecast shifts back to 2005, and the character of the decline itself could be much different as the cycle lows are not as close together. An interpretation could be made that an orderly decline in 2005 would unfold in comparison to the sharp spike bottom implied by the 2006 cycles that bottom together in Figure 2–1. What is the correct period to use if both the nearby market interpretation and extended views can be changed so easily by just a minor period adjustment of 85 to 89 in these cycles? In reality, one period is not more correct than the other; we can see from these charts both had predictive value in 1998. However, both periods will be wrong if new price data are ignored and the periods defined today are not later adjusted for the markets' natural growth and decay attributes that will develop between now and 2005.

In Figure 2–2 the major low that developed in July 1995 was missed all together by the cycles using periods of 52, 85, and 89. We will address this particular low shortly, but let's stick with growth-decay attributes within the markets for a moment. As soon as the phrase *Growth and Decay* is used, most traders will know that we are heading into a discussion about Fibonacci ratios. Let me offer the bottom line for this methodology up front: Fibonacci cycle projections will not provide us with the definitive answer when we ask, "What is the most important cycle within the market I trade now?" It is not good enough to tell a trader that both the 85- and 89-period cycles on a monthly chart are correct. We need something that will give us a higher probability than a six-month window of time

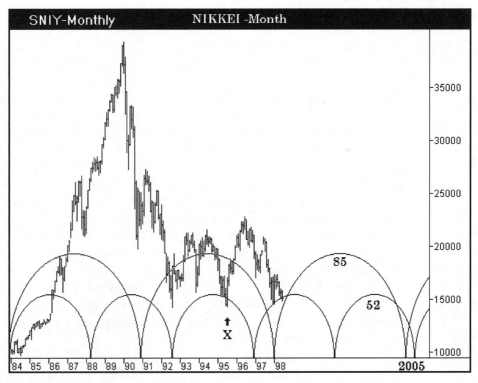

FIGURE 2–2

from which to determine a major market bottom. While Fibonacci ratios alone will not provide us with the definitive answer, this mathematical series of numbers does offer an essential component in our quest to recognize what has immediate significance. The number series is certainly of value, but conceptually the Fibonacci sequence may have an even greater impact.

As a professional trader and student of the markets, one cannot escape an encounter with the remarkable Italian mathematician, Leonard of Pisa, better known as Leonardo Fibonacci. But did you know Fibonacci was not his name? That was a nickname, an abbreviation of "filius Bonacci." If you are new to Fibonacci but can accept the bottom line of his theorem without the background discussion for proof, know that your financial livelihood will be very much tied to the ratios 0.146, 0.236, 0.382, 0.500, 0.618, 1.00, 1.618, and 2.618 and that they will directly impact your P/L.

Why? These ratios have been around for a very long time. Leonardo Fibonacci wrote about them in his book, *Liber Abaci,* in 1202, but the number sequence from which these ratios are derived were in use around 4700 B.C. when the Egyptians built the Great Pyramid of Gizeh. The slant edge of the Great Pyramid is almost exactly 0.618. To create the number series, add the first number to the second, the second to the third, and you develop the sequence: 1, 1, 2, 3, 5, 8, 13, 21, 34, 55, 89, 144, 233, 377, and so forth. These specific numbers will be of value to you as periods for moving averages and within indicators. The ratios themselves come from the fact that any given number over 3 in the series is approximately 0.618, or 61.8 percent, of the number that follows it. Any adjacent number in the sequence over 5 is approximately 1.618 times the number preceding it. Between alternate numbers, the higher will be approximately 2.618 times the first, and the lower number between alternates will be approximately 0.382.

The really interesting aspect about these ratios is that they are found in anything that has a growth and decay developmental cycle. Plants, animals, vegetables, minerals, and—you guessed it—markets. As all living entities do exhibit these exact same expansion and contraction ratios, Leonardo's mathematical theorem is viewed as a Law of Nature. It should not be surprising that these ratios are frequently respected within the markets. Markets expand and contract and so abide by the same Law. If you want to know more, head to the Internet and start surfing. You will undoubtedly discover the original question concerning rabbit population growth and see that Leonardo Fibonacci and Darth Vader shared the same style of dress. But let's move on to see how the Fibonacci number sequence applies to cycles in the markets.

In Figure 2–3 we are still viewing the Japanese Nikkei Index, but we have dropped down to a weekly chart. A symmetrical fixed-period cycle is charted that displays corresponding cycle bottoms at market lows near the end of 1993 and the

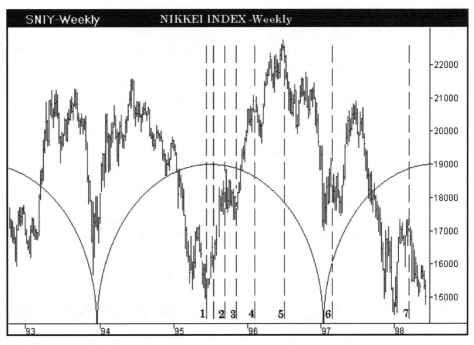

FIGURE 2-3

start of 1997. The same chart also shows vertical broken lines that are numbered 1 through 7. The 1995 low marks the starting anchor for the vertical series of lines. Each vertical time line plotted is derived from a Fibonacci ratio. These lines are called *Fibonacci time cycles*. At points 1 and 3 the line bisects a market low. Points 2, 4, 5, 6, and 7 all mark pivot points preceding a market pullback. That is the thing about Fibonacci time cycles that will be troubling for a trader—not knowing if he or she is approaching a market high or low. True, a pivot implies a market trend reversal so assume a reversal from the present trend. But take a closer look at point 6. That is a significant Fibonacci cycle projection that denotes a market high. The Fibonacci cycle at point 6 immediately precedes a cycle low in the symmetrical cycle that accompanies the price bottom in early 1997. That just adds a lot of conflict. Which cycle method will be proven right? In hindsight the symmetrical cycle bottom was stronger, but the Fibonacci time cycle was also correct—it just did not amount to much of a trend reversal at point 6. The question of knowing what the magnitude or strength of a signal will be is the heart of the issue for a trader.

If we plot a second Fibonacci time cycle with the starting point at the market bottom near the close of 1993 (not on the chart), a Fibonacci time cycle from that low would not coincide with any other cycle marked in Figure 2–3. The additional information just becomes noise. Many of us have witnessed an in-depth Fibonacci time cycle analysis that failed. The work was not flawed—it was just that the fire cracker after having been ignited did not produce any consequential reaction. All the right ingredients seemed to be present, but then nothing happened—a dud, or worse a reaction opposite to our expectations. Multiple Fibonacci cycles projected from numerous market lows reveal confluence points where different ratios overlap one another or form very tight cluster groups. The cumulative effect when cycles of varying periods or Fibonacci frequencies overlap to form a clustered group should mean a high-probability pivot and trend reversal for the market. While this is true for Fibonacci retracements derived from price, it is far less accurate for Fibonacci time projections.

The inaccuracies and weaknesses we all experience as traders with both symmetrical and Fibonacci cycle analysis may be caused from an oversight. The oversight is ignoring the basic premise that nothing is static; therefore, rescaling for cycles forming within multiple time horizons cannot be defined from linear or symmetrical periods. It is possible that the calendar of time itself is incorrect, a pos-

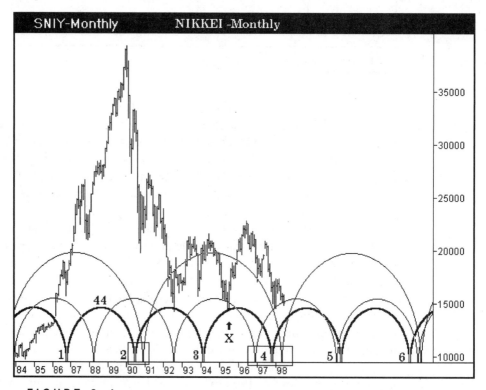

FIGURE 2-4

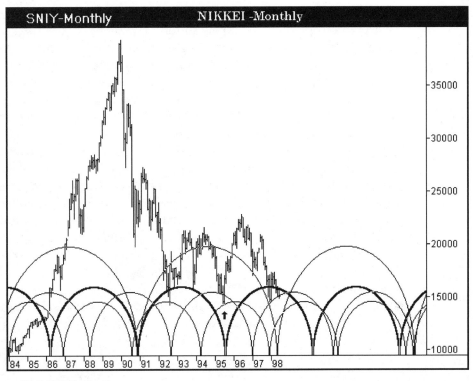

FIGURE 2–5

sibility that has led others to explore lunar calendars and other measures of time. However, the solution is likely a combination of all these methods, thereby creating a variable period. *Fibonacci ratios denoting expansion and contraction can be used themselves as exponential factors to weight symmetrical periods in conventional cycle analysis.* If you can weight a cycle projection, so too can you adjust an indicator. You may be thinking, "And just how are we going to do that?" Stick with me on this one as I promise to show you the results in charts using the tools we currently have today, though the application will be different.

Figure 2–4 returns to the monthly bar chart for the Nikkei Index. The same two cycles displayed in Figure 2–1 are repeated in this chart showing 52 and 89 periods. In Figure 2–4, a 44-period cycle has now been added, and the heavier line helps to locate the new period in this chart that captures the market low that was missed in January 1998. The 44-period cycle was selected as it also captures the price low that coincides at the cycle bottom marked at point 1. At point 2 both the 44-period and 89-period cycles have a close proximity and contribute to the meltdown drop into the 1990 low. The cycle bottom at point 3 is late for the price low, but the same cycle period is also slightly early for the January 1998 bottom where three cycles are beginning to form a cluster now near point 4. We do not know which cycle period is most important, but clearly the market lows that coincide with the cycle bottoms clustering at point 4 are all significant. We still have the price low at point X that remains unidentified by any of the cycle periods selected up to this point. We will need to add one more cycle to capture this low.

The cycle that is now highlighted by a heavier line in Figure 2–5 is a 56-period cycle. It marks the important low that occurred in 1995. As you study this chart, you might begin to think this is somewhat similar to Gann. There are so many cycles plotted that surely you are bound to hit one of them. Well, you will find later in this book that with Gann it will become a question of knowing which relationships are of greatest significance and learning how to filter out the others. So too in this case when a lot of cycles have been plotted. We need to know how to view a select number of cycles in this chart that will have far greater importance.

Figure 2–6 has all the cycles we have been building upon in the prior charts. But now look at what happens when you use the Fibonacci cycle in a different way. Anchor the tight starting cluster of Fibonacci ratios between the two cycle bottoms plotted in 1986. Then let the Fibonacci series extend forward in time from this anchor point. You are not using a price low, but the symmetrical cycle bottoms clustered at the start of the chart, to project the Fibonacci cycles. Not only do the resulting Fibonacci cycles fall entirely on market lows but they are also lows of tremendous significance. Point 1 shows you the anchor point to start this projection. Point 2 is two periods late, but it is much earlier than the symmetrical cycle that is closest to it. Point 4 defines a major price low that is not even portrayed within our cycles plotted in this chart. Point 5 marks what promises to become the most significant of all the cycles preceding this cluster of numerous symmetrical cycle bottoms. As for point 6, it is the end of the tight cluster of cycles that will mark a capitulation bottom.

The chart in Figure 2–6 is visually very busy with all the overlapping cycle lines, and it allows no room for applying additional methods we may favor. Can this information be displayed in a manner that offers a much cleaner representation of these results?

At first glance the Stochastics indicator in Figure 2–7 will appear normal as it is plotted with the 120-minute Dow Jones Industrial Average (DJIA). However, this particular Stochastics formula is not using a fixed period, but rather a variable period. We will discuss how to select the correct fixed period in the next chapter. Let's say a 13-period Slow Stochastics is favored. The fixed period can then be weighted by the Fibonacci series, which produces a variable period. As a result, the indicator has been smoothed, and it plots the cumulative effect of the cycles described in Figure 2–6. Now that we have graphically cleaned up Figure 2–6, we can see that there is a lag, which is viewed as a problem in this Stochastics chart. However, the smooth oscillation displayed by the Stochastics indicator is clearly informative.

In Figure 2–8 a custom indicator called the "Derivative Oscillator" is introduced to you. (A discussion of the indicator's formula and interpretative guidelines will be deferred until Chapter 14.) Figure 2–8 shows a "var" Derivative Oscillator, letting you know that a variable period has been applied within the standard formula. (The use of a variable or weighted period in any indicator will not be discussed beyond this chapter to avoid confusion.) Figure 2–8 shows that the Stochastics lag that was present in Figure 2–7 has been significantly improved. (Just view price bottoms at this time to stay within the context of evaluating cycle lows. The oscillator peaks will need to be addressed in a different discussion.) The last, or far right bar, in both Figures 2–7 and 2–8, captures the freefall that was unfolding in the DJIA on June 12, 1998. The Stochastics indicator does not show a trend change, and prices are still on the way down in Figure 2–7. In Figure 2–8 the Derivative Oscillator shows an

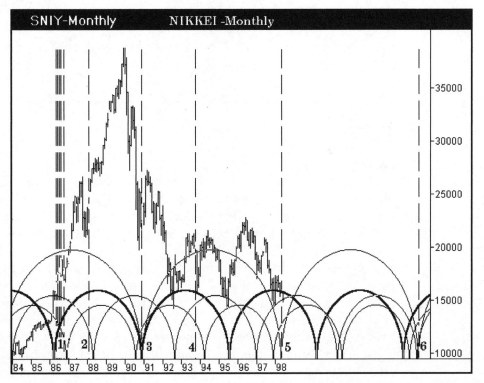

FIGURE 2-6

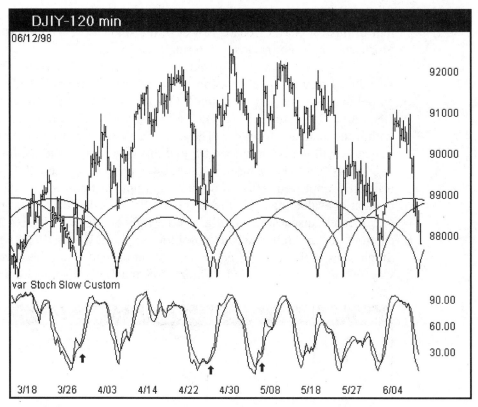

FIGURE 2-7

oscillator extreme, and price has formed a spike bottom or key reversal. The oscillator low at this point is at a precise objective (see also Chapter 14). Figures 2–7 and 2–8 show that it is possible to visually incorporate all the concepts discussed previously in this chapter into one indicator. The cycles plotted with prices in these figures help the reader compare traditional methods combined with the weighted oscillators.

We have discussed two kinds of cycles: symmetrical and Fibonacci. We have discussed the use of applying a weighted factor to a fixed symmetrical cycle period to produce a variable period that will help us isolate the more significant cycles developing in an expansion and contraction environment. But we have still not answered the most important question, "How can we tell what trading signal is the most significant and will have the highest probability for success?" To answer this question, we need to use multiple time horizons to filter out lower-probability signals generated within any one individual chart. In

Figure 2–9 are two charts for Yen/$. The 240-minute chart on the left is compared to the same market on the right in a 60-minute time horizon. To help isolate similar time horizons, a box has been drawn in both charts, with the labels 1 and 2 inserted above them. The areas within boxes 1 and 2 cover the same time frame. Within these two boxes there is but a single occasion when both oscillators offer a buy signal for dollars against the Yen. The signal occurs as the oscillator rolls up in both the 240-minute chart and 60-minute chart at the same time. The dotted vertical line will help you compare the timing of the oscillator signals relative to the position of the market. Therefore, the answer to our question about probability is to chart more than one time horizon and look for signals that occur simultaneously.

We have come a long way in our discussion about cycles. We will use this information about market cycles to determine what period to use for Stochastics and MACD studies in the next chapter.

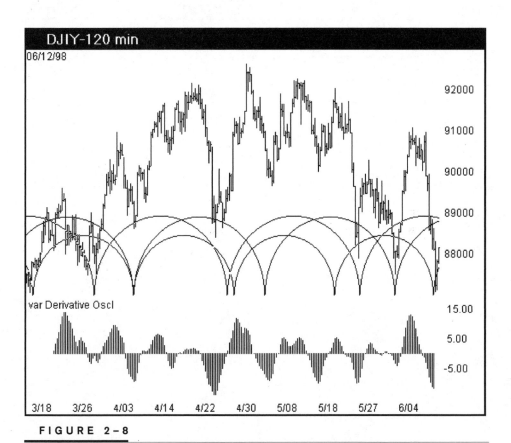

FIGURE 2–8

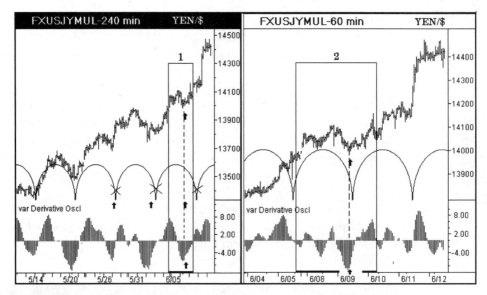

FIGURE 2-9

CHAPTER 3

Choosing and Adjusting Period Setup for Oscillators

As the Stochastics indicator is one of the more widely used studies in the industry, it is a good place to begin a discussion about how to set up initial periods. As mentioned in the first chapter, quote vendors use the same default periods for their studies. Stochastics is generally one of the first studies that novice technical traders will add to their market data, allowing the professional trader to use this knowledge to their advantage for short-horizon market moves.

The S&P 500 futures market can be graphed in one-minute time intervals. Clearly, this would be a ridiculous time interval for trading cash currencies as the data has no structure when plotted and the market does not operate within that time boundary. However, the S&P is an entirely different "animal," and there is a large group of us who operate as off-floor traders and hold positions for only a short period of time.

Figure 3–1 is a 2-minute chart of the September S&P on June 12, 1998. The data are so well defined that I could remove the labels on the time and price axis and lead you to believe that the chart was a 60-minute or daily bar chart. If the data in your market are not as well defined in the short time horizon, don't drop down to these extremely short time intervals. Also, please keep in mind that the 2-minute chart is used only after extensive analysis of longer time horizons from monthly charts on down to the shorter time intervals. I strongly recommend that you not use tick charts as you will be forcing a fixed number of trades into a single bar as opposed to plotting the trades that occur over a fixed unit of time. Your indicators will have numerous failures, and if you use chart patterns at all, you will be working with distorted chart formations. If you need to look at your data in a different format, use Point-and-Figure charts. Intervals to consider using in the S&P are

100 by 3 and 50 by 3. Why those particular periods? These setup periods for Point-and-Figure charts are popular with the floor traders in the S&P pit. Which leads us right back to Figure 3–1 because if our market can be influenced by a known entity that could shift the timing for our own position entry or exit, we should monitor that element if at all possible. If there is a favored analytic method used by a large group of traders like a specific period for Point-and-Figure charts, Candle-Stick charts (which are followed by a large audience for Asian markets), or simply a common error used by inexperienced traders in mass, that knowledge can be used to your advantage.

The 2-minute S&P chart in Figure 3–1 was deliberately set up with the vendor's default periods so that the retail sector could be monitored. In the morning if my market opinion is bearish, I may delay entering my own market order if the timing coincides with the technically inexperienced trader operating within the "Stochastics Default Club." I would then sell the market when my own indicators have given me permission the next time around at a more favorable level. The reverse is also true. In the afternoon session if I am looking for an opportunity to buy, I might delay my order if the timing is moments away from the Stochastics Default Club. There clearly has to be other concerns present first, such as an Elliott Wave pattern and momentum indicator combination in my own charts to suggest

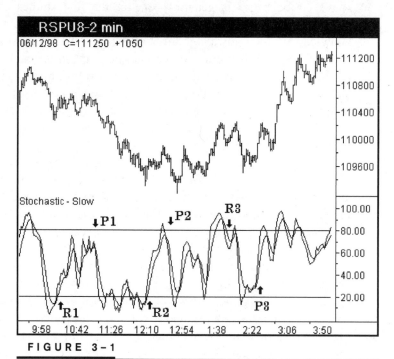

FIGURE 3–1

that something could be out of sync. But then looking at a Stochastics study that is deliberately set up incorrectly can be of interest. In Figure 3–1, a few signals are marked to show an R for the retail sector most likely entering the market. The P in the same chart denotes where professionals are using the retail trader's volume to establish more favorable entries for themselves. The Stochastics Default Club will enter on cue as the indicator crosses up through the 20 line and will sell as the indicator crosses below the 80 level. They are doing just what their user's manual told them to do and what they see demonstrated on CNBC by some guests. If Stochastics gives the retail sector three signals in a row and offers divergence or a W bottom in the indicator like the chart displays at R2, they will generally come out in larger numbers and squeeze out some of the weaker market positions with size (large position size), producing a three-wave corrective move. The professional traders generally will not let the Stochastics Default Club off the hook graciously because the professional orders will likely be entered before the Default Club charts have had an opportunity to trigger a reverse signal. That is because we are making our trading decisions from different periods and from different time horizons. Add the range rules for oscillators, and we would be entering orders from entirely different zones from the same chart. Coining the phrase "Stochastics Default Club" is not meant to be disrespectful, as I was once a member myself when I started. Maybe it is just a rite of passage. There is no experience quite like the emotional swings of being trapped on the wrong side of a runaway fast market shortly after your indicators gave you permission to boldly step in front of an oncoming freight train. Splat. It isn't too long before basic survival instincts motivate us to find a better way.

How do we go about finding the right period to use? And what will happen when everyone uses the same method to define the right period? Won't we be establishing a "Modified Stochastics Club"? Well, forming a new club will be harder to do as dominant cycles are not symmetrical, and it will be harder to identify the correct cycle to use than one might suspect. However, Stochastics is very forgiving if the period used is just slightly off the mark. By solving a different problem, I found that this solution would also prevent a trader from operating within a Stochastics Club unknowingly, even if the trader at the desk beside us followed the same final steps. So for now just accept that a solution will be offered after the foundation has been established.

Stochastics is based on the observation that, as price decreases, the daily Closes tend to accumulate ever closer to their extreme Lows of the daily range. Conversely, as price increases, the daily Closes tend to accumulate ever closer to the extreme Highs of the daily ranges. This concept holds true whether we are trading from a 2-minute bar chart or a monthly time period. George Lane used this observation to develop his overbought-oversold oscillator, which shows this relationship.

Stochastics is a two-line oscillator that uses %D as the primary and %K in a shorter interval to offer a leading indicator to %D. George Lane uses a three-line oscillator by plotting %K, %D along with %D-Slow as a confirming indicator. The Slow Stochastics gives a smoother sine wave than the Fast Stochastics. By varying the period used for the primary oscillator %D, different results will occur.

In Figure 3–2 the weekly DMK/$ chart is offered. The method for defining the correct periodicity for %D is to study the time horizon in the chart from which you are making trading decisions and determine the best cycle for that chart. The data in this chart have been compressed so that as much data can be seen on the screen for this weekly time horizon. We need to see only price lows so the temporary distortion of the data is inconsequential. In this chart a cycle of 118 is identified. This cycle is close, but it does not fit the price lows exactly for reasons discussed in the preceding chapter. Therefore, bias your cycle placement so that the cycle bottoms align most accurately with the price lows in the most recent data, and let the price lows farthest to the left of the chart fall slightly out of phase. Most will establish cycles from left to right and let the price lows closest to the current bar fall out of sync. That just doesn't make much sense.

Use the periodicity that is 50 percent of the cycle length you identified. As a 118-period cycle is acknowledged in the weekly chart, a 59-period would be used

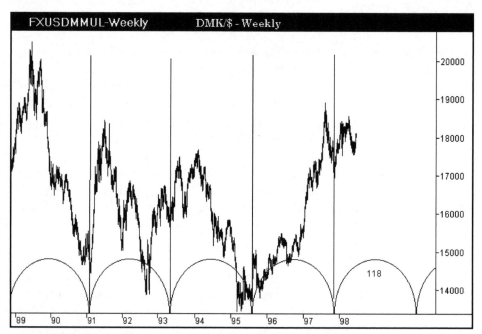

FIGURE 3–2

for %D. That's all there is too it. Right? Wrong. How do we know that the 118-period cycle is the correct one to use? In Chapter 2 we developed a chart that needed 4 cycles just to mark some of the more significant market lows. As we are never going to stumble on the ideal cycle to use in most cases, here is a useful way to evaluate the period you selected.

The compressed *x* axis can now be expanded so that the data appears normal on the screen. Then add the Stochastics study to the chart using a 59-period interval. While the results in Figure 3–3 are correct, I do not like the results from this period because there is insufficient movement in the indicator and the oscillator does not display the range rules discussed in Chapter 1. So the first efforts have established a period that is too long. If I repeat the process of arbitrarily plotting a best-fit cycle and taking a look at the period results in the Stochastics formula, it could take several hours to find something I really liked. So let's use the computer's smarts to see what it can come up with as the period to use.

Professional charting products all have an optimization feature. In Figure 3–4 the Omega TradeStation software offers us the ability to optimize a period when you want to edit the default value. Omega TradeStation uses a default value of 10 in their Stochastics Crossover System, but their default value is different when you select Stochastics as an indicator to be plotted in a chart. Regardless,

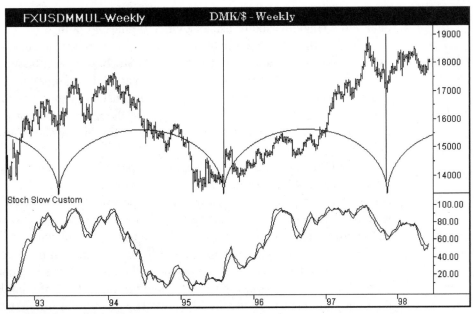

FIGURE 3-3

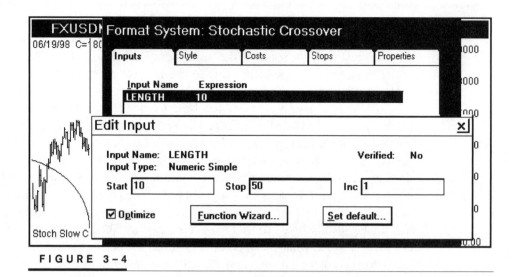

FIGURE 3–4

we know that the 59-period is too long and the default of 10 will be too short. Instead, let the computer run through an optimization range of 10 to 50 in increments of 1 unit to identify a better period. Curve-fitting technical indicators that are used in unconventional or specialized interpretative ways are not recommended. But in this situation we are consciously trying to curve fit the historical data into a single period to use as a guide or starting point.

The optimization feature for the Omega TradeStation Stochastics system will use the buy-sell signals generated when the Stochastics oscillators cross through the 80 and 20 levels. Vendors have to demonstrate the same logic defined in their user's manual. As we do not want to use Stochastics in such a manner, the profitability test results they will offer as a part of the optimization process will be of no value to us. The period identified through the optimization process may be of some interest, however.

The computer optimization suggests a period of 36 is the best value to use for %D. Working backward, we know that the cycle will be double the Stochastics period. The computer is indicating that a 72-period cycle will be dominant in this weekly DMK/$ chart. After setting a 72-period cycle, comparable price lows can be identified. The computer may have found a better cycle, and this is tested when the data are compressed to show the full historical range in the database. Having passed the first test, we can go ahead and add a Stochastics study using a 36 period for %D. The results in Figure 3–5 should immediately offer confirmation that the right period has been identified. How? The range rules discussed in Chapter 1 are now present. The four boundary lines discussed in Chapter 1 to mark the upper and lower levels for a trending bull and bear market have been reduced in this chart to show only two: the lower range for a bull market and the upper resistance zone for a bear market.

The price data show that the computer gave us buy-sell signals when the indicator crossed through the 20 and 80 levels. This is not how George Lane advises us to use his indicator, and we can see that these signals offer poor results. He advises trading only with the trend when using this indicator—that is, to buy or sell when permission is obtained from divergence analysis and when the "permission" signal is accompanied on lower volume. However, when the correct period is identified for the Stochastics Oscillator, it will contain trend information by traveling within the ranges that were detailed in the first chapter. While the oscillator character between RSI and Stochastics will be different, the signals to buy or sell will abide by the same range rules. The Stochastics indicator in Figure 3–5 has been marked to show the buy-sell signals generated when you apply range rules. The signals are occurring in the direction of the market's trend. Every point marked with a buy or sell signal was discussed in the first chapter with the exception of three. There are two buy signals along a trend line drawn on the oscillator that occurred in 1996. The addition of trend lines and moving averages is of great value and will be discussed in greater detail separately. The other signal is the Stochastics peak that has the word "Elliott" above

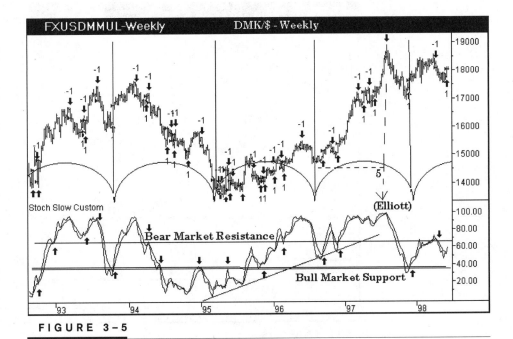

FIGURE 3-5

it. Permission to sell is not given by Stochastics just because it is at an extreme high. However, the rally that unfolds from the low identified with a dotted line to the high is a distinct five-wave advance that someone using the Elliott Wave Principle along with Stochastics would have known to act upon, or to at least unwind, or scale back a portion of a long dollar position. The Gann trader would also have known to do likewise as the market formed a key reversal from a major Gann objective. We will cover some of these complementary techniques separately at another time.

Are you curious to know how the 2-minute S&P chart in Figure 3–1 would have been altered by using the setup procedure just outlined? Let's take a look at Figure 3–6. The default value for %D has been changed so that the indicator can convey the range rules outlined in Chapter 1. Figure 3–6 shows the changes that occur in the buy-sell signals when the correct period is used and when the range rules for oscillators are applied. The interpretation is different from the chart in Figure 3–1.

After discussing how to identify the correct %D periodicity for Stochastics, the reader will likely ask, "When should the period be changed?" It is generally recognized when Stochastics is used without range rules applied that a shorter period can be used to anticipate a signal. In strong trending markets, don't halve

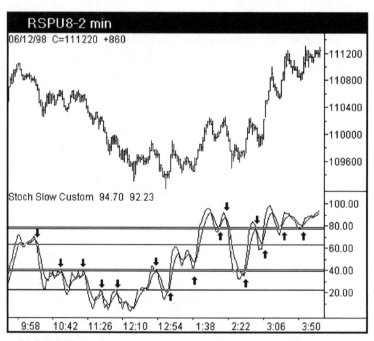

FIGURE 3–6

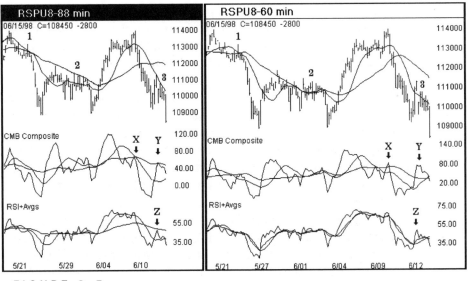

FIGURE 3-7

the Cycle, but rather, use the full Cycle, and only seek permission from the indicator when it offers signals with the trend. Once you begin to use the range rules discussed for oscillators in bull and bear markets, you will not want to change the period as your range rules will not be present.

Early in this discussion the question was asked, "Will we not be creating a new Modified Stochastics Club if everyone uses the same procedure of using half the cycle length?" First, people will find different cycles, but second, you will want to make one last "tweak." What you will want to change is the time period for creating the bar chart. I've not encountered others that do this. You will find it is not only an effective way to make an adjustment but it is also the easiest way to catch that an adjustment is required.

Figure 3–7 is a comparison between an 88-minute and 60-minute September S&P 500 bar chart. In both charts two oscillators are plotted. The bottom oscillator is a 14-period RSI, and the middle oscillator is a custom formula I developed called the Composite Index as it is a formula that is a composite of two studies. Both oscillators have two moving averages plotted with them, and two averages are plotted with the price data. The only difference between these two windows is the time interval used to create the bar charts. In the 60-minute bar chart, the moving averages appear to be incorrectly defined as the price highs near points 1, 2, and 3 are all exceeding the nearby averages. However, in the 88-minute chart the same data points are directly below the moving average at points 1, 2, and 3. Now take a look at what also occurs in the oscillators: The oscillator pivot points marked at *X, Y,* and *Z* in the 60-minute chart are not very helpful. But the exact same indicators in the 88-minute bar chart trigger signals easy to interpret and are right on their mark when the market is at a very difficult decision point for a trader.

How did I know 88 minutes would work at point 3? When I sit down in front of a chart, the first thing I check is the relationship of my fixed-interval averages on prices in the oldest data on the left of the screen. In this case, the 88-minute period of time was set up several weeks ago, and the key pivots were still working on the left-hand side of the screen. Therefore, I would not make a change. As the current data coming into the chart is the most critical, the assumption is made that if the signals are true on the left, then I should be able to see accurate signals form in the real-time data entering the screen on the right. In a 2-minute chart, the far left or oldest data is clearly missing its mark. Change the time period of the bar chart. I look at the old points to see if a 3-minute chart is a better fit...maybe a 1-minute bar chart. What surprises me most is that I nearly always land right on or within a minute of a Fibonacci number. Keep an eye on the old data as it relates to its moving averages. This is really important: Consider only the price data and moving averages; never try to adjust the indicators plotted below the data. Let the indicators fall wherever they will. When you encounter bar charts in this book created with unconventional time periods, this is the method by which they were derived. It is very rare that I change the favored periods for specific markets. Clearly, I can use this adjustment only within intraday periods, and I rarely exceed 240 minutes.

You probably want to know what moving averages were used on the price data in these charts showing the S&P. Right? Sorry, that's the one area beyond our discussion. Gann analysis is extremely important to me. The averages used on price are based on research that defines the high-frequency correlation points between the Gann price objectives and the intersection of the averages. The averages themselves are never used for trailing stops. Many have commented to me that one should never write a book that details methods known to work well in markets in which the author derives his or her income. I disagree with that view. In my opinion, the methods can be passed on, provided that the risk management and price projection methods used with the indicators are not entirely revealed. I will provide several price projection methods, but Gann is my primary price projection method, so forgive me if on occasion our discussion suddenly runs into a closed door. The only door closed to you is the specific Gann price projections that I use. But you will understand more clearly why when we take a look at W. D. Gann's methods later in this book.

We need to cover times when you will want to change the periodicity of an oscillator. In the following example, a shorter period is deliberately used to move an oscillator freely between 0 and 100. In the first chapter a strong case was made that oscillators do not travel between 0 and 100. In this case we will set up a condition so as to look for a specific oscillator formation and ignore all other squiggles the indicator may produce. In Figure 3–8 is an 11-period RSI calculated from the September S&P 500 futures market and charted in 88- and 13-minute intervals. When you look for a market top, use this chart combination to find just one pattern for confirmation between the two time intervals. In this example the 88-minute chart is forming a second peak with divergence near the 80 level. The same price high in the 13-minute chart forces the RSI to be pressed into the same 80 level boundary. That's all there is to this signal if you need only the last trigger after everything else you monitor is in place. This method will help the timing of entering a position. It is not used to exit a position as I don't hesitate when a target is realized for any reason. Ignore the fact that the oscillators roll to the bottom of the screen; in fact, don't even look at this screen combination until you are interested in using it to buy the market. The RSI is not interpreted in any other way except to find the extremes to sell or buy into within a specific time period. Ensure that you enter stops the same time the order is entered. This concept works well with longer time horizons such as monthly-weekly chart pairings. Some markets such as currencies require longer trading pairings more suitable for that market. Figure 3–9 shows

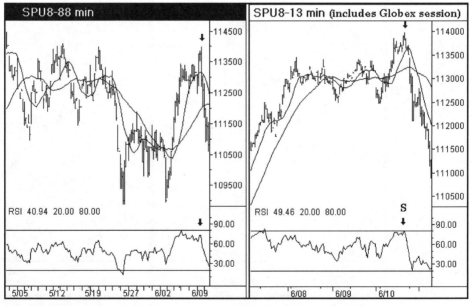

FIGURE 3-8

the Yen/$ applying a 360-minute and an 89-minute chart that completes a full sell/buy signal for this time horizon.

Does one have to use an RSI to apply this method? No. Other oscillators can be used. In Figure 3–10 Stochastics indicators show a time and market cross comparison of similar indices. In this case the DJIA is charted with an 88-minute interval versus the September S&P 500 in a 2-minute interval. The arrow on the 2-minute chart shows what kind of market action can result when these align at an extreme. If you get caught in one of these S&P infamous "back drafts," or washouts, it can ruin your whole day if you are caught on the wrong side in an intraday time horizon. This method has saved me from stepping on hidden landmines in this market on numerous occasions. In Figure 3–10 you are witness to a 6-handle short squeeze that is a vertical rise in the 2-minute bar chart. The market rally developed just moments before a 15-handle collapse in the S&P.

Many of the short-horizon chart examples throughout this book are actual real-time trading screens of which I have taken a quick snapshot view in order to capture the analytics and prices moments after a position was established or closed. In this case I was selling into the 1104 level based on the charts in Figure 3–10. The advance from the bottom was thought to be an Elliott Wave pattern that

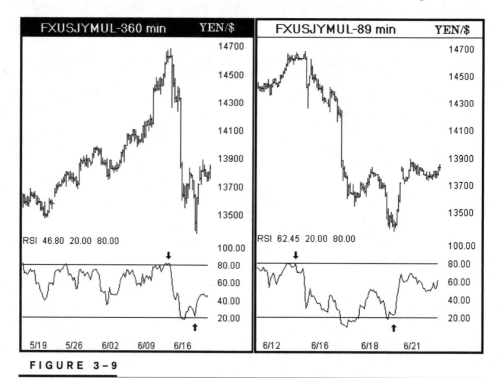

FIGURE 3-9

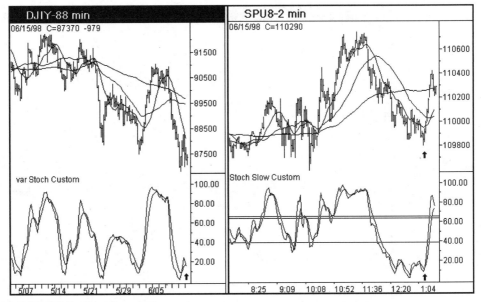

FIGURE 3-10

we will look at much later called an *Expanded Flat*. It would mean that the market would rally sharply and reverse just as quickly. By just the press of the print key on my computer, the entire screen is recorded without interfering with the collection of real-time data. Various utility software packages function differently, but they all allow a later evaluation of the exact screen that was used to enter the trade. We will be discussing some surprising observations derived from this method when we address indicators on indicators and moving averages. Ever wondered how you could have missed such an obvious market signal when you looked back? It is very possible that it was not there in real-time.

How do you set the periodicity for other indicators? The RSI will be set at 14 periods because it has a specific price projection capability that we will discuss separately.

MACD is favored by position traders as the indicator's travel is very smooth. Smoothed indicators, however, have a severe lag that needs to be addressed by plotting two separate studies. MACD is simply two moving averages, one slow, one fast, plotted in a separate window below the price data. The spread of the two averages can be plotted as a histogram that will detrend the differential of the two averages. The histogram will cross the zero line as the faster moving average crosses through the slower average, making it easier for a trader to see a precise crossover point.

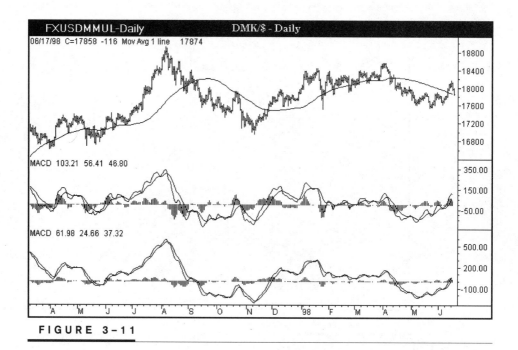

FIGURE 3-11

The MACD requires three periods that serve to smooth the oscillators' travel. *A single MACD study should never be used alone.* At minimum you will need two MACD studies. If a single study is used, the MACD in a downtrend, for instance, will generally develop late buy signals and premature sell signals. So two studies are needed. The default periods of 12-26-9 are offered as a starting guideline by the originator of the study, Gerald Appel. A short moving average pairing might be near 6-19-9, and the longer study may use periods closer to the default like 13-26-9. As markets tend to correct faster than they advance, you may need four MACD studies: two MACD studies using a faster moving average pairing for declining markets and two MACD studies using slower moving average pairings in rising markets. So the bear market studies may need two studies with periods near 6-19-9 and 13-26-9, while the bull market may need two studies that use 5-24-8 for one, and 5-34-5 or 19-39-9 for the other. You will have to do your own testing to find the pairing combinations that will serve you best. It becomes critical to know what trend is present so that the correct study combination is applied. To determine trend, Gerald Appel tends to favor a 50-day moving average on prices. As you can see from this discussion, the smoothed oscillator requires some specialized handling, as do all oscillators. The objective of this discussion is simply to caution you not to use a single study for MACD and then to do your homework to find the best moving average pairings for your particular market and time horizon.

I learned about the need for two MACD studies while attending a lecture given by Gerald Appel at one of the Telerate Technical Analysis Seminars offered each year. As I strive to use methods that ultimately offer noncorrelated signals from varying techniques, I do not use the MACD because Stochastics and the RSI are better indicators for my needs. This doesn't mean that I view the MACD unfavorably. Rather, the specialized applications I favor in other oscillators are not greatly enhanced if the efforts are duplicated by adding the MACD. Position traders using Stochastics with the MACD for their signals will want to devote more time and research to their selected indicators. Although the MACD study does not suit my purposes, the underlying premise behind the construction of the MACD indicator and the use for multiple studies will be advantageous to many readers. So don't skip over a technical method just because you may not have an immediate application for it. In this business it pays to be a jack of all trading tools and a master of some.

As the lecture about the MACD progressed discussing the use of multiple studies and periods, it led to an idea that produced a new chart formation. In Figure 3–12 an RSI is plotted with multiple periods. Because it looks like a wave, the study variation is named the "RSI Wave." It shows the indicator using the multiple periods as a timing signal and as a defining method for some key support and

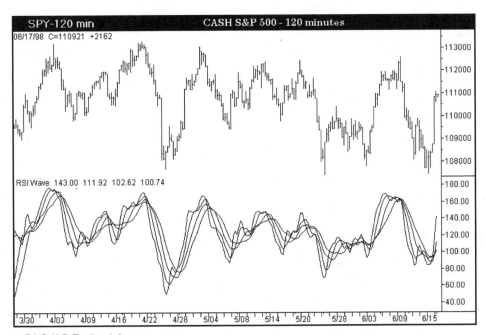

FIGURE 3-12

resistance areas in the market. The RSI Wave was an idea that grew from the thought that the multiple MACD indicators being described might be plotted all together in a single window. I have never looked further to see if the idea could be of merit for the MACD; but it is useful when applied to the RSI and Composite Index oscillators I currently favor. The underlying premise behind the formula for the MACD study also lead to an entirely new indicator that will be discussed in Chapter 14 called the "Derivative Oscillator."

CHAPTER 4

Dominant Trend Lines Are Not Always from Extreme Price Highs or Lows

We all have preexisting mental patterns that will dictate just how constrained our capacity is to learn new ideas or expand our visual perception beyond the conventional. Our ability to see the critical trend lines in prices or within our indicators will be affected by how strongly we hold onto our preconditioning. This chapter requires an active participation from you to gain the most from it. Please grab a pencil and a straightedge before we move on, and resist the temptation to turn the pages to see the solutions for the different problems. By not looking at the solution, you will consciously learn how you work within boundaries. How you attempt to find a solution is as important as the solution itself.

Let's begin with a visual puzzle that you may have seen previously. Even if you have seen this puzzle before, do try to draw an answer as it will be the visual solution to a chart problem that follows. The first puzzle is in Figure 4–1, and it displays nine squares. Here is your task. Read the instructions carefully: You must connect all nine squares by drawing four straight CONTINUOUS lines *without lifting your pencil* or RETRACING a line. You may cross over one of the four lines that you draw, but you may not retrace its path.

Turn the page and complete the puzzle before reading further.

The addition of grid lines in the background of the nine squares is intentional. It was also by design to frame the grid lines within a box that is again surrounded by an outer perimeter border. Not only does it make the puzzle harder, but it also more closely approximates what we are all actually staring at for hours on end. The puzzle is displayed on paper in the same dimensions as a computer screen. The chart's border and the frame of the computer screen all serve to precondition us. Whether you view charts with grid lines or not will make little difference. The impact in our minds to this configuration of nine squares is that we immediately try to create a

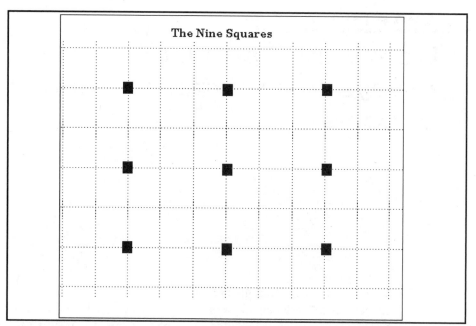

FIGURE 4-1

square and try to circumscribe it with four lines, leaving the center square untouched. The key to solving the puzzle requires that we get out of the boxes that we create for ourselves and that others have designed for us. The solution is in Figure 4-2. You may feel this is an unfair quiz because the solution requires a line to be drawn beyond the left boundary beyond the grid pattern. Read the directions closely a second time. At no time did the instructions state that you had to stay within the area marked with grid lines or stay within *any* boundary. Within the "rules" of trading markets, it at no time states that we may not scroll our data screen to the left to see if older data just out of view might contain the price pivot that is the solution to the market's current movement. Ready for another one? Good.

In Figure 4–3 we have a 120-minute chart of the Dow Jones Industrial Average. Just like the puzzle to connect the nine squares, now you will be asked to connect the nine dots. The dots are labeled 1 to 9, and the dots, of course, are the extreme price highs or lows that have been numbered in the chart. Here is your task. Connect all nine dots using only FOUR trend lines. You will not need any data out of view to draw the four lines this time. Do not turn the page until you attempt to find a solution. If you get frustrated, look at the solution for the nine squares on the opposite page. The four trend lines that will connect all nine points in the DJIA chart will be very similar to the pattern that was drawn for the nine squares. Now try to connect the dots.

You probably had a tough time if you tried to draw trend lines that always started or ended at the price high in this chart. The solution for connecting all nine price lows and highs requires seeing that two major trend lines bisect one another just left of the price high and that the critical trend that connects points 4, 5, 7, and 9 originates from the intersection of the trend lines and not the price high. We have been told that a trend line is created by drawing a line that connects two price highs or lows and when the market tests the trend line a third time, it is considered a confirmed trend. Hogwash! Erase that programming because it is misleading. It is not wrong, but markets do not operate entirely within the limitations of elementary geometry. Preconditioning can lead us down the wrong path and guide us in the wrong direction.

There isn't a trader among us that doesn't enjoy a good story. So let me digress a moment and share with you a funny story that was first told in *Aerodynamic Trading*.[1] This is a story that illustrates just how preconditioning will influence our ability to make decisions.

The story begins on a hot summer's day as I was driving along a narrow country road through the mountains of northern Georgia. The Centennial Olympic Games were approaching, and I had recently relocated from New York. There is quite a culture difference between New York and Georgia, but Georgia is beautiful, especially in the north where the Appalachian foothills lead to the mountains. Driving along, I approached a narrow bridge on the winding road. Near the last bend in the road before the bridge, another car was coming toward me, around that turn. As we passed, the driver made gestures with his arm out the window and yelled, "HOG!" He quickly drove by, and I became very upset that he seemed so angry with my driving. I was clearly on my side of the road, and I had not taken, or hogged, more than my fair share. Was it my New York plates that prompted him to use the familiar gestures of a Manhattan taxicab driver? Without more time to think, I made the last sharp turn toward the bridge. I narrowly missed hitting the largest hog I had ever seen in my life! The immense porker was standing right in the middle of a single-lane bridge. That driver's one single-word warning had produced a string of emotions, artificial images, and false assumptions. The reality? There was a pig in the road—a "Hog!"

We need to use the guidelines we have been given concerning trend lines as a starting point only. Training and experience condition us to connect extreme highs and lows easily to form trend lines, but this preconditioning may prevent us from seeing more meaningful information that will allow us to act sooner from more subtle chart symmetries and formations. Let's take a closer look at some

---

[1] Constance M. Brown, *Aerodynamic Trading* (Gainesville, Georgia: New Classics Library, 1995).

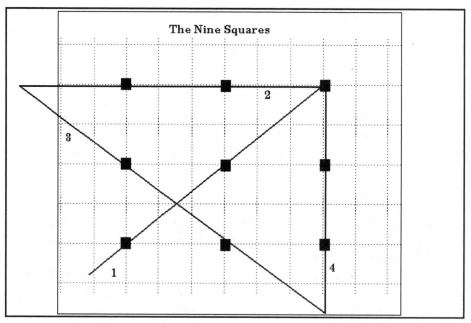

FIGURE 4-2

of the critical points in this same DJIA chart now marked with new labels in Figure 4–5.

From point 1, draw a support trend line to connect points 3, 4, and 5, and then mark a resistance level at point 6 prior to a decline. The important aspect to this trend line is knowing how to work with the spike or key reversal at point 2. More often than not, in my experience, the spikes are better left ignored in favor of connecting the high or low that immediately follows the spike. At point 2 the spike drops through the trend line, but the market low that follows in the next bar is on the trend line that defines support for points 3, 4, and 5. Point 7 has become the key to this puzzle as the descending trend line of greatest importance originates from the apex just left of the price high. The apex was formed by connecting points 1 to 5 and then 8 to 11, then extending the trend lines as far as possible in both directions. Always extend trend lines as the point where trend lines bisect may mark the timing for a market turn.

I will repeat myself to emphasize this point. Not only do you want to extend trend lines forward to find a price level for future market support or resistance but also to find the location where trend lines bisect because that point will frequently project the *timing* of a market turn before it has occurred. In Figure 4–6 a daily chart of the S&P 500 futures market shows trend lines that have been extended forward as far right as possible. Each trend line is numbered at its point of origin. All the trend lines in this chart, with the exception of trend line 4, illustrate the prior discussion in that it can be seen that trend lines should start from the price extreme that is *behind* the key reversal or spike rather than from the actual price low or high. Study the origins of these trend lines carefully. On your own, you should evaluate how the market reacts to touching the trend lines because the information is very straightforward to interpret.

Frequently traders overlook what happens in the market when two trend lines cross over one another.

In Figure 4–6 there are seven trend lines that cross over at 10 different points within the chart. Let's start by looking at point *a* where trend lines 1 and 2 cross. A trend line must be tested by the market a third time in order to use an intersection

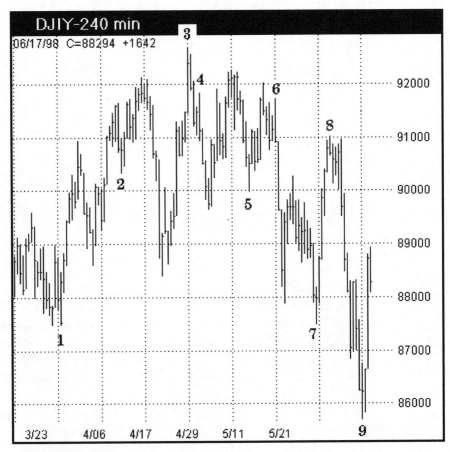

FIGURE 4-3

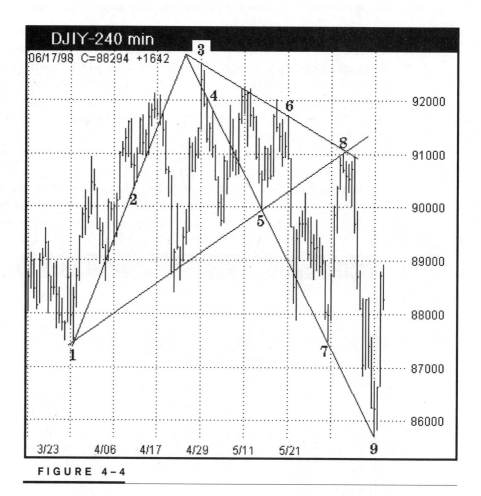

FIGURE 4-4

point as a warning that a market turn may develop. Trend lines 1 and 2 have both been tested three times so the crossover at point *a* was a valid alarm to watch for a possible trend change. When trend lines 1 and 4 cross at point *b,* the market is testing trend line 4 the third time, and the crossover can also be used as a possible timing signal for a reversal. Trend lines 1 and 3 cross at point *c* and would have been useful in alerting a trader to watch for a trend change near this time period. The operative word here is *near* this point as our other tools must provide us with the actual signal to buy or sell.

The intersection of two trend lines is a wake-up call that we need to examine our other indicators very closely. Just past intersection *c,* trend lines 3 and 4 cross. The crossover is not labeled, and someone will wonder why it has been omitted. Trend line 3 has been deliberately drawn incorrectly to illustrate where the higher probability point is located from which to draw a trend line. So please skip past this intersection and move to point *d*. At point *d* trend lines 2 and 3 intersect. The intersection is marked with an *X*. Move your eye upward to the price high in December 1997 marked *X*. The intersection at point *d* is very premature. Either this intersection has been incorrectly drawn or it is one that did not work very well. While the intersection is close to a pivot in the market as a price high does follow shortly, there is a problem with trend line 3 that we will look at separately in a moment. At intersection *e* trend lines 4 and 6 cross. Trend line 6 is being tested for the third time by the market and can be used as a timing signal now as well as a support level. Moving along to intersection *f* where trend lines 5 and 6 cross will emphasize that the crossover is a timing signal for a market pivot and not just a support or resistance price objective. The market has a minor setback that corresponds to point *f* and is of value only as a timing signal as the market does not use these trend lines as a support level. Point *g* is not a timing

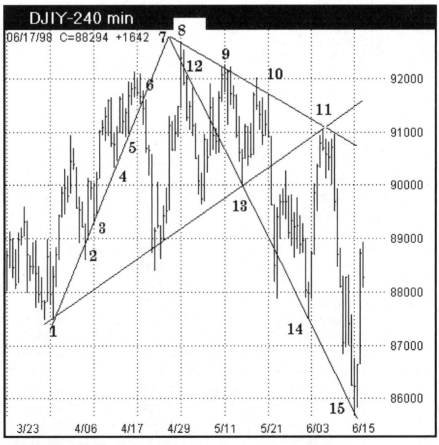

FIGURE 4-5

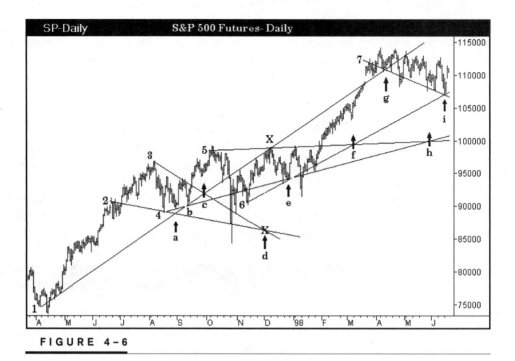

FIGURE 4-6

signal as the price levels near *g* have been used to establish trend line 7. However, point *i* where trend line 7 crosses 6 is an extremely important time projection for a possible trend reversal. The final point on this chart, *h,* is where trend lines 4 and 5 cross. This point illustrates why the intersection point is suggested to be a time estimate for a possible market turn, not a precise forecast. Use other indicators and methods in conjunction with this method. I should add that I use this method only in longer-horizon charts, such as daily, weekly, and monthly bar charts. It is this tool that helps me keep my perspective when I view shorter time horizon charts. It is the 2-by-4 across the head that I need sometimes to warn me to back up and take a closer look at the longer-horizon charts when I become too fixated on the shorter-horizon view.

Let's go back to trend line 3 that produced the only questionable timing signal in this daily chart. In Figure 4–6 the origin of trend line 3 is at the price high just one bar behind the actual market high. However, earlier it was stated that in my experience key reversals and spikes should be ignored when you start to draw a trend line. Look what happens in Figure 4–7 when the price high *behind* the key reversal is used to start the trend line. The key reversal itself is a market failure above the trend line. That is exactly what a key reversal is: a market failure. The angle for trend line 2 has not been touched in Figure 4–7 from where it was placed in Figure 4–8. However, changing the origin of trend line 3 alters the timing when trend lines 2 and 3 cross. The new intersection becomes a very significant change. Now the crossover of trend lines 2 and 3 mark one of the more important market turns as it was the start of the rally in 1998. Draw trend lines so that key reversals and spike pivots are consistent for what we already know them to be: market failure patterns that denote a possible trend change.

At the end of this chapter there will be a few more chart quizzes for you to try. Trend lines that you see drawn in a finished chart will rob you of the opportunity to evaluate where the lines might have been drawn using your own mind's eye. So know that a few more quizzes will be offered. But first we need to discuss trend lines on indicators so that they can be included.

Oscillators, like price data, can have extreme highs connected to define areas of resistance or oscillator lows connected to define areas of support. However, as with trend lines on price data, there is another way that will produce targets of greater significance for oscillators. The end result will show that the oscillator will be respecting these trend lines more often than just a conventional line that connects extremes. Here is the difference: Draw trend lines only from oscillator peaks or troughs that mean something to us. Therefore, draw trend lines from oscillator peaks or troughs that form bullish or bearish divergence with price. As recommended for

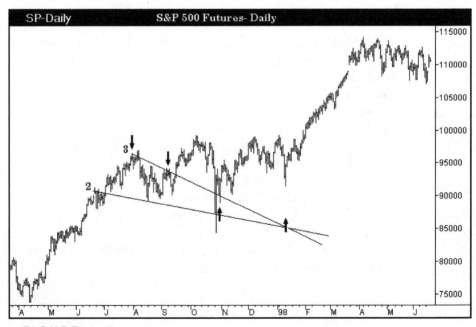

FIGURE 4-7

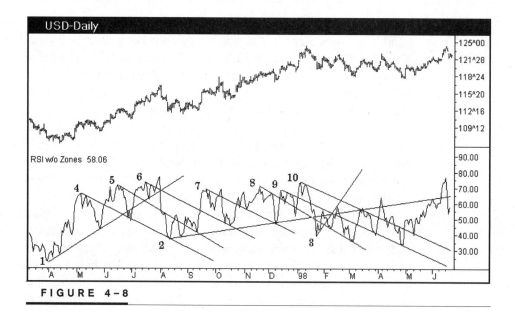

FIGURE 4-8

trend lines on prices, we will extend the trend lines as far forward as possible on oscillators.

Figure 4–8 shows a daily chart for U.S. Bond futures. All the trend lines are drawn by using two oscillator lows or highs that formed divergences with the closing-price bars. Trend lines 1, 2, and 3 are bullish divergences with price. The oscillator makes a higher low when the corresponding closing price makes a lower low. Trend lines 4 through 10 are all associated with bullish divergences. The first and second oscillator peak form lower highs, but corresponding closing prices are higher. While Figure 4–8 uses this method of drawing trend lines on the RSI, the method can be applied to any oscillator.

Before we move away from Figure 4–8, it should be noted that the scale used to plot RSI or any oscillator is important. The range RSI plotted in Figure 4–8 is altered from the standard default of 0 to 100. If the normal range for an oscillator is 0 to 100, vendors will always plot the indicator using this maximum scale. You want to see the indicator as large as possible. So if the range is within a bull market, you might change the default to a range of 25 to 90. In a bear market the scale might be 15 to 70. You never want to limit the details available for interpretation by compressing the scale of your indicator. In addition, the computer system you use should allow for an oscillator to be viewed in at least 50 percent of the computer screen's height. Otherwise, you are likely to be working from a ticker-tape-size indicator that fits in a small narrow band at the bottom of the screen. On such a scale, it would be difficult to differentiate an electroencephalogram versus the RSI.

The most one can hope to interpret from either chart displayed in this manner would be that neither had become a flat line! The same can be said for published chart books that add for our convenience a squashed indicator at the bottom of the page. These charts are for people who want to know only when an indicator is at an extreme. There is limited value in viewing indicators in this manner.

Let's move forward and discuss using horizontal trend lines on oscillators. There are two kinds of oscillators: those that have been normalized and will confine the travel of the indicator to stay within a range such as 0 to 100, and those whose formulas allow movement to any extreme. There is great value in using one of each type of oscillator to compensate for a rather serious problem inherent with normalized oscillators such as the RSI and Stochastics.

The following question illustrates the problem with normalized oscillators: "An atom always moves one-half the distance from its current location toward a fixed object. How many times will it have to move from a distance of 1 mile presently to reach the fixed object?" As the atom moves only one-half the distance, it will not reach the fixed object until the diameter of its own size represents more than one-half of the remaining distance. The rate of travel toward the fixed object will become extremely slow the closer the atom gets as the distance covered is smaller and smaller. This is how normalized indicators function, and it is why a normalized oscillator at an extreme oversold or overbought position can appear locked while a market produces a meltdown or ballistic rally against what would seem impossible to the oscillator.

In Figure 4–9 an 80-minute bar chart of the Japanese Yen per U.S. Dollars is displayed. Below the price data is the Composite Index. The Composite Index is a custom formula that will be discussed separately, but for now it is important to know that it is a formula that has not been normalized. This oscillator is capable of traveling below zero or above 100. Plotted below the Composite Index is the RSI using a 14-period interval. There are several key oscillator lows that have been labeled with the letters *a* through *k*. In the Composite Index a horizontal trend line has been drawn to connect the oscillator lows at points *a, b,* and *c.* A similar horizontal trend line is drawn on the RSI using points *f* and *h.* Why was the line drawn at points *f* and *h* and not from the low at point *g* for the RSI? If you look to the far left, the RSI tested the same level as *f* and *h* once before. In addition, we are using this horizontal trend line in a different way. The horizontal line needs to be drawn at the level that shows the greatest number of oscillator lows. The line is then viewed as the normal range for the oscillator within present market conditions. At point *g* the RSI makes a minor violation of this trend line. A trend line that the market used as its major support level will nearly always be tested.

In the case of interpreting the RSI, one could establish a long dollar position at point *h* as the old range is being tested. Keep in mind that oscillators plot

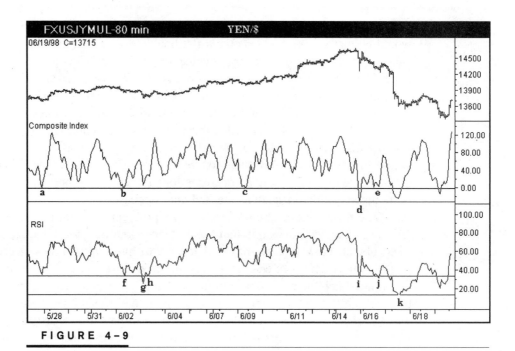

FIGURE 4-9

prices only on the close, and a sharp spike down that closed at current levels
would have the same oscillator position. This is not a buy-sell signal. Now move
your eye to point *i* on the RSI. The low the RSI makes at *i* can be interpreted as
a test of this trend line. The same market move, however, moved the Composite
Index to point *d, which warns that the market conditions are changing.* What follows from point *d* is an advance, and the Composite Index then pulls back as the
Yen strengthens (chart prices decline). While the Composite Index forms a W, or
double bottom, at point *e,* the RSI once again tests the trend line at point *j.* If only
the RSI were viewed, the second test at point *j* could easily be interpreted as a
completed correction in an slightly overextended, but secure, uptrending market.
Instead, the Composite Index has warned that market conditions may be changing,
and once the prior support level is tested at point *e,* the character of the market
should be carefully observed.

In this situation the oscillator advances from point *e* without the price data
following proportionately. If you pick up only a single notion from this book, let
it be the following: *When an oscillator advances or declines disproportionately
to the markets' movement, you are on the wrong side of the market if you are positioned with the oscillator.* In market downtrends, oscillators will travel rapidly
upward as a market correction develops, and the opposite will be true for uptrend-

ing markets. In Figure 4–9 the Composite Index begins to advance rapidly beyond point *e,* and though the oscillator is capable of advancing, prices fail to exceed minimum objectives for a rally. Intervention then occurs to support the Yen showing that the market drop could have been technically forecasted. The RSI does not warn that conditions changed until after the fact at point *k,* which is too late.

If the oscillator low at point *d* is a new extreme move for the indicator, a horizontal trend line should be drawn and maintained on the chart. If the prior range resumes and this oscillator low scrolls off the screen to the left, it will no longer be in view. However, over the life of the market or contract, the level will be recorded. Should the market drop to new extremes, it is frequently to these prior levels, and the old horizontal trend line would once again become visible. The same should be done for oscillator peaks.

One last comment about trend lines on oscillators: It was demonstrated how the intersection of trend lines drawn on price could be used as an indication of the timing of a market reversal. This is less so for oscillators unless a change is made. To increase the probability of trend lines' forecasting market turns from an oscillator, the indicator should be plotted by hand. The reason for resorting to manual drafting is that the oscillator scale versus time will be linear. Computer screens are not linear. The *x*-axis and *y*-axis are never a 1-to-1 ratio for their grid lines. A computer with approximately 240 characters side to side will only have 24 lines from top to bottom. This will vary with screen resolution. If the effort is made to chart

F I G U R E   4 – 1 0

oscillators by hand for longer-horizon work, it will be found that intersecting trend lines will have greater accuracy and importance than those drawn on price or indicator by a computer.

The time has come to test some of the concepts discussed in this chapter. There are no wrong or right answers concerning trend lines, but one method of drawing a line could prove to be of greater value to the trader than another. There will be two charts from which you can test your own eye.

Figure 4–10 is the German DAX Index. Find these trend lines:

- The four major trend lines on price that show why the double top in prices has occurred in the most recent data
- Two significant levels of support for this same market with which to identify the nearby objectives for a pullback
- In the RSI, the trend lines that mark the levels of greatest current interest for this indicator

Figure 4–11 displays the trend lines that I would have favored for this chart. There are numerous small arrows to show you that once a trend line is started, the angle of the line is set by using key points that fall in the middle or midsection of the chart in an effort to minimize errors that would occur in the most recent data. The *T* under the RSI pivot is a time projection that has become a support level.

FIGURE 4–11

When we address price objectives, we will reverse-engineer a price target from the oscillator. Clearly, if the oscillator could decline to point *T*, it would be of value to know beforehand at what market price the oscillator would realize point *T*. That is a topic we will approach at another time.

Let's move on to the last trend line quiz and discuss Figure 4–12 displaying a 20-minute bar chart for the September U.S. Bond market. This time you have the Composite Index and the RSI plotted against price. We have discussed drawing trend lines on oscillators that diverge with prices, but trend lines can also be drawn from divergences between indicators. In Figure 4–12 a few key bullish and bearish divergences between the oscillators are already marked so that you may be introduced to this concept. As a short-horizon trader, you have two critical questions to answer:

1. What trend line is present within the price data to have caused the bond market high in the last bar to stall? The market has already exceeded the nearby moving average displayed on price; visually you will want to see why the market has not advanced further (marked with a black arrow on the price scale).

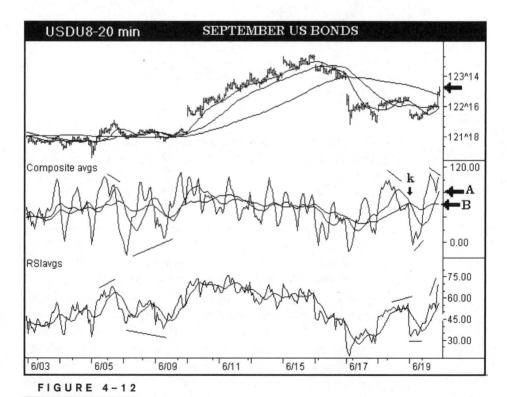

FIGURE 4–12

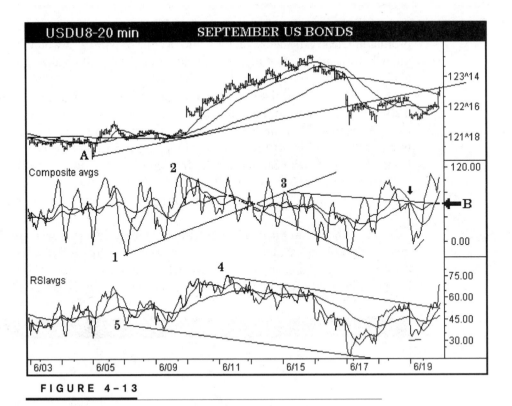

FIGURE 4-13

2. If the market pulls back from this trend line that caused the market to stall, what moving average in the Composite Index, marked with arrows *A* and *B,* will the oscillator likely decline toward? If you know the moving average that is most likely to be the target, you will be able to calculate a price objective before-hand or recognize the price level once the indicator has declined. The Composite Index graph has an indicator peak marked with a black arrow. The peak *forms underneath the point where two moving averages cross over.* This is a major signal that will be discussed in the next chapter. The trend line you draw on the Composite Index should bisect this important peak. (The RSI in this case is used to find the divergences that form in the Composite Index. You will find that the trend lines on the RSI will be less informative as to the preceding questions.)

In Figure 4–13, trend line *A* marks the reason that prices have stalled at current levels. Trend lines 1 and 2 on the Composite oscillator are drawn from divergences between the RSI and the Composite Index. Trend line 1 is derived from a major bullish divergence formation, and projected forward, it actually identifies the oscillator peak of greatest value to start trend line 3. As trend line 3 originates from a peak that respects trend line 1 and crosses the peak marked with the black arrow, it is moving average B that would offer a price objective for bonds.

Both the Price and Oscillator windows have included moving averages. In Figure 4–12 the RSI displays only a single moving average so that the RSI can be more easily seen. In Figure 4–13 both averages calculated from the RSI are displayed. Using averages on indicators is extremely valuable and will be the topic for discussion in the next chapter.

CHAPTER 5

Signals from Moving Averages Are Frequently Absent in Real-Time Charts

"How did I miss such an obvious signal like that one?" Chances are that you did not miss the signal; it may not have been present when you were considering the trade. Many traders suspect that signals may have appeared differently to them in real-time, but few take the time to really explore the character of the indicators from which they trade. What do I mean by the "character of an indicator"? The character of an indicator is how it moves across the computer screen relative to other indicators or data. The character is also the psychological change we experience because the computer changes the y-axis scale to display for us a range defined by the maximum high and low within a fixed number of bars. As new data enters on the right side of our screen and old data scrolls off on the left, new extreme highs or lows in price or an indicator may lead to a new y-axis scale to accommodate the data.

Technical analysis software allows traders to scroll backward to view historical data (*scroll*—not click the page number and press GO, which is not a technical analysis system). Scrolling offers an interesting means to observe indicators. Scroll forward from the first bar in your database as *FAST* as possible toward the most current data. It will be important to scroll forward and watch the movement that occurs nearest the new data entering the screen on the right. Clearly, not much will be gained from a monthly chart as the objective is to scroll through as many new data points as possible for this exercise. As an example, view a 15-minute chart that has 500 bars in its history. The character you will see in your indicators in a 15-minute bar chart will be a subset or micropicture for what will develop in longer time-horizon bar charts for the same market. In a sense you will be animating the still pictures that are normally viewed as static charts except for the changes that occur in the most current bar.

By not looking at specifics and animating our indicators, just for purposes of observation, we are able to see that the undulations of our indicators may dramatically change their relative positions and scale as new data is added to the right-hand side of the computer screen. Traders must know if the indicators they trade from rescale or operate within fixed boundaries. Do the indicators we use as graph additions on prices or other indicators shift their positions over time?

As mentioned earlier, I often take a snapshot or freeze-frame picture of an intraday trading screen just after an order has been entered. The purpose is to allow a later evaluation of why the trigger was pulled at that precise moment to enter or exit the trade. Figures 5–1, 5–2, and 5–3 are all intraday charts. Figure 5–1 is a 3-minute S&P bar chart. A good point of reference is the 11:06 time grid mark on the *x*-axis. Figures 5–2 and 5–3 are much longer intraday bar charts for different markets that remain anonymous. All three examples have an oscillator high or low that is marked *T*1 in the left window and *T*2 on the right. In each figure pairing, you are looking at the exact same indicator and market. *T*1 shows the appearance of the indicator at time 1. The *T*2, or time 2, label is the same indicator peak or low viewed at a later time. Slow Stochastics, MACD, or for that matter *any* indicator that has a smoothed variable in its formula calculated by applying a moving average, is capable of experiencing the dramatic changes demonstrated in Figures

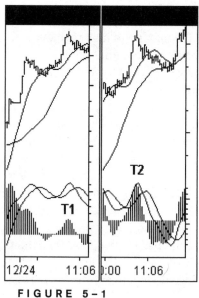

FIGURE 5 – 1

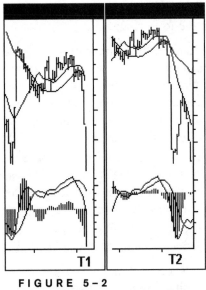

F I G U R E   5 – 2

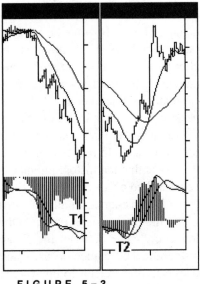

F I G U R E   5 – 3

5–1 through 5–3. The degree to which you will see such a dramatic shift will depend on the following:

1. Consider the formula of the indicator and the type of moving average that is used. Does it use a simple or exponential average, for example? The impact on the current period will be affected by the type of weighting applied to the number of bars being averaged. The smoothing technique selected will also determine how significant it will be for the current bar when extreme ranges drop out of the moving average calculation.

2. The time period or number of bars to be averaged remains the same, but the time interval is volatile. Also, the fewer the elements averaged, the greater will be the displacement that occurs. Short moving averages are extremely dynamic.

3. The size of the window you have chosen to display an indicator will define the number of bars used to chart the y-axis scale.

In Figures 5–1 through 5–3, the charts are all narrow-width windows displaying a limited number of bars at any one time. This was deliberately done to exaggerate the distortion possible with indicators plotted from intraday data on a computer using Microsoft's *Windows 95/98* platform. As soon as we are given the ability to define our own dimensions for a chart's size, our natural tendency is to overdo our adjustments. If you like your trading screens to display a mosaic of numerous small windows at one time, just beware that you may want to enlarge a single smaller window to full screen size before making a final judgment.

In Figure 5–1 the oscillator peak is nowhere near the moving averages charted above the oscillator at time interval $T1$. However, at time interval $T2$, the exact same oscillator peak appears much larger in scale and has moved directly under the moving averages, allowing an interpretation in hindsight that the oscillator was peaking directly under resistance. In real-time it was not. The reason $T2$ is so different from $T1$ in Figure 5–1 is that the histogram indicator with the highest peak to the far left of $T1$ has now scrolled off the screen and the computer has rescaled the y axis to plot the histogram. (The histogram in all three of the figures is the spread or differential between the two moving averages on prices that are charted in the top window.) There is also a dramatic change between the $T1$ and $T2$ moving averages relative to the oscillator histogram. The change occurs when the look-back period for the averages no longer uses extremes in their rolling forward calculations as the oldest data drops out of the formulas for simple moving averages. Simple moving average periods using the common Fibonacci numbers of 5 and 8 are extremely vulnerable to displacement. They are of great value, but a trader should be cognizant of the dynamic character of shorter-period simple moving averages and make allowances in their interpretation of them in real-time environments.

In Figure 5–2 a sharp market decline develops. The most recent bar at $T1$ records the oscillator and moving averages as they appeared in real-time. Stochastics, RSI, and MACD—in fact, most indicators—use the closing price to calculate the indicator. Some indicators do not see current bars as they cannot calculate the position of the indicator until the next bar forward. In Figure 5–2 the indicators for $T1$ are actually off by one bar because of the nature of their formulas, and they do not know that the market is in a freefall. The averages near $T2$ have been recalculated, and it appears that ideal support was tested by an oversold oscillator in hindsight. This was not the case at $T1$, and what complicates the matter is that the histogram is the differential of the two moving averages on price. So now $T1$ is at least two bars behind. The MACD operates in this manner. $T1$ was in fact an oscillator at an extreme low equal to the low of a prior oscillator extreme recorded a few weeks earlier for the same time interval charted.

Recall the discussion about using a horizontal trend line to mark historical displacement extremes of maximum resistance and support for oscillators. In this case an "extreme" trend line marked a couple of weeks earlier would reappear as the computer rescales the y-axis. When markets are in extreme conditions, I will use indicators that have been expressly tested for extreme situations only and ignore those that are known to perform poorly in a different climate. Sometimes the same indicator is used, but the interpretation can be different. *In this situation only the histogram is viewed and the averages are ignored.* An oscillator tracking intraday data that are currently at an extreme position that has not been seen in over two weeks is a major piece of technical information. Add an Elliott Wave pattern or a price projection system to this oscillator extreme, and we know a signal to buy exists at $T1$ that could lead to a sharp sling-shot rebound. As the oscillator had declined to the extremes made over two weeks ago and had entered a new range for the indicator, it would also be known that the oscillator would most likely decline to test the prior support lows that defined the range for the last week. Such an indicator move would likely produce a new price low. If you did not know how this indicator performed in different market situations, a trader might have sold at the precise low of $T1$ just prior to a short squeeze rally. The breakout trader is the most vulnerable to this type of trap. It will also be a high-risk scenario for the Elliott Wave trader who relies on price patterns alone. By understanding the high-probability patterns that develop in oscillators, we can anticipate the next indicator signals before they even appear on the screen.

Once market direction is anticipated, price projection methods can be applied, allowing trades in the market from both sides or at least allowing a market position to be entered with the larger trend that has a minimal capital exposure because we can use tighter stops. There are specific oscillator patterns that will warn us that such a rebound is a countertrend rally in addition to the range rules defined for oscillators. There are oscillator patterns that will be discussed in the price projection section of this book that will offer confirmation that the larger trend will resume.

In Figure 5–3 the oscillator at *T*1 shows bullish divergence compared to the new price lows that develop. Once the oscillator extreme to the left of *T*1 scrolls out of view, the moving averages jump up and move to just under the oscillator at point *T*2. It may seem hard to believe that *T*1 and *T*2 are identical indicators that are being viewed at a later time.

This demonstration does not discredit technical analysis; it does, however, discredit some display setups and warns that extremely short horizon trading is even more vulnerable to these differences between real-time trade decisions and postmortem evaluations. Most analysts are unaware of the dynamic nature that surrounds the current bar on our trading screens. But the analyst or trader that does have an intimate knowledge about the indicators used and understands how their quote vendor calculates and incorporates current data into their formulas will be able to forecast the future travel of their indicators and the market.

It is important to recognize that indicators on prices, or indicators on other indicators, are dynamic and will change their positions once the most recent bar moves to the left and becomes a part of the historical record constantly building. In some cases, we must knowingly jump in front of the indicator signals because we know they will appear perfectly aligned once 10 bars or so of new data have been added to the screen. As an example, we may decide to buy when the market has declined to an objective but the price data remains much higher than the moving average that was being monitored. The knowledge that the moving average will in fact shift upward into a permanent position will allow a trader to pull the trigger with confidence because the signal in real-time can be correctly interpreted. While the shift will appear minor in weekly charts, the capital exposure in question will be far greater, so weekly position traders are not excluded from this discussion, *especially if they use moving averages to define initial or trailing stop placement.*

We must know how our indicators are constructed, the impact of our trading time horizon on these indicators, the scale that is normal for charting an indicator, and then, how the indicator responds in normal and extreme market movements in real-time conditions. It is only after endless hours of careful observation that these indicator changes become finely woven into the fabric of our intuition.

Is intuition a gut feeling, some sixth sense, or inner wisdom that some traders are blessed to have had since birth? I think not, as a direct knowing without conscious use of reasoning can come only after extensive training and preparation. Intuitive knowing is the essential key for success in fast-paced environments. We do not have the luxury of time to think. Three-time Super Bowl Most Valuable Player Joe Montana once stated, "If I ever stopped to think about what happens after the ball hits my hands, it might screw up the whole process." Yogi Berra, baseball legend, stated, "How can you think and hit at the same time?" Both sports legends had to practice thousands of times until their actions became intuitive. As traders, if we have to worry about how an indicator might change with the passing of time, the critical timing of making the trade will be destroyed and will minimize the results. We need to know our indicators through such elaborate study that what we learn becomes effortless and automated. The easiest part of our job is to pick up the phone and say "Buy" or "Sell." Some readers will be disturbed by the dramatic displacement of the indicators displayed in the first three figures. If this information about indicator dynamics is new to you, it will open the door to many hours of hard work that must be done. You will need to resolve the questions this discussion will undoubtedly leave behind with you about your own indicators in real-time scenarios. Answer the indicator questions before the markets answer them for you. Either way, the questions will be answered over time.

It is also helpful to apply indicators to markets that we normally do not trade so that we can experience how our indicators will respond to market movements and conditions that we may not be accustomed to viewing. This will train and prepare us for those occasions when our principal market changes its character and begins to adopt some other markets' action. An example would be the recent transition that occurred in the 1990s in the S&P 500, which now acts more like a commodity market than a financial market as it did in the 1980s.

With the knowledge that moving averages on oscillators or prices will be dynamic in real-time conditions, we can now move forward and discuss using moving averages profitably. There are numerous discussions elsewhere in published books that detail the different kinds of moving averages and comparisons of how to use alternatives to closing prices. I have elected not to cover ground here that has already been well traveled. But if you need to reinforce your understanding of the different types of averages used in our industry, a good reference can be found in Perry Kaufman's book *The New Commodity Trading Systems and Methods* [1]. For now, our discussion will focus on applying moving averages to three oscillators: Stochastics, the RSI, and the custom oscillator Composite Index. Adding moving averages to traditional plots for the RSI or Stochastics will require some custom setup changes to most quote vendors' software.

In Figure 5–4 are the PowerEditor formulas required to add moving averages to Omega's *TradeStation*. Other vendors will gladly convert these equations for you to fit their system's charting conventions. The periods that work best for you should replace the unknown variables *X, Y,* and *Z* within the first lines that state

---

[1] Perry J. Kaufman, *The New Commodity Trading Systems and Methods* (New York: Wiley, 1987), pp. 58–90.

```
Indicator:  Stochastics+Avgs
Input: Length(X),PERIOD(Y),PERIOD2(Z);
plot1(FastK(Length),"FastK");
plot2(FastD(Length),"FastD");
plot3(Average(FastD(Length),PERIOD),"Plot3");
plot4(Average(FastD(Length),PERIOD2),"Plot4");



Indicator:  RSI+Avgs
Input: LENGTH(14),PERIOD(Y),PERIOD2(Z);
Plot1(RSI(Close,LENGTH),"Plot1");
Plot2(Average((RSI(Close,LENGTH)),PERIOD),"Plot2");
Plot3(XAverage((RSI(Close,LENGTH)),PERIOD2),"Plot3");
```

FIGURE 5-4

LENGTH(X), PERIOD(Y), and PERIOD2(Z). The RSI will be using a fixed period of 14 for reasons that will be addressed later. Now that you know how the charts can be constructed, let's take a detailed look at the results and interpretation.

In Figure 5–5 the Weekly German Deutsche Mark per U.S. Dollar is charted with a Fast Stochastics study that includes two moving averages. When a Slow Stochastics is used, or %D is smoothed, it is smoothed by a moving average. This chart alternative simply offers more flexibility and was taught to me by George Lane; the originator of the Stochastics formula, and by Andrew Cardwell, who is the world's authority on using the Relative Strength Index. Both of these industry leaders add two moving averages to their oscillators because doing so adds tremendous clarification and depth in the oscillators' interpretation that may otherwise be easily overlooked.

In Figure 5–5 the Stochastics study has a short- and longer-period moving average. We begin the chart evaluation at point 1, which is where the Stochastics study has rolled up to test the point where two moving averages are crossing over one another. If the shorter moving average is crossing down through the longer period, the signal is bearish if the indicator fails at this intersection. In real-time the shorter moving average would most likely not have crossed the longer-period average, but Stochastics would still be failing under the averages. The sharp angle of descent in the shorter-period moving average would be accurate, and one can easily see that an intersection would form if the oscillator failed to break above the longer average. At point 2 the moving average is tested by Stochastics after the indicator breaks above the longer average and fails. The important difference is that at point 2 the Stochastics indicator is staying above the shorter average, and in previous attempts the Stochastics indicator was below the short-period average. As we know, short-period moving averages will shift upward into their permanent chart positions from the real-time chart position, and the Stochastics indicator would have been slightly higher than the short-period average, giving a stronger signal than what is present in this chart.

Point 3 shows a double top in the indicator *under the longer moving average*. An M pattern in the indicator can be interpreted as a double top provided the pattern forms under the trending average. Is Stochastics really under the average at point 3? The slower component of Stochastics remains under resistance so it is viewed as a market failure signal. At point 4 the faster component %K breaks below the moving average, but the slower %D stays above the average. The angle of ascent in the shorter period is important as it is soon to intersect the slower

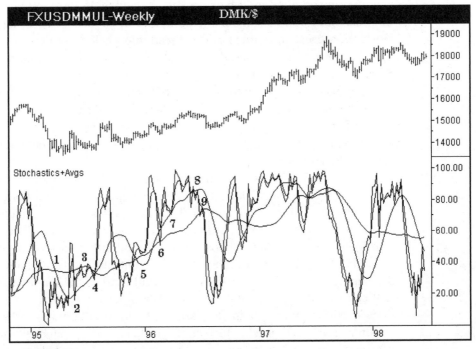

FIGURE 5-5

moving average. Therefore, point 4 occurs at an intersection and is a stronger signal. Oscillators frequently respond to such formations in the same way as one would jump from a trampoline. The market accelerates from signals like point 4, as the dollar does in this chart. The oscillator then travels into highs that form an M-pattern top and then breaks sharply. Note where the oscillator stalls briefly near the averages and then breaks below. This break requires the use of more than one method and a knowledge about the normal character of currency markets. Using the Elliott Wave Principle, a trader would suspect a series of first and second waves are developing. Whether you knew this or not, a trader should know that currency markets commonly form deep retracements early in their transition to a trend change. Second waves very often retrace nearly all of the early first waves.

There is an extremely important juxtaposition in the Stochastics oscillator lows that develop just prior to point 5 compared to point 4. The oscillator low at point 4 is higher than the current Stochastics position, but the prices on close for these corresponding lows are higher. Therefore, the indicator is becoming oversold at higher price levels, which denotes growing market strength. At point 4 the oscillator stays above the longer moving average for the first time, and it is a trader's last warning that the trend reversal is now in force. The Stochastics pullback at point 5 is at the support zone for a bull market, testing the 45 level in this situation. The information at point 5 is overwhelming that the dollar wants to attempt a rally. However, because most traders do not read information from the Stochastics other than divergences at extremes, they would not be aware of this important signal. The Stochastics indicator then jumps upward and pulls back a second time to test the longer moving average. Notice at point 6 that the %D component of Stochastics is above the shorter moving average while %K tests the slower moving average. This relationship would have been important in real-time as more likely the %D would have been testing the longer average. The signal is the same, but the shift in hindsight could have been anticipated.

At point 7 Stochastics remains above both the moving averages, which is where it would have been in real-time as the angle of ascent for both averages has been in force for some time without change. At points 8 and 9 a gradual trend shift develops as the indicator rolls under the averages. As the oscillator then breaks sharply to the screen lows opposite point 2, but with prices staying much higher than what formed at point 2, the decline is confirmed to be a correction within a developing uptrend. Points 1 through 9 detail most of the important patterns that will be seen between moving averages on a Stochastics study. Note the series of three W bottoms that form in Stochastics after the oscillator low in 1996. The third W forms near the 75 level, which conforms to an earlier statement that one would have permission to buy the market when the Stochastics pulled back to the 75 level in an uptrend. Confirmation of the signal is present because the two moving averages have a positive differential; that is to say that the shorter-period average is higher than the longer period. This is a price projection that accompanies this pull-back and it will be discussed later. But in a quick summary the market has only attained half the distance it will achieve from the prices that developed at the oscillator lows in 1996 up to the price highs that followed prior to the current buy signal in Stochastics. We'll go into more detail on price projections at another time. Let's take a look at a chart applying the RSI indicator.

The weekly DMK/$ chart is again displayed in Figure 5–6, but this time with a 14-period RSI that includes two moving averages. The two averages in this chart use the exact same period, but one is a simple moving average while the other is an exponential moving average. In my own charts I will use one fast simple moving average and one slower exponential moving average. In Figure 5–6 the signals are discussed for the RSI as the indicator relates to a single average. You need to decide if you prefer to use the simple or exponential moving average formula. In Figure 5–4 the true formula I use was given to you, but Figure 5–6 shows that you may elect to use two exponential averages or two simple averages. It becomes a matter of how you want the real-time displacement to be handled relative to this indicator, which can be determined only if you evaluate the differences on your own.

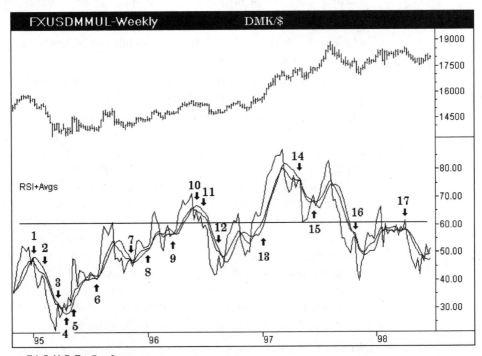

FIGURE 5–6

In Figure 5–6 a horizontal line near the 60 level has been added to help your eye see when the RSI is failing at the upper zone for a bear market or using the zone as support in a bull market environment. The same market and chart was used with just the RSI when we discussed detecting trend reversals in the first chapter. This chart interpretation adds another dimension of detail. Points 1, 2, and 3 are all RSI pivots that occur below the moving average. Points 4, 5, and 6 are also straightforward, showing the RSI pivots developing above the averages.

The RSI at point 7 is more difficult to interpret in this chart. Is point 7 a failure to exceed the averages that will lead to a market decline? This is the same point that was so distinctive and clearly a buy signal for Figure 5–5 when the Stochastics were discussed. So is something wrong with the RSI, or is this a contradiction between oscillator formulas? What is wrong is that the slower exponential RSI is not displayed in this chart, but if it were present, it would show that the RSI was forming a buy signal at the same time as the Stochastics. But the difficulty is not in the omission of an average; *it is in making a blatant observation about an oscillator relative to a moving average without giving it further consideration once the first interpretation has been made.* How often are we satisfied because we have formed "an answer" to the puzzle at hand, after which we confidently move on to something else?

There is a wealth of information developing at and around point 7 that has been overlooked:

1. The two RSI oscillator lows that straddle the high at point 7 form bullish divergences with prices.

2. This divergence is occurring above the 40 to 45 support zone defined as the lower range for a bull market.

3. In addition, the price level on close associated with the oscillator peak at point 3 is the *same price area* that forms the bullish divergence oscillator lows surrounding point 7. An oscillator that once formed a peak at a price level that later develops an oscillator low is a market that has found a former resistance level of great significance and the former area of resistance has become support. These signals can occur at extreme oscillator lows, or they can develop in the midpoint of travel and become hidden signals. The hidden signals are in fact far more powerful than the patterns that form at the oscillator extremes because they are frequently confirming signals that developed earlier in the same chart or within the chart time horizon that is longer than the present chart. In other words, this signal in a weekly chart may be confirming a signal that formed in the monthly chart much earlier.

With or without the slower moving average on the RSI, the signal is bullish. The pivot high at point 7 is just a stall for time. We need to consider this signal that develops in the lows surrounding point 7 further. It was stated above that frequently these hidden signals are confirmations for an earlier signal located in a longer-horizon chart. It is this transfer and confirmation of signals from long time horizon charts right down into shorter time horizons that increases the probability of the signal in the shortest time horizon used to decide when the position should be entered. A similar formation seen in a 60-minute chart may in fact be the last hidden warning of a ballistic rally that has been building within a market for months. The progression of signals that develops from month, week, day, intraday charts, and through the different time horizons we use for trading a market is in essence a domino effect. A few dominos' being out of sequence is the warning we need to find an alternative path that a market may travel in order to realign all these domino signals into their correct sequential order. This is how more complex market corrections can be detected before they develop and how patterns such as time-consuming triangles versus sharp quick pullbacks can be anticipated before they develop.

Often I have been asked, "How could you have possibly known a complex correction would have developed instead of a fairly quick simple one?" It is this struggle to understand how all the pieces of the domino puzzle will fit together that brings results. This aspect of fitting different time horizons together into a sequential order is exactly what I do in my analytic work between international markets. An example of how this method is applied is offered in Appendix A, where the Yen/$ has been identified as the key to understanding the next major move for the American S&P 500 Index. The indicators in fact were ignored for the S&P in favor of believing that the Yen/$ would be the first trigger signal that would cause the chain reaction of falling domino signals throughout the Global financial complex and ultimately dictate the short-horizon direction for the S&P 500. Our markets are interlinked and complex. Companies that strongly believe each market is an independent entity have not kept pace with the expanding Global communication highways that are tying us all more closely together. Technical analysis offers us a universal language to assimilate the masses of fundamental reports printed in foreign languages. Without the techniques offered by technical analysis, we could not possibly process all the Global fundamental factors in time to make a correct decision about probable market direction. It is for this reason that the number of people using technical analysis is growing.

Returning to Figure 5–6, points 8 and 9 show oscillator lows over a moving average that are easily interpreted as buy signals preceding a dollar rally. However, take a look at the oscillator pivot low that forms between points 8 and 9. The oscillator low is below point 8, though at a corresponding higher price. This is confirmation of an uptrend as the oscillator became oversold at a higher price showing market strength. Points 10, 11, and 12 all form oscillator peaks below the average.

The averages again clearly make the indicator easier to interpret. The reentry signal to buy the market does not actually develop until point 13. An exit signal forms at point 14. When an M pattern forms under an average in the oscillator, it is generally viewed a major sell signal; similarly, a W just above an average would be viewed as a buy signal. In this situation the M pattern declines to the 60 level and uses the old resistance zone for oscillators in a bear market as a support zone, adding confidence that the market will remain in an uptrend. At point 15 confirmation develops, and the rally resumes with renewed enthusiasm. Points 15, 16, and 17 all become important considerations for a major trend reversal that was discussed in Chapter 1. The saving grace for the U.S. Dollar is that the oscillator after pivot high 17 leads to the support zone defined for a bull market, the 40 to 45 area for the RSI. The danger area for the dollar will come if the next advance fails to push the RSI through the 60 level. Such an oscillator pattern could lead to a long-term bear market for the dollar as the DMark strengthened.

Up until this juncture, global rates have been largely ignored in the chart examples. Let's correct this imbalance now and focus on a daily chart for

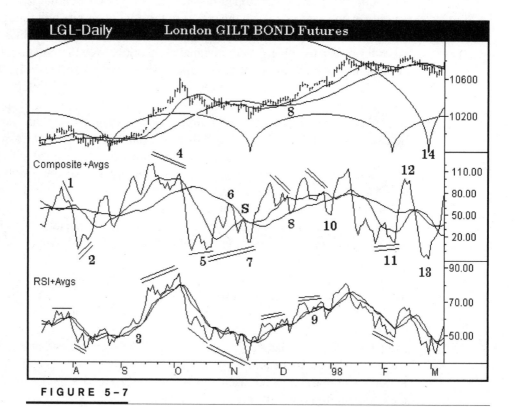

FIGURE 5-7

London's Gilt Bond futures market in Figure 5–7. Now we are beginning to apply all the techniques discussed at great length in the first five chapters. Averages are added to prices and oscillators. Cycles have been identified. (In Figure 5–8, we will add trend lines to this same market to see how they might contribute additional information to the details we obtain from Figure 5–7.) Figure 5–7 includes the RSI with two averages that use the exact same period, but one is simple and the other is exponential. As I mentioned earlier, I would normally use a longer period for the exponential moving average on the RSI, but in this market the longer average makes it hard to see the RSI in a black-and-white image. So the two averages in the chart allow you to explore the differences between simple and exponential weightings. The RSI uses a 14-period interval. The middle indicator is the Composite Index with two simple moving averages added to the oscillator; one short and one longer period. Starting at point 1 on the Composite Index, there is a sharp divergence between the angle of the peaks that form in the RSI. Bearish divergence at an extreme is a sell signal that leads toward bullish divergence between indicators at point 2. The RSI remains below the short-period averages, but it declines only to the 45 level in the RSI, indicating a correction in a bull market. The Composite Index has unlimited range between its upper and lower displacement, so range rules will not apply to this indicator normally. At point 3 the RSI is testing the averages, and the Composite Index is maintaining its distance above the shorter moving average. Both signals are correctly bullish for London Bonds. Moving along to point 4 is bearish divergence between the Composite Index and the RSI. The RSI travels under the double line, staying above the moving averages, and it offers no warning. The cycles on price remain up. There are only two warnings present in this chart that a decline will soon follow. The first is the bearish divergence between the RSI and the Composite Index; the second is the price advance from the bar marked with the first cycle low into the high that corresponds to point 4 in the Composite Index, which is a very clear five-wave rally, applying the Elliott Wave Principle. The fact that the Composite Index has topped warns that a correction is nearby. Point 4 is marked to show that no matter how much detail and experience one can develop with a single indicator or method, we are assured to be blind-sided by the market if we do not develop multiple noncorrelating methods. In this case, the RSI is clearly at an extreme, but it offers no further information about the degree to which the bond market will decline or of its timing. The correction allows both oscillators to alleviate their overbought condition, and the first bounce in the market is foretold by a bullish divergence between indicators that forms at point 5.

At point 6 the Composite Index fails to exceed the long-period moving average, which is a little easier to read than the formation that forms in the RSI. Move to the oscillator peak that develops at point *S* in the Composite Index. The

Composite Index is directly under the crossover point of two moving averages, which warns that the buy signal at point 5 is premature. The RSI has a similar warning as it is unable to exceed the moving averages. The RSI then declines to new lows, but the Composite Index does not form a bullish divergence a second time at point 7 with the RSI. Point 7 coincides with a cycle low in price that is important coincidental evidence.

Following point 7 in Figure 5-7, both oscillators break above their moving averages before prices are able to exceed their own averages. This is a lead that should not be missed. Minor divergence between the Composite Index and the RSI leads to a pullback toward point 8. Point 8 in the Composite Index holds above the longer moving average. At point 9 the trend in the RSI is not broken, but it leads to a push that forms a divergence with the Composite Index. Point 10 is an oscillator low that has broken the averages in the Composite Index. However, note that point 10 is lower than point 8, but the oscillator is at a higher price at point 10. The market has become oversold at a higher price level, denoting strength. The RSI forms a similar pattern between the new low and point 9. The RSI is the first to cross back down through the averages, offering the first warning.

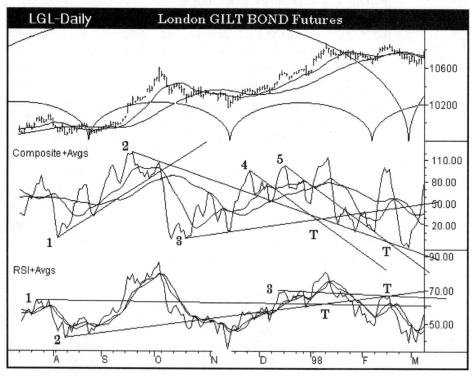

FIGURE 5-8

At point 11 a bullish divergence develops, and a rally soon follows into point 12. Point 12 is an M pattern in both the RSI and the Composite that warns that the cycle low approaching at point 14 will soon be seen. The oscillators then form a W bottom at point 13 that coincides with the cycle low at point 14. The cycle at point 14 is clearly a cycle that could be viewed in a weekly chart, and it is significant that the oscillators form a signal near this same cycle bottom.

Now take the same market and add trend lines from the oscillator lows and highs that have formed bullish or bearish divergences. Figure 5–8 shows that many of the pivots in the oscillators that were not discussed in Figure 5–7 have major support or resistance now at previously overlooked pivots. Trend lines 2, 3, and 5 on the Composite Index have become extremely valuable additions. Trend lines 1, 2, and 3 have also become valuable as drawn on the RSI. While it would be difficult to see all the notations drawn in Figures 5–7 and 5–8 in one chart that is black and white, the lines are easily differentiated with systems that use color.

Now that we have a strong arsenal of tools from which to define market direction, we are ready to discuss various price projection methods, which is necessary because knowing the market direction alone is insufficient.

PART TWO

Calculating Market Price Objectives

CHAPTER 6

Adjusting Traditional Fibonacci Projections for Higher-Probability Targets

Fibonacci retracements: Easy, right? Just take a measurement of the distance traveled by a market from *obvious* price extremes—for example, from an extreme price low to the market high—then calculate the corresponding price levels that represent a retracement equal to the Fibonacci ratios 0.382, 0.50, or 0.618, relative to the total distance. Very straightforward, but in practice traders soon discover that their limit orders at these retracement levels are frequently missed. Worse, protective stops tucked safely below or above these Fibonacci price objectives are washed out of the market, forcing a trader to accept greater risk or be left behind entirely. Yet many traders confidently go forward without considering a change to their method as they know Fibonacci retracements must *always* be calculated from the extreme price highs and lows. Right? Wrong!

During trading tutorials that I have given, I have found that most experienced traders feel they have mastered Fibonacci calculations. They politely listen to the explanations and nod their heads in understanding and agreement to variations. However, time again the same traders with a solid understanding of the principles run into extreme difficulty when we move over to real-time trading screens to apply the methods. The problems begin when traders stop looking at the clues and signals the market has to offer because they are confident they know beforehand how a market will conform to our methods. *Markets will conform to our methods?* Unlikely. The market is the Master, and we must accept the role of being the lifetime student to survive. Is there to be no allowance given to the rescaling changes that occur as a market rally or decline accelerates? No adjustment considered for a market beginning to compress its scale prior to a trend reversal or within a time-consuming consolidation? The "Theorists" cannot adapt to changing market conditions because they are unable to modify their ideal textbook example. Yet markets are dynamic, and the concept of one size fits all cannot possibly apply. Traders unable to evolve beyond textbook basics will be victimized often by a market and will be spared the fate of becoming market roadkill only if solid money management skills are applied.

When we lose the student or beginner's mindset, we tend to blind ourselves to any new information so that our methodology or confidence is not challenged. Theorists rarely become exceptional traders because academic examples are only the milestones from which we begin to learn. The "Money Producers" are the traders who have evolved beyond the basics and discovered the variations that make the textbook examples work *more often* in real-time market environments.

Figure 6–1 is a 60-minute chart of the September T-Bond futures market. Most traders will calculate the Fibonacci retracements from the extreme price high and low marked on the left chart to project the price objective for the correction at *R*, the retracement target. The traders that made this calculation and entered buy orders at or immediately above the 0.618 retracement calculation were left behind when a sharp rebound resumed in the direction of the larger trend. The first observation is that bonds are in a bull market in this chart and *we do not want to see a full 0.618 retracement* from the extreme price high and low. A full retracement would tell us the larger trend was losing strength. The chart on the right-hand side

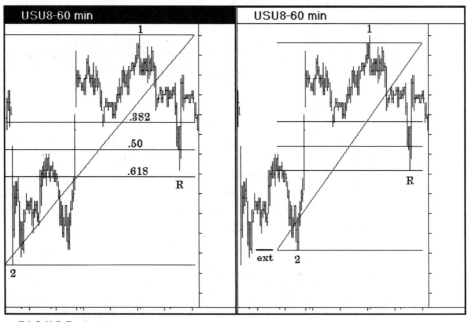

FIGURE 6 – 1

of Figure 6–1 shows the Fibonacci retracement calculations based on the secondary price low at point 2. While the high could have been used, *it will nearly always be more accurate to ignore the spike or key reversal in a chart.* The two closest price bars just behind the price high at point 1 have tested the same price level twice. That is the more significant price level from which to make the Fibonacci calculations. Why use the spike from some poor trader's error after the floor ran their stop or bid the market up with a poorly timed market order? Their mistake should not become our mistake also. The price projection to determine *R* in fact becomes the exact level for the bond market reversal and was identified when more thoughtful price levels were used to calculate the retracement objectives.

If the price high was not used at point 1, why did I not crop the key reversal signal at point 2 and use the slightly higher price low just prior to point 2? Because the price low at point 2 in effect is a second test of a level that truncated a prior spike. Extend the price level at point 2 backward and you will see the significant market action that formed above this level earlier. The market is telling us that point 2 is significant. What is interesting is that both charts in Figure 6–1 have identical 0.382 retracement price objectives. Both traders working from their calculations will think they are seeing confirmation by the market if the first retracement ratio at 0.382 is tested and becomes support briefly before it is broken. However, the trader working from the left chart will in fact be working from an incorrect 0.618 retracement calculation.

In the next example a 240-minute bar chart displays the September S&P 500 futures contract in Figure 6–2. A strong advance has developed, and we want to find a retracement target when the market is near the market highs at point 1. With such a bullish move, do not calculate the retracement from a secondary low just near to the extreme price low, as there is no chance to reenter a new position if the calculations are made from such conservative pivot levels. In fact, if the market developed a deep decline, it would challenge the bullish outlook of the nearby trend. So make the calculation from the origin of the strongest leg up; in this chart it is the price low marked "point 2."

As in the first example, when the price high is used, the calculation for *R* falls short of its mark as the market fails to realize the 0.618 retracement. This chart shows a market accelerating. Some will correctly read the market's inability to realize the 0.618 retracement in the left chart as a bullish signal denoting underlying market strength. They will know this only in hindsight after the market has developed a rally from the price low at R. Had the calculation been made from more observant pivot levels, a precise target could have been defined that would make it easier to identify the market bottom in real-time conditions. In the right chart of Figure 6–2, point 1 is the price high just behind the extreme price high, thereby truncating the spike itself.

FIGURE 6-2

If you look very carefully, point 2 in the right-hand chart has been adjusted slightly to align with point a. Now points a and 2 mark a level that was both resistance and support for the market. This level is always of greater significance than a single pivot level. There are other signals to confirm that points 1 and 2 are correctly defined because point b respects this same mathematical grid. *If the market has shown respect in the past to a Fibonacci grid drawn on the chart, the chances are much higher that it will also respect those levels in the future market action.* Point R is the retracement we wanted to project as a future price objective, and the market stops exactly on the 50 percent retracement level. If we missed the price low at the 50 percent target expecting a 61.8 percent retracement, we would see the second warning of building market strength when the market rallies and then pulls back to the 0.382 ratio at point d. Before we move on, consider the price high marked point 1 and the low labeled point 2 as the order you want to use for establishing these anchor points. We are attempting to define the retracement targets within a bull market. Therefore, the calculation must start at point 1, the high, and drag the Fibonacci grid downward toward point 2. Otherwise, you will never see the market's internal signals that occur as was demonstrated at points a and b.

In Figure 6–3 we continue viewing the September S&P 500 futures market but add the complexity of the Globex session. The thin overnight computer-traded session is added to the day session in 10-minute bar chart intervals. The first observation is that this is a downtrend. (In reality, a time frame such as 60-minute chart should dictate what the actual trend is within a 10-minute chart. So assume confirmation of a downtrend for this discussion in both time horizons.) The first anchor to begin a Fibonacci retracement grid will be from a price low, which is where we begin and then we work upward toward a price high. The chart on the left shows the outcome of the Theorist who uses the price low at point 1 and the extreme price high at point 2 to project the retracement that will occur at point R. The first thing the trader using the price extremes should have observed is that the 0.618 projection for pivot R was a low-probability calculation. The market did not respect the Fibonacci retracements plotted in any prior price bars. The critical warning signs are ignored that develop at price low a1 and price high k. It is not a surprise that the market's retracement falls short of its objective at R. The cycle is repeated in the left chart when the price lows at points 3 and 4 are used to make a Fibonacci assessment. R2 appears to be just a minor violation through the 50 percent retracement level when the market begins to rapidly descend once again. Not bad, but we could have called the exact pivot level had we used more intelligent points for the calculations and avoided a possible error interpreting the night session.

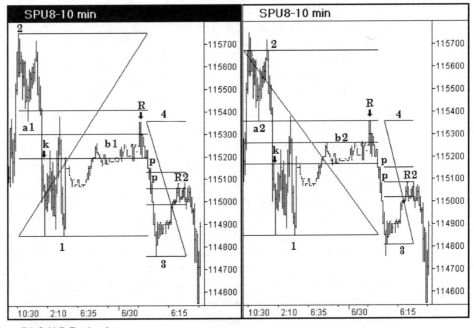

FIGURE 6-3

Look at what occurs when we make the same calculations after cropping the spikes and reading what the market has to offer. The right chart in Figure 6-3 uses the same price low at point 1—not because it is the obvious price low, but because it is a double bottom. The price high, which is a secondary retracement at point 2, is used to crop the price spikes. The level at point 2 has been tested three times by the market. It not only truncates the spikes, but we now see the price reversals at points a2 and k respect the same Fibonacci ratios that we have just added to the chart. The critical objective and primary reason for calculating the Fibonacci ratios for pivot R soon mark the exact pivot that coincides with the 0.618 retracement. Now take a look at the price action in the thin Globex session near b1 and b2. The left chart can be read near b1 as weakness when the market slips through the 0.382 retracement and fails to achieve the 50 percent level. The spike that develops at R may not have been anticipated, enticing the trader to step in before the last exhaustion spike. This is not a major problem in this example because it displays only a 2 handle error, but a similar pattern and error from a weekly chart would be very expensive.

The grid drawn in the right chart of Figure 6-3 gives a very different look. The market through the night session advances to the 50 percent retracement level and then becomes range bound between the 38.2 and 50 percent retracement levels. A test at the 0.618 ratio at R can be sensed prior to the actual decline. To calculate point R2, we should truncate the spike and use the secondary higher low at point 3. The price high at point 4 is the same as was used in the left chart, not because it is the price high but because this key reversal occurs at a price high that was formerly used as a price low at point a2. We are viewing a support level that later became resistance for the market. There is additional evidence being offered that confirms that the correct anchor points have been used to calculate the Fibonacci grid in the right chart. Observe the minor pivots that develop at internal levels marked with a p. When a comparison is made of the same levels in the left chart, the price levels at p have no relationship to the Fibonacci grid drawn. They do have a relationship to the grid drawn in the right chart. These subtle innuendoes cannot be overlooked.

The Globex night session was deliberately included with the S&P data as this market is now respecting price objectives defined in the overnight session more so than from data only from the day session. It means our dilemma on how best to handle the Globex data has been answered for us with time; we truly have to use charts displaying both sessions to define accurate price objectives for this market. I have found this to be true for multiple price projection methods.

Beware that several professional charting products on the market limit the trader from using Fibonacci calculations beyond elementary applications. As an example, CQG for *Windows* will draw their Fibonacci ratios in such a manner that the grid will project backward or away from the future price objectives that you need to monitor when you start from a price low and move the mouse upward and to the left toward an older price high. In a downtrend, when a corrective rally target is required, you must start from a price low and move the mouse upward toward the high. This direction is required to allow assessment of the internal price pivots as they relate to the Fibonacci grid being drawn. In uptrends, when a corrective decline is anticipated, always start from the price high and move down toward a price low.

CQG can change their graph default so that their ratios travel across the entire screen, but that will create a lot of interference on the screen that is unnecessary and hinders the use of multiple Fibonacci grids and bidirectional overlays. To use multiple Fibonacci grids, you need a fast one-click option to change the color of an entire grid. The reason is that similar colors will disappear on the screen when they overlap one another so different colors are needed in both high and low intensity. The low-intensity colors allow the grid to visually drop behind the price bars so you don't have to view a neon sign that conflicts with the market data.

Beware that the starting default Fibonacci ratios that your vendor offers could be wrong. They should be set at 0.382, 0.500, and 0.618. Some systems such as CQG use starting default values of 0.382, 0.618, and 0.750. Change the defaults if necessary before you use them. Also there is a need to be able to pick up the entire Fibonacci grid, maintaining the aspect ratio of the original grid, and move it over to an entirely new location on the computer screen. Why? We need to measure Fibonacci swings and use the old Fibonacci ratios to project the targets from a new pivot point. Many systems force you to delete the old grid and redraw it. How do you redraw a grid in a new position with the same aspect ratio of an older calculation? You cannot do it unless you can relocate it. Fibonacci swing price objectives are derived from prior market moves. We will discuss this price projection method in Figure 6–5 within the next few pages.

One last comment about differences among charting products. All the charts in this chapter will display a Z pattern because a diagonal line is drawn from the selected start and ending levels. The diagonal line allows you to pick up the entire grid without changing it so that you can relocate it to a different position on the screen. It is one of the most valuable trading tools we have for making fast accurate price projections. We will look at this aspect in more detail as well.

The Z pattern in these charts allows the user to click on a corner of the Z pattern and adjust or relocate the start or ending levels from which the grid was drawn. Most systems that draw just Fibonacci lines are permanent and cannot be altered once drawn. However, once a grid is established, you have to be able to make a minor adjustment. This becomes very important after you draw a second and third Fibonacci grid and want to determine the confluence or overlapping levels where multiple Fibonacci calculations begin to cluster together.

I frequently have to make a minor adjustment to find these levels that overlap. Forcing a trader to erase the grids and redraw them makes the system unusable for a trader who uses Fibonacci in a more advanced manner. A lone voice requesting change will be told that the systems in question fit the needs of the masses. Precisely the problem; we need flexibility so that we can operate in a manner that is smarter than the masses. I have to admit that Omega Research's *TradeStation* and their offline product *SuperCharts* handle Fibonacci ratios particularly well. A system strong in one area will be very weak and have its limitations in another. *TradeStation* has its own shortcomings elsewhere so it always comes down to choosing between lesser evils. The ideal system that offers both exceptional data management for international markets and flexible technical analysis capabilities does not exist in today's market.

The chart examples in this chapter have addressed only intraday bar charts. Let's shift our focus now to a longer time horizon and use an Index so that we know the spikes in the chart were not caused by pit locals running stops or other aspects associated with short-horizon trading. The recommendation to truncate the spikes for Fibonacci retracement calculations will hold true in longer time horizon charts of real market action and for synthetic indices.

The daily AMEX Computer Technology Index is displayed in Figure 6–4. An Elliott Wave interpretation is added to the chart, but I am jumping ahead as we have not discussed the Elliott Wave Principle. If you are not familiar with wave interpretations, please view the wave counts as a convenient way for me to refer to numerous market pivots in a complex chart. The labels define the termination points of "waves," but you can view these same labels as the identification marker for the price pivots. The discussion that follows will not require a knowledge of the Elliott Wave Principle at this time.

The points used to calculate the Fibonacci grid show that the price spikes have been truncated. The high that was used to calculate the Fibonacci grid is a level that was tested twice on either side of the key reversal spike. I actually considered the price low at point 2 at first when I was preparing this chart, but the internals did not offer any confirmation, and it became easy to see that the better level to use was the price low just to the left of point 2. Take a look at the levels marked with black arrows, then the secondary low one bar past a′, the market test at c′, and then again at e′ (the bottom of wave e′ of 4). Each of these price pivot levels shows respect for the Fibonacci grid added to this chart. The subtle confirmations indicate that the target being projected for R (or wave 5′ of c down) is a high-probability objective. As the decline develops from the high, the 38.2 percent retracement marks the bottom of wave 3′, and the 50 percent retracement defines the price low for wave 5′ (of c) at R highlighted with a black arrow.

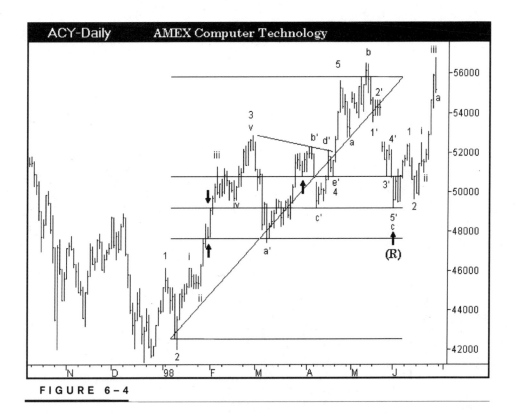

FIGURE 6-4

The more time you spend observing the internal market pivots relative to the Fibonacci grid added to a chart, the more accurate your price objectives will be. Over time you will see for yourself that the spikes that form in a market should rarely be used for calculating Fibonacci retracements.

We have discussed only one method of calculating price objectives by utilizing the Fibonacci number sequence. Another common practice is to calculate Fibonacci price swing projections. Contrary to the discussion about ignoring spikes for retracement calculations, we will want to use the price extremes for swing projections *and will then make further adjustments by adding or subtracting gaps that may be present in the price data.*

We will use the daily AMEX Computer Technology Index in Figure 6–5 to show how to calculate Fibonacci swing price objectives. A swing projection will always require three market pivot levels: two highs and one low to project a decline, or two lows and a high to project a rally target. In Figure 6–5 we will use the top of wave 5, the bottom of wave a, and the top of wave b to project a Fibonacci relationship relative to the distance traveled by wave a. (The distance

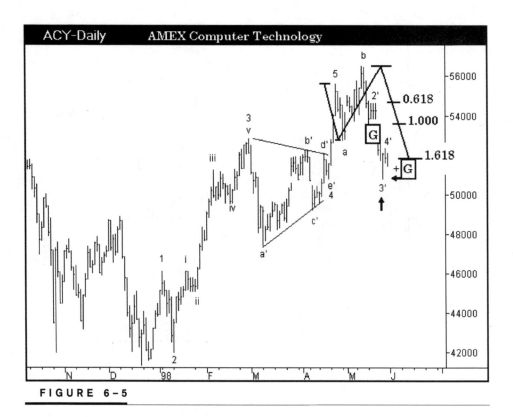

FIGURE 6−5

traveled by wave a is the distance between the price high at point 5 to the price low at a.) The ratios 0.618, equality with wave a (1.000), and 1.618 are projected from the high that marks the resolution of wave b up. While the 0.618 relationship is ignored by the market on the way down, it does become important resistance for three days just below the 0.618 Fibonacci level. A decline then follows to the 1.000 target (an equality market decline from the high relative to the distance traveled by wave a) that marks the exact price low for wave 1′ down. The label for wave 1′ had to be removed in Figure 6–5, but it is still present in Figure 6−4 if a quick reference is needed. Then the 1.618 relationship with wave a seems to be held briefly for one day, and then it is broken. The spike forms below the 1.618 price projection, and wave 3′ down finds a bottom below this projected support level.

Is the 1.618 projection incorrect? No, the market developed a gap after the 1.00 objective was realized, and if we subtract the differential of the gap from the initial 1.618 price objective (add the differential for a rally projection), it shows that the gap adjustment now defines the exact price low for wave 3′ down. If wave 4′ up had entered into the gap and partially filled the gap, *only the remainder of the gap should be used to make this adjustment.* When calculating the 2.618 relationship, include this gap adjustment just described and any other gap that may occur if the adjusted 1.618 price objective is broken. This should be done for all markets and for all time horizons. If you compare wave 3′ down in Figure 6–5 to Figure 6–4 at wave 3′ down, both methods offer the exact same price objective for wave 3′ down, though the methods used are very different.

If you did not know how to apply the Elliott Wave Principle, how would the non-Elliott trader have known that the market low at 3′ was not the final bottom?

Figure 6–6 displays the Composite Index and the RSI with their corresponding moving averages with the daily price data for the AMEX Computer Technology Index. The Elliott Wave interpretation has also been transferred from the price data to the pivots that correspond in the indicators. The indicators are not being given wave interpretations, but the effort is being made to show the juxtaposition of price label to the corresponding oscillator position. Let's first address how the non-Elliott trader would have also known that the market low at 3′ was not the final bottom.

While the price low at 3′ declined to a 0.382 retracement target, the oscillator lows corresponding to this price low did not display bullish divergence or signal a market bottom. When a new price low develops to the bottom of wave 5′, the

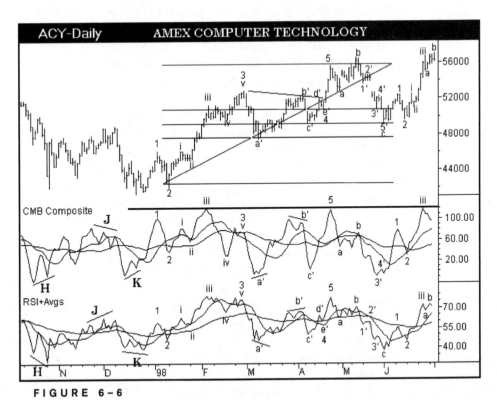

FIGURE 6-6

indicators diverge and offers the first visible buy signal. The safest buy signal for this market is at the bottom of wave 2 down, which is to the right of the oscillator divergences. The Composite Index corresponding to the price low at 2 on the far right is testing the support level where two moving averages are crossing over one another. We discussed in prior chapters how this indicator formation frequently leads to a strong market move.

You may want to come back to this chart after we have discussed the Elliott Wave Principle. The trend range rules for the RSI mark a trend reversal in this chart. Observe how the market reacts to the extreme oscillator trend line highs. Note how the market reacts and frequently changes direction when the Composite Index and RSI indicators diverge from one another. These are all review topics from prior discussions.

If you are familiar with the Elliott Wave Principle, you will be extremely interested in the transposed wave count that was been added to the indicators relative to the structure that developed in prices. As an example, waves iii, 5, and iii all top at the same oscillator level. The resolution of the triangle at wave e′ of 4 corresponds to an indicator signal that is extremely important in the RSI. If you are lost now because this is your first introduction to "waves," you will discover later that the Elliott Wave notations just add a sense of proportion and scale to the methods you currently use. Indicators can tell us a rally is approaching, but the size and scale of the advance will be difficult to assess without the use of the Elliott Wave Principle. The methods of R. N. Elliott will work for some and not for others.

Figure 6–5 began the discussion of how to calculate Fibonacci swing projections. The most common projections are 0.618, 1.00 (equality with a former move), 1.618, and 2.618. You may not realize that you can easily make these projections on your computer screen if your software allows you to reposition Fibonacci calculations. In Figure 6–5 we discussed how to calculate the Fibonacci swing objectives for a market decline. Now we will determine the primary objectives for a market poised to make a new historic high.

Figure 6–7 is an 88-minute bar chart of the September S&P 500 futures contract on July 9, 1998. This particular example is being created in a real-time context. The calculations being described for you are being written before the outcome of the market move is known to both the author and the reader. Let's begin by creating a Fibonacci grid from a price low and high. The first or original grid will become our template for calculating the Fibonacci price ratios 0.618, 1.00, and 1.618 for the next rally relative to the first advance.

Figure 6–7 shows the rally selected to calculate the first Fibonacci targets. Now draw a second grid right on top of the first. The Z customarily seen in all the prior Fibonacci charts is now an X because there are two grids drawn on top of one another. Both grids will become transparent and disappear if the grids are the same

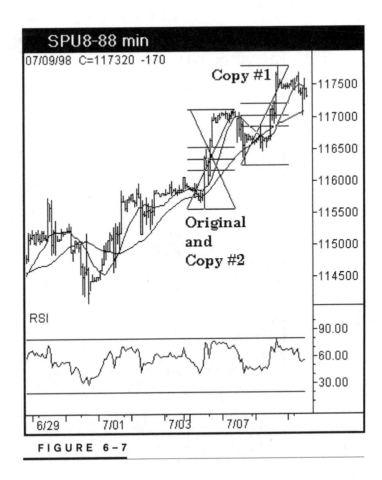

FIGURE 6–7

color. Therefore, use a different color so that overlapping Fibonacci lines can be seen. This is the purpose for which we are doing this calculation. Now pick up or grab the duplicate or copied Fibonacci grid anywhere along its diagonal axis with the computer's mouse, and move it. In this example the Fibonacci grid "copy 1" shows that the market advanced an equal distance relative to the first advance. We can see this relationship into the present high. As the market has already realized this target, we need to find a higher objective if the market attempts a new high. Where will the market go? Figure 6–7 shows an X as the original Fibonacci grid has another copy overlapping the original for a second projection. The second copy was made to project where the 1.618 price objective is located relative to the original move.

Figure 6–8 has relocated copy 2 so that it is now added to the top range of copy 1. By adding a second copy, we have an exact price objective drawn at the

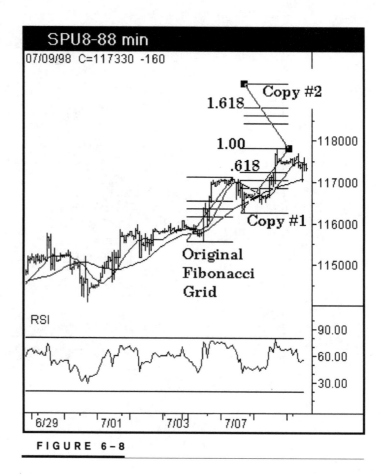

FIGURE 6-8

1.618 relationship. The top line for this new Fibonacci grid is at a 2.00 target. A 2.0 level is of little interest, but 2.618 is of interest, so you could do this a third time if desired. I usually wait to see what develops at a 1.618 target before adding any more grids to the trading screen. You'll see why in a moment. In Figure 6–8 there are small square boxes on the extreme corners of copy 2. These squares, or handles, let you know the grid is active and that you can place your mouse cursor on one of these handles and extend the width of the grid. If you move the mouse up or down, the Fibonacci retracements would change to adjust to the new price high or low. In this example you do not want to change the height as it must remain an identical aspect ratio of the first grid. If you make an error by accidentally changing the height, you can always pick up the grid and overlay it with the original one to ensure that the ratio did not change and then move it back to the projection position. Are we done? Do we now have the most probable price objective identified if the market advances? No. We can do better. We can improve our target accuracy by adding additional price projections from different pivot points.

We have been discussing how to calculate Fibonacci retracements and swing projections from a single market move. However, both of these methods have greater precision when more than one Fibonacci grid is calculated. Let's look at what occurs when multiple retracement calculations or swing projections are made from as many *meaningful pivot levels* as possible for a market.

In Figure 6–9 we still have the price projections on the screen from the steps we discussed for Figure 6–8. However, we want to create a second swing projection, and we start by drawing a Fibonacci grid at position 1. This is a larger market advance for the next calculation, and it begins from a different price low. Clearly the resulting Fibonacci ratios will be entirely different than those obtained from the first projection. Our next step is to draw a duplicate grid right on top of

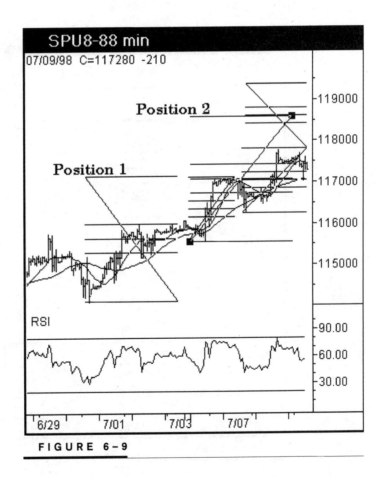

FIGURE 6–9

position 1, then pick it up with the mouse and move it into position 2. If you look closely, the new grid at position 2 has the square handles on the corners to show which grid is currently active. (Also the Z pattern within the Fibonacci grid becomes valuable as a guide to see the start and ending price levels of the grid.) Here is what becomes extremely important. The 1.00 or equality price projection identified from the Fibonacci grid at position 2 (the upper range for position 2) has a confluence level now with the first calculations that were made. The 1.00 projection in position 2 overlaps the 1.50 price target created in Figure 6–8. Therefore, the important price objectives are 1.00, the former high, and 1.50—**not 1.618.** The 1.618 objective will be too high. When you have overlapping Fibonacci projections that form a cluster, you have found the price objective of greatest significance. Failures at these levels or the lack of respect shown by a market will provide invaluable information about the bigger picture.

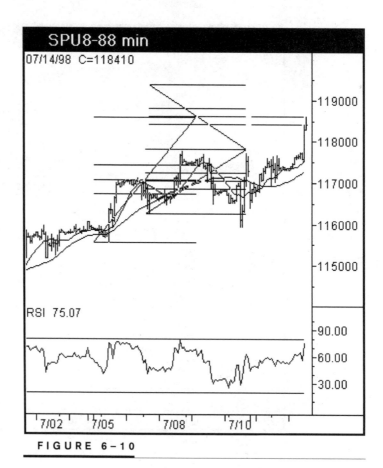

FIGURE 6–10

Five days have passed since the explanation for Figure 6–9 was written. It is now July 14, 1998, and a breakout rally into new highs has occurred in the September S&P 500 contract, which can be seen in Figure 6-10. The chart shows the market consolidated under the old high for several days. The old high was the 1.00 objective we identified from Figure 6–8. We then projected that the 1.50 relationship would be the next target if the market successfully penetrated former highs. The time stamps in the top left corners of these charts are real. There was no hindsight selection criteria to find a perfect example to explain a theory. I will admit that more calculations were done than just those described in Figures 6–8 and 6–9. Gann and RSI objectives were defined that confirmed for me in advance that a void that was suggested in Figure 6–9 just over the old high was formidable. The void is the absence of resistance levels between two major targets. In this case the old high and the 1.500 objective from Figure 6–8 and the 1.00 target (same level) from Figure 6–9. Below the 1.500 objective is a minor resistance level at 1.382. The market breaks out above the old high and produces a fast market condition right to the 1.382 line that has been extended for your comparison from our original calculations. The market then pushes up to the major objective and again shows respect to our projected target. The spread between target zones can define slippage exposure for traders, and this will be discussed in further detail in the next chart. The progression of steps we described in Figures 6–8 and 6–9 would now be repeated as new market pivot levels have been added to our trading screens.

What would have happened if the market failed to acknowledge these objectives? Of course there are times this will happen, and it means that the math grid we developed from selected pivot points is incorrect. When the market shows us that our first target is wrong, it should begin an immediate frenzy of activity to re-create all these calculations from every logical level to identify the pivots the market is actually working from presently. It is for this reason that the views of a trader or analyst in a longer horizon cannot be imposed and forced on the market action in the shorter time horizon. If the resistance or support grid developed for a 15-minute chart begins to step off course, then they are the first steps to warn us that the longer time horizon may also be changing direction through these subtle grid failures. Analysts and traders who marry their long-horizon market opinions and look only at short-horizon data to seek confirmation of their views will always find the confirmation they seek. They are willing to acknowledge only that evidence that supports their views, and it is easy to quickly dismiss contradictions. Therefore, be assertive in defining the longer-horizon direction for a market, but use the shorter-horizon data to be judge and jury to continually challenge that opinion. Should the 15-minute chart step off track and then your 60-minute and perhaps a 120-minute chart, know that your longer-horizon market view that was favored needs to be revisited before it is too late.

The math grids we develop from Fibonacci projections or other methods are all fractals within a larger framework. The more attentive we are to the smaller pieces of our financial puzzle, the more accurate we can be about the entire financial complex of intermarket relationships globally. When I step down to a 2-min chart in the S&P futures, it is because my risk is so great that I need to fight for the identification of every major pivot. As long as I know the identification of each pivot and the grid work that the market is tracking, I also know my longer-horizon view is not being challenged. The time of greatest risk is when we have just finished scaling into our full market position. Even if we scale our size in proportions of 50, 30, and 20 percent without ever adding to a losing leg within the total position size, the S&P can turn around so fast and viciously that we can find ourselves underwater within minutes. If the very short horizon framework starts to fall apart and the origin of the new pivots forming cannot be defined quickly, I will unwind the position until I know I am back in sync with the market's movements and mathematical framework displayed on my computer screen and in the Microsoft *Excel* tables. The drawback to putting this much effort into defining the mathematical proportions of a market is that you are restricted to trading only a few markets. It is extremely labor intensive.

I am told by traders employed by institutions and money center banks that I have a strong reputation for price projection accuracy. But what people do not realize is that the support-resistance price tables that I create are derived from three noncorrelated price projection methods. Each independent method was derived from overlapping *seven* different time horizons. Then I compare the major clusters that result from the three different methods. When clusters from independent methods overlap, it marks the price objective of greatest significance. In Figure 6-10 the 1.50 Fibonacci projection we made earlier was respected by the market. This could define a minor contraction in this market's larger trend. In addition, a target zone from longer time horizons and 3 methods is approaching near the 1198 level. Confluence in objectives from monthly and quarterly charts is rare.

The three methods I use are Fibonacci, Gann, and the RSI. I will give you only two of these methods: Fibonacci and the RSI. It is similar to the concept of pinpointing the origin of an earthquake through triangulation measurement. You need three points that intersect to define precise longitude, latitude, and minute coordinates. Two methods will get you close. However, the method of triangulation assumes each contributing element is of equal importance. Not so for triangulation of a market price objective. The method of greatest accuracy and importance among these three is without question Gann.

That is why I am willing to disclose this method of price projection. While the basics are revealed, keep in mind that I use adjustment factors for gaps, I truncate spikes, and I have other adjustments not described. Trust me, I am not giving away my own price accuracy advantage and jeopardizing my clients in our investment pool. It was necessary to say this to reassure them. But I am confident that the concepts are of value even if only a single projection method is adopted. Risk management will dictate how fanatical you will become about price objective accuracy. An analyst that gives me a target range of 5 handles in the S&P is asking for an estimate in my opinion. I cannot operate within a 5-handle estimate as it is hard to effectively manage risk. A target in the S&P is a target zone no wider than 1.50 S&P points for a major zone containing numerous targets. Sometimes a target range no wider than 0.40 in the S&P can occur from 20 independent calculations. That is incredible when you consider that the S&P is trading at a price level of 1186 at this time. An objective no wider than 1.50 in the S&P as a percentage of the trading range would seem impossible to some. Yet I have consistently demonstrated to traders monitoring our Web site[1] that it can be done.

The point is that you can define precise objectives for a market if you want to put in the hours of work. Though the S&P 500 Index has doubled in only a few years, the target zones that develop from overlapping objectives remain narrow target zones. If overlapping targets exceed 2.00 S&P points, I no longer view them as a confluence area of clustered targets. They are too spread out. This remains true despite the volatility that now occurs in this index. The T-Bond contract rarely has major target zones that exceed a window of ^05 ticks for a major price target. Rarely will the T-Bond market violate this narrow target window. Spot currency objectives can also be expected to respect narrow target zones of 0.0070. The Deutsche Mark has greater accuracy potential than the Swiss Franc. The Yen is about the same as the Swiss Franc, and I have no opinion about the Sterling as I do not calculate targets for this market. I think the toughest currency market for which I have ever been asked to define a price objective was the Thai Bhat/Lira cross. We were able to define extremely narrow target windows using the techniques described. Cross rates are very labor intensive as each Fibonacci grid needs assessment to define the start and ending points for the targets. Cross rates have some unique adjustment factors as well because of the character of the chart patterns. The technique of triangulation to forecast financial market objectives is perhaps a book in itself, and this is only an introduction.

One aspect that safeguards these methods of multiple target overlays is that there are few willing to sit down at the end of a trading day and put in nearly four hours of additional work to find the next day's targets with the help of a computer! When a contract rolls into a new front month, it can take a full day of preparation to identify the new math grids from which to trade. To those who are as crazy as I am about multiple projection techniques, let me caution you that when you roll over

---

[1] Aerodynamic Investments Inc.: Web site address: http://www.aeroinvest.com.

to a new contract, the old grids cannot just be given a conversion factor to create the grid template for the new contract. Knowing that up front will save you a lot of money. You will find that we have to let the new contract dictate its own grid. It also means that we may not be able to trade the first day of a new contract with confidence because there will be insufficient data points with which to create a multiple grid from reliable intraday data.

The bottom line is that, if we want price objective accuracy, we have to put in a lot of work. The easiest step is picking up the phone and entering the order. Sadly, too many traders just skip to the easiest step as some of the methods described are very time-consuming and labor intensive. Some traders have told me they do not have time to put this much effort into defining a market objective because they have to enter the order. *Tilt.* Something seems out of sync with that logic.

We have discussed multiple Fibonacci swing projections; we now need to cover how to create multiple retracement levels and define why the extra effort is worth it. Figure 6–11 displays the chart for the daily Yen/$ spot currency market. The chart will look different from those in previous figures. I have transferred the *FutureSource* data, which is my data feed for *TradeStation,* into an ASCII file that is then plotted by Microsoft's *Excel* spreadsheet on a different computer. We'll go through this export-import process step by step in the next chapter. When multiple Fibonacci retracements are plotted from numerous pivot levels, the individual

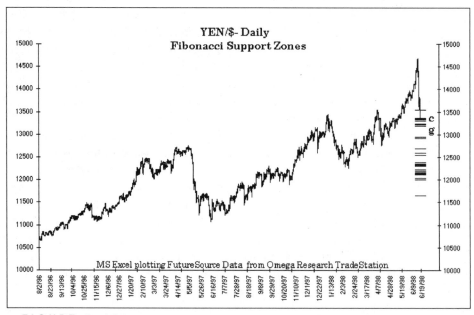

FIGURE 6-11

price objectives begin to cluster into tight support or resistance zones. They will also define areas within the market that have limited or no support or resistance.

On June 19, 1998, the Yen/$ formed a significant decline in a daily chart after government intervention to strengthen the Yen occurred. The market bottom displayed in the far right or most current bar was on the first major Fibonacci support zone. It became a long-horizon price low for the dollar in the daily charts. A major support zone forms when *different* overlapping Fibonacci ratios cluster near one another. The *Excel* graph was deliberately compressed so that as many data points in history could be displayed at one time. (Some of the calculations, however, are from price lows to the left of the display screen.) By removing the start and ending price levels that define the range that was used to create the Fibonacci calculations and only plotting the retracement ratios themselves, such a chart can be created.

The chart in Figure 6–11 shows that the dollar declined to a single, or minor, Fibonacci support level and then dropped to the next support zone that was a clustered area of targets marked c. There is a gap between the first minor support level and the strong Fibonacci cluster marked c. Gaps between clustered target zones will warn us in advance what the character of a decline will be like if the first support level is broken. The absence of support levels warns us that fast market conditions will develop without friction and prices will accelerate toward the next zone of support or resistance. Notice the gap under the next support zone that is marked with a *g*. That area is also a high-risk fast market trading range for the Yen/$. *Multiple Fibonacci retracement objectives can therefore calculate slippage exposure.* Many times I find that I am unable to enter a position because, if the target zone is broken, I know the slippage exposure for filling my stops is beyond my risk management parameters. Therefore attaining a price objective alone is insufficient reason to pull the trigger. I also have to know that there will be a gracious out if I am wrong. That can be extremely frustrating at times. But this is a game that has no finish line, and longevity can come only from correctly assessing your risk.

A custom macro can be written in Microsoft *Excel* to develop similar charts. However, the specific price levels from a spreadsheet table are of much greater value for trading than just a hash-mark on a chart. We give out our *Excel* spreadsheets to only those who attend our trading seminars. If you would like to read more about multiple Fibonacci price projections, I recommend Joe DiNapoli's book.[2]

---

[2] Joe DiNapoli, *Trading with DiNapoli Levels* (Sarasota, Florida: Coast Investment Software, 1998).

CHAPTER 7

Price Projections by Reverse-Engineering Indicators

In the first five chapters we discussed ways to increase our probability of correctly interpreting indicators to determine market direction. Many of the techniques gave us the means to identify precise targets for our *indicators*. As an example, we know a trend line drawn from oscillator pivots that form bullish or bearish divergence with prices, or another indicator, is a significant area of future support or resistance for that indicator. If we know the chart position toward which an indicator is focused on traveling, then we are left with one unknown variable: the price level required to drive the indicator to that projected chart position. Therefore, we are about to embark on a discussion of reverse-engineering our indicators to define a price objective.

Technical analysis software products do not give us the ability to reverse-engineer our indicators to solve for an unknown future price. At least not at this time. However, Microsoft *Excel* does provide us with the means to expand the functionality of our real-time quote systems. It is not difficult to create a chart or project the price within Microsoft *Excel*; the difficulty is exporting the raw data from the real-time quote system into a format that could be imported and recognized by Microsoft *Excel*. As the discussion about reverse-engineering an indicator will be useless if you cannot import your data file, I'll get you past this horrendous hurdle by displaying a step-by-step demonstration of how to accomplish this task. This procedure will export real-time FutureSource data files used by Omega Research's *TradeStation* into an *Excel* application. I suspect the procedure will be similar for any data vendor supplying a live data feed for use with *TradeStation*. There will be variations for different real-time charting products, but as long as the platform is

Microsoft *Windows 95/98NT,* and not DOS, these steps should be easy to modify for your specific vendor's system.

The objective of this exercise is to import the data and the indicators displayed in Figure 7–1 into Microsoft *Excel* for further analysis. Figure 7–1 displays the *TradeStation* chart of the daily Yen/$ with the RSI and two moving averages on the indicator. We discussed how the moving averages were added to the RSI graph in a prior chapter. From the range rules we discussed in Chapter 1, we know the major support level is at 40 to 45 for the RSI in a trending bull market. This chart clearly shows an upward trend for the dollar versus the Yen, and the RSI produced an oscillator low near the 45 level at point 1 in Figure 7–1. We will make the assumption that the RSI will return to this important level of support from current highs in anticipation of a significant decline. As we know the level the oscillator will most likely target, we need to solve for the unknown variable y, the price that is required to push the RSI down to point 2 in this chart.

Figure 7–1 shows a Data Window below the chart. Display this window by clicking the left mouse button on View from the pull-down menus on the top of the *TradeStation* screen, and select Data Window. The data window will correspond to the active chart you were last viewing. So make sure that if you have

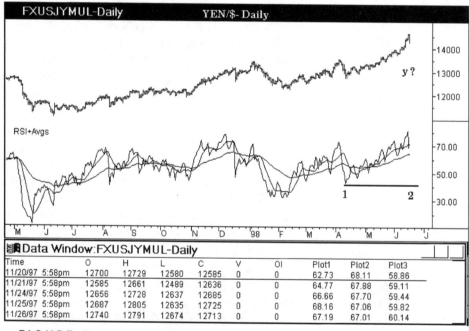

FIGURE 7–1

multiple charts in one *WorkPlan,* you have the correct data and indicators displayed. Most likely you will not have all the data visible in the data window. Move the mouse cursor to any position within the header bar that has the title Data Window, and click the right mouse button. A small menu will appear, and you will need to put a check mark beside Show All Data. Press enter, and the data window will now contain several new columns that include your indicators. One severe limitation to note: *TradeStation* will transfer only six columns of indicator data. In Figure 7–1 we have the RSI and two averages. Three columns have been used. If you have more than one indicator, you will likely have to do this procedure a couple times as it is very easy to exceed the six-column limit of *TradeStation.*

Now move the mouse cursor back into the title bar Data Window of Figure 7–1, and right click the mouse. The small window menu that offered Display All Data will also display Send to File.... This is the last option on the bottom of the pop-up menu. Double click the mouse, or select Send to File, and press enter on the keyboard.

Figure 7–2 displays the window that will open after the last step. This is a very important step. A file name has to be entered in the empty box. I am transferring the file to a floppy disk in drive A: because I use a different computer for my offline analysis work. You may want to use the same computer. Type the drive letter, directory if needed, and then name the file with no more than eight letters. No spaces or fancy characters—just use letters. *Then you must type the extension .txt after your file name.* Excel will know this is a text file because you added this extension. Do not allow the computer to designate a default extension, which it will do if you do not type .txt. You will be stuck at this step for ever more. Another quirk to mention: If your directory or floppy disk already has a file with the exact same name, in this case yen.txt, *TradeStation* will merrily beep at you that it transferred the file to the disk, when in fact it will not overwrite a file with the same name. *TradeStation* will not warn you that the file was not overwritten and revised. You'll go through all the steps that follow and discover the old file is still the one in memory.

Once you have decided on a file name, press enter or click OK as illustrated in Figure 7–2. That was the last step from *TradeStation.* Now we need to import the saved text file into Microsoft *Excel.*

From START>PROGRAMS>EXCEL, open the *Excel* spreadsheet program so that a new screen is displayed. Select from the top menus FILE>OPEN. The screen displayed in Figure 7–3 will appear. You will need to change the default file type on the bottom left to All Files (*.*). Then select the directory or drive where the data file was saved. In this example the file is on the floppy disk I used to move the file over

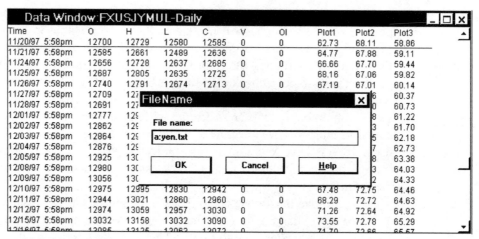

FIGURE 7-2

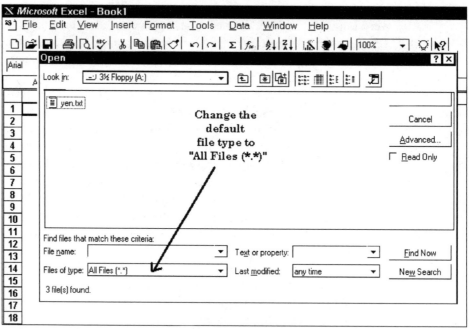

FIGURE 7-3

to a different computer. The text file yen.txt will be displayed in the window. Double click on this file name to open it.

Excel will display the Text Import Wizard that will walk you through the three steps required to import this file into a recognizable format for the *Excel* program. Step 1 of 3 is displayed in Figure 7–4. Ensure that this screen has the following selected: Original Data Type is Delimited, Starting Import row is 1, the File Origin will be Windows (ANSI). These are my defaults, but not necessarily yours, so check them. You are ready to click the next button.

The second step is displayed by the Text Import Wizard. The options to select in Figure 7–5 will be Delimiters—select Comma, and be sure to uncheck any others. I always have to uncheck the Tab box. The Text Qualifier should be the quote symbol. It may be your default as I never seem to need to change it. Click the Next button, and move on to the last step.

In the Data Preview group, click on the column of data that has the dates. The column should be highlighted and may already be highlighted when this screen first appears. Then we move to the Column Data Format options on the top right. Click on Date. (General is the default that needs to be changed.) The last step is to

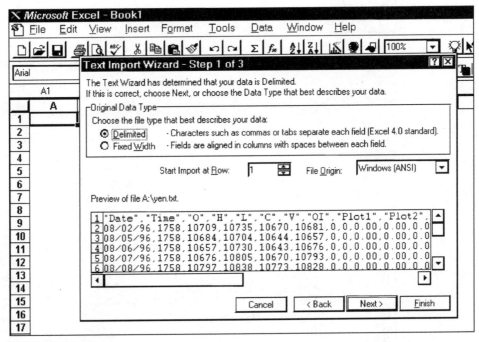

F I G U R E   7 – 4

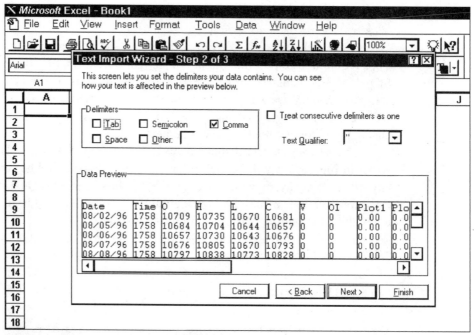

FIGURE   7-5

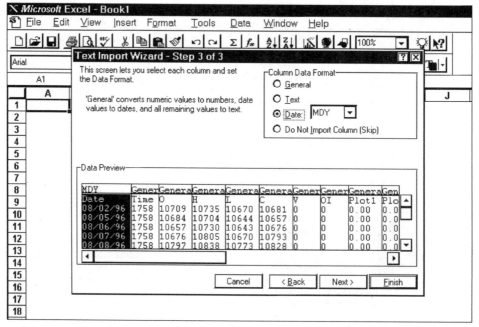

FIGURE   7-6

select MDY in the list for American users or DMY for the rest of the world. Now just click Finish.

Voilà! It has been done. Your data and indicators have just been transferred into *Excel*. I would suggest saving the file immediately as an *Excel* file rather than as text. I will leave you at that step knowing that you have data from which to learn how to create charts. It's up to you to learn how to use *Excel*. The charting is relatively easy. Just know that some of the reverse-engineering projections require you to know the indicator formula and to have *Excel* generate the results, rather than just plugging in the indicator values from *TradeStation*. It will depend on how elaborately you want to use this method. I'm not really an *Excel* Wizard, and I frequently have to contract a programmer to teach me how to do something that I am attempting. All my macros have been written by professionals contracted to develop them. But once the steps are spelled out for me by a pro, most often a university student, the whole universe opens up to offline projection techniques.

Figure 7–8 displays the data and the RSI in an *Excel* chart. We knew the target for the RSI was point 2; it was the same indicator level that developed at point 1. Now we can solve for *y* and determine the price that will move the oscillator to point 2. The projected price for the Yen/$ is at 133.72. *Excel* can draw

	A	B	C	D	E	F	G	H	I
	Date	Time	O	H	L	C	Plot1	Plot2	Plot3
2	12/6/96	1758	11227	11301	11177	11290	52.15	57.23	56.92
3	12/9/96	1758	11299	11354	11286	11343	55.62	57.48	56.86
4	12/10/96	1758	11344	11373	11301	11338	55.21	57.05	56.79
5	12/11/96	1758	11338	11338	11262	11281	50.66	55.74	56.52
6	12/12/96	1758	11282	11364	11245	11313	53	54.61	56.37
7	12/13/96	1758	11312	11402	11274	11390	58.15	53.56	56.45
8	12/16/96	1758	11397	11433	11367	11385	57.71	53.79	56.5
9	12/17/96	1758	11382	11420	11342	11384	57.61	54.19	56.55
10	12/18/96	1758	11385	11395	11327	11362	55.47	55.07	56.5
11	12/19/96	1758	11360	11420	11336	11408	58.92	55.82	56.61
12	12/20/96	1758	11407	11441	11403	11430	60.49	56.36	56.78
13	12/23/96	1758	11423	11435	11387	11410	58.3	56.7	56.84
14	12/24/96	1758	11415	11457	11407	11457	61.8	57.94	57.06
15	12/25/96	1758	11445	11473	11440	11468	62.59	59	57.3
16	12/26/96	1758	11467	11510	11447	11494	64.46	59.71	57.61
17	12/27/96	1758	11492	11617	11472	11530	66.93	60.73	58.02
18	12/30/96	1758	11557	11626	11555	11622	72.24	62.36	58.63

FIGURE 7-7

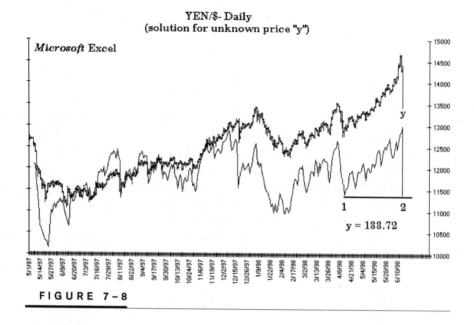

YEN/$- Daily
(solution for unknown price "y")

FIGURE 7-8

these new levels on the chart if desired. The last bar in this chart is the hypothetical projection.

Figure 7–9 returns us to *TradeStation* and the actual market move that developed on June 16, 1998. The price low that the market recorded was 133.67, based
on FutureSource's contributors reporting Spot currency trades. Your vendor might
be slightly different for the same extreme low because it is a cash market quote.
Regardless, the estimate and the actual market price low could not have been much
closer. The oscillator is just slightly higher than our original assumption and has not
formed a perfect double bottom. The reason is that the market required more than
one day to realize the objective. While it took four days for the market to realize the
price objective thereby having an impact on the oscillator, it did not modify the
price objective. This is not a method you will want to use for short intraday market
moves. It is a method to consider when a significant market extreme needs to be
identified in case the worst-case scenario develops. To determine a corresponding
price, you can pick any indicator level you want. In fact, you can use any other indicator to reverse-engineer a price objective.

One of the most valued indicators I use to reverse-engineer an indicator to
project a market move is displayed in Figure 7–10. In the chapter that addressed
trend lines, it was recommended that a horizontal line be plotted to mark the historic highs and lows for an indicator. This helps to keep in perspective that an
oscillator extreme displayed in the chart window is in fact a lifetime extreme or

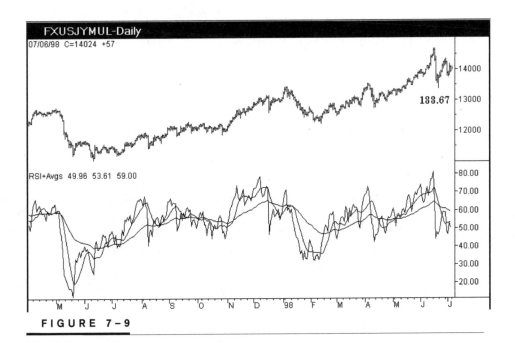

FIGURE 7-9

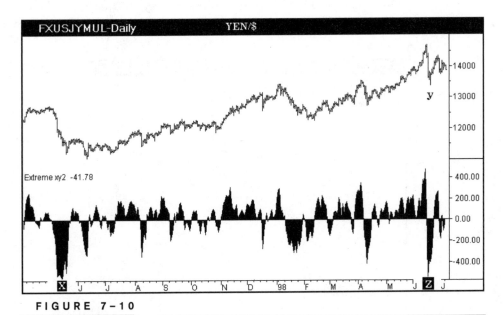

FIGURE 7-10

a lesser displacement that remains unchallenged over a long period of time. I will view a year of daily data and pick the maximum displacement extremes to establish a worst-case market scenario.

In Figure 7–10 the extreme oscillator low at point X was clearly the maximum displacement in this daily chart of the Yen/$ prior to June 16, 1998. The weekly chart warned that it was time to make a projection by solving for the unknown price variable y. The chart shows the actual displacement in this indicator when the market intervention on June 16, 1998, occurred. The oscillator at point Z was displaced a equal distance to that which occurred at point X. The price projection from this indicator that used an entirely different oscillator was 133.40. The chart itself shows the actual market move at point y that formed a market bottom at 133.67 low. What is this magical indicator displayed in Figure 7–10? Extremely complex, years of research and high-tech computers were required to develop it. Well, not really. The oscillator in Figure 7–10 is just the difference between the closing prices and a simple short-period moving average of price. I made it look really fancy by plotting the same differential as a histogram and a line chart. The zero line is where the closing price crosses this simple moving average. Not so high-tech after all, but it works like a charm.

The reason the oscillator extreme was used to project a price extreme in June 1998 was that the weekly Yen/$ chart displayed in Figure 7–11 was recording a maximum displacement equal to the one seen in 1995. When a market records

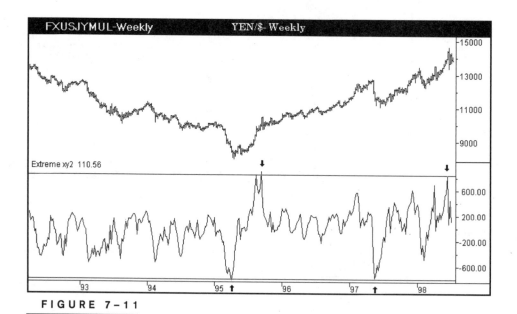

FIGURE 7–11

a displacement equal to the extreme unmatched over a three-year period, that's of great interest. The indicator in Figure 7–11 is the exact one used for Figure 7–10: the differential between market closing prices and a simple short-period moving average. The difference is that the displacement was just plotted as a line this time and the histogram and zero axis were not added. When you plot a moving average of prices as an oscillator, you are in reality just detrending the moving average, or in this case the differential between closing prices and the average. A detrended indicator is frequently easier to read when extremes occur.

If the market realizes a price objective derived from reverse-engineering an indicator, and the indicator challenges the former historical displacement as occurred in Figures 7–10 and 7–11, what happens next? First, use the extreme that just occurred to define an intraday projection for the next. In other words, assume the indicator is capable of making a double bottom the very next day as the market attempts to follow through on the prior day's emotional environment. The level you calculate for price $y+1$ day will be the intraday pivot point that will likely precede a ballistic market move in the opposite direction. If a bow is pulled back with just a little extra effort after extreme tension has been realized, the arrow might be projected at a slightly faster speed. The market is similar. If the market produces an intraday move equal to $y+1$ day, you better not be greedy and expect more from the market. A spike key reversal nearly always follows. As a spike follows and the close for the market is much higher, the oscillator will never show you a double bottom in the indicator. It will develop only on an intraday basis. The indicator will now be off the extreme low or high. My experience has been that you then need to allow, using this method, a minimum of three days to pass before calculating an extreme. The reason is that the indicator includes a simple moving average and needs about three new price bars to incorporate the new extreme displacement into the indicator formula and in effect reset the price projection capability of the indicator.

Recall from the moving average chapter that some indicator formulas will shift to a permanent position. Knowing an indicator shift could develop when new data enters the screen will explain why we need to refrain from using any indicator utilizing moving averages for price projection purposes until after it as shifted into its permanent chart position. Generally three days is long enough. In the meantime, use other indicators because the market will consolidate in a couple days or produce a sharp countertrend move away from the extreme.

This method may be tested by a market only once or twice a year. However, I tend to calculate my primary trading markets for worse-case projections on a regular basis. It is used on the days that a shock wave hits the market with unexpected news. Usually the support or resistance table I have defined for a single day's session is quickly exceeded, and I then know the worst-case price projection is the more probable target. It is a price objective that offers a secure milestone when others become engulfed in total panic and chaos. It's really comforting to sit calmly with a price objective in hand when others are madly scrambling around you trying to figure out where the market's unexpected move could be heading. The preparation is well worth the effort.

As a final note for this particular application of price projection in extreme environments, S&P traders should calculate both the Cash S&P and Future price extremes. In a meltdown or ballistic advance, only one index will realize the extreme projection. Usually it is the futures market, but I have been grateful to know that Cash realized an extreme without Futures and take the appropriate action to unwind immediately. That is a significant signal that means step to the sidelines whenever this technique has a price objective realized.

Let's take another look at applying reverse-engineering. This is a little more esoteric and admittedly used only when other methods seem to be conflicting. In Chapter 3, Figure 3–12, introduced a method of charting the RSI with multiple periods called an *RSI Wave pattern*. Figure 7–12 offers another example of this chart technique where the Weekly Toronto TSE 300 Index is plotted with the RSI Wave indicator study. The wave-plotting technique shows that an indicator can use its own formula plotted multiple times with different

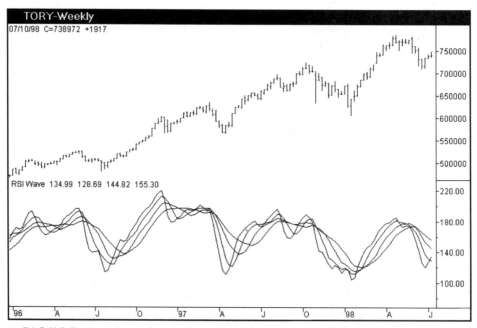

FIGURE 7–12

periods to define support-resistance levels for the indicator. Any charting method that is able to define a support-resistance target is a candidate for reverse-engineering. We need to solve the unknown market prices that will move the oscillator to specific indicator formations. To reverse-engineer this indicator in Figure 7–12, you will now need to know the formula for the RSI. It has been modified. The study in Figure 7–12 is producing an oscillator travel between 100 and 220. Clearly the RSI formula has been modified from its normal range of 0 to 100.

Indicators that use only closing prices in their formulation are blind to extreme price movement. On occasion, to reduce this bias in these formulas, I will first create three indicators derived from the High, Low, and Closing prices. Then the results are averaged. In Figure 7–13 a function is created called "RSIHLC." The RSI equation will use a 14-period setup for each study. But the RSI is calculated using High, Low, and Closing prices. When the formula was being developed, it was found that the close should be given a weighted factor. Markets that rarely produce extreme highs and lows beyond a standard deviation of 1.8 can use a weighted factor within this equation of 2 times the closing price. In Figure 7–13 the sum of the RSI calculated from Highs, Lows, and two Closes are then divided by 4 for the average. Markets that have more frequent highs and lows beyond a standard deviation of 1.8 should not use two closing prices as a weighted factor. Use the sum of the RSI calculated from using Highs, Lows, and Closes; then divide by 3 for the average.

Another approach is to imbed a volatility variable into the formula that will accommodate the characteristic difference between declining and rising markets. We will defer that discussion until a later time when volatility bands are plotted with indicators.

The average obtained in the Function window of Figure 7–13 is then smoothed by creating four simple moving averages with short periods within the Fibonacci number series. The reverse-engineering technique is used to define the price level that will cause the shortest average (in this case a 2-period average of RSIHLC) to test one of the other Fibonacci averages plotted. The areas of greater interest, and frequently the only ones I calculate, are the price levels that will drive the shortest-period average into an area where the three slightly longer period averages begin to converge. It is the narrowing of the spread between these four averages that warns of upcoming trend changes. Trend continuation requires no price projection as the study itself is easy to read. A shorter-period average will test a slower one and not break the trend formation. Not all time horizons or markets should be plotted with this wave pattern technique. If the indicator study is not as distinctive as the one shown in Figure 7–12, it is an inappropriate study for the time horizon you are charting.

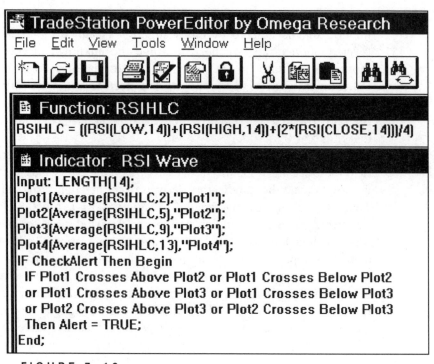

FIGURE 7−13

Ultimately you will need to select three price projection methods that are all noncorrelated. Reverse-engineering, in my opinion, is more appropriate for preparation in the event of extreme market moves, and it is not a method I would use for day-to-day market forecasting. So let's move on to another price projection method that uses an indicator for forecasting. However, this next method requires no reverse-engineering techniques or sophisticated computer skills. It also has the added bonus of being able to measure the probability of realizing the price objective obtained from the method.

CHAPTER 8

Price Objectives Derived from Positive and Negative Reversals in the RSI

The Relative Strength Index is more than a momentum oscillator from which market overbought and oversold conditions can be identified. This indicator has the ability to forecast future market levels from specific indicator patterns called *Positive and Negative Reversals*. The price projection characteristics of the RSI were not discovered by J. Welles Wilder, who first developed the RSI formula, but by Andrew Cardwell who is recognized by many to be the world's leading authority on the Relative Strength Index. It is because of Cardwell's focused research on a single indicator that we now have this method of price forecasting. What is of particular interest is that the signals Cardwell first identified within the RSI formula are present in other oscillators. His work with the RSI has actually opened the door to a new method of using oscillators in general for price projection.

While Cardwell has been giving lectures around the world since 1989 to select audiences about his price projection techniques derived from the RSI, he is not widely known, and his methods have not been formally published. His lectures are similar to the writings of W. D. Gann. There is so much detail in his lectures and charts that it is easy to get lost in the volume of information he extracts from every single RSI squiggle. As I believe no method should be used in isolation, my intention is to focus on the polished gem within his methodology: his approach of calculating new price objectives for a market.

I am managing my own offshore investment pool today because of the guidance and technical foundation that was given to me by four mentors who are industry leaders. Andrew Cardwell and George Lane, whom I turn to for help about momentum indicators and issues that address survival in this industry; Joe DiNapoli for Fibonacci applications and trading guidance; and Dave Allman who taught me the Elliott Wave Principle. Had I not crossed paths with these four industry leaders, I am confident I would not be in the position I am in today.

The three methods I use for obtaining a price objective for a market are Gann, Fibonacci, and Andrew Cardwell's Reversal signals derived from the RSI. Cardwell's methods are perhaps the least known, and I will attempt to correct that oversight now as he has made a major contribution to the field of technical analysis.

Readers of this book can look back on the days when it was a struggle to recognize bullish and bearish divergence between price data and indicators. It will help if you recall those earlier days now and know that with time the signals we are about to discuss will be very easy signals to see; but it will not happen overnight or without some effort. It took me nearly a year to be able to quickly observe the most blatant signals, and perhaps another year to pick out the more hidden and subtle innuendoes within the RSI. Even three years later Cardwell could still point out signals and information that I had overlooked. We can push each other now on equal footing when discussing our analytic work, but it has

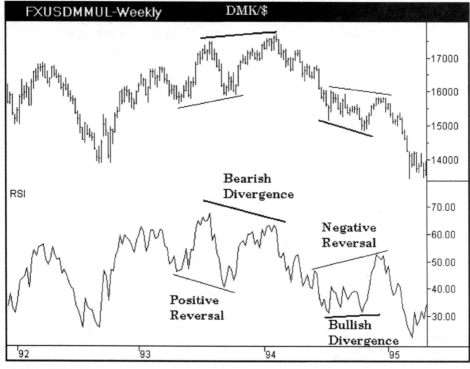

FIGURE 8-1

taken me nearly nine years of practice and experience to come to this milestone. So if you find you are struggling at first, don't be discouraged.

In Figure 8–1 we are looking at a weekly DMK/$ chart. To capture your interest, let me cut straight to the bottom line for this chart. When the market was at 1.5957, the price projection method we will evaluate produced a price target on close of 1.7537. The actual close for the highest price bar was 1.7540. Interesting? Well, there is more coming. From the market high in Figure 8–1, the final market bottom of the decline that follows ends at the last price bar in this chart on the right. The RSI developed four price targets as the decline unfolded from 1.7537. The objectives were 1.6610, 1.6424, 1.5157, and a final target on close of 1.3676. The actual closing price for the decline that formed the week of April 21, 1995, was 1.3678. A difference of 0.0002 in a decline that unfolded from 1.7537 to 1.3678. Have these numbers piqued your curiosity? Good. Let's take a closer look at how these price objectives were obtained.

Figure 8–1 uses bold lines to mark the bullish and bearish divergences present in this weekly DMK/$ chart between the price data and indicator. Bearish divergence occurs when the market forms a new price high that is not confirmed by the indicator. In this chart the RSI is clearly at a lower peak when the price high is recorded. Conversely, bullish divergence will occur when the market makes a new price low and the indicator does not. This must be firmly rooted now within your technical skills before moving on. If you are still training your eye to recognize divergences, skip this chapter entirely until a later time as I promise you, that those who see divergences now will forget what they look like by the time we are through.

Figure 8–1 conveniently has both bullish and bearish divergences in the same chart and displays examples of the new RSI signals that offer price projections. The new signals are called *Reversals*. There are *Positive* and *Negative Reversals*. In a Positive Reversal, the RSI will develop a new oscillator low relative to a former indicator pivot when the price data is at a *higher* level. Tilt? I know, it is hard to put into words too as it is such a visual pattern. But look at the Positive Reversal in Figure 8–1. It makes perfect sense that this indicator pattern would be bullish as the oscillator is becoming oversold when the market is trading at a higher level. This tells us that the market is building underlying strength when this indicator formation is present. Conversely, a Negative Reversal develops when the RSI is able to attain a new high relative to a prior oscillator peak, but the closing price associated with the new oscillator peak is at a *lower* price level. As the oscillator is becoming overbought when prices are at a lower level, it warns that the market is beginning to erode and become weaker.

In Figure 8–1 there is labeled a Positive Reversal pattern that forms from fairly blatant oscillator lows. *Reversal signals do not have to be at oscillator peaks and troughs that form extremes.* The Negative Reversal in Figure 8–1 shows that the first RSI peak is not at an obvious extreme pivot. However, the second RSI pivot high on the right side of this Negative Reversal signal is clearly associated with a lower price. This will be clearer when the price projection method is discussed. When an RSI Reversal signal occurs within the larger trend for the oscillator, it is called a *Hidden Signal,* and they are much stronger market signals than Reversals that form at blatantly obvious pivot extremes.

The Positive Reversal in Figure 8–2 is the same signal introduced to you in Figure 8–1. It now has three oscillator pivots labeled: two oscillator lows I've arbitrarily called pivots W and X, then an oscillator high marked Y that is the highest-momentum extreme located between points W and X. Frequently the momentum high will not be the price high as oscillators form divergences with price. We will always look for the momentum peak that is the highest level for the Positive Reversal price projection calculation. Keep in mind that the closing price for a price bar is used, not the high or low, when we want to know the associated price for the oscillator pivot. The Negative Reversal also has three oscillator pivots labeled W,

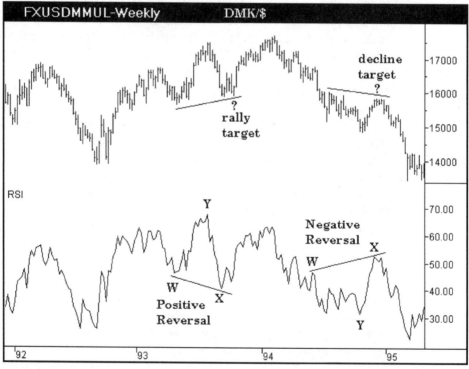

FIGURE 8–2

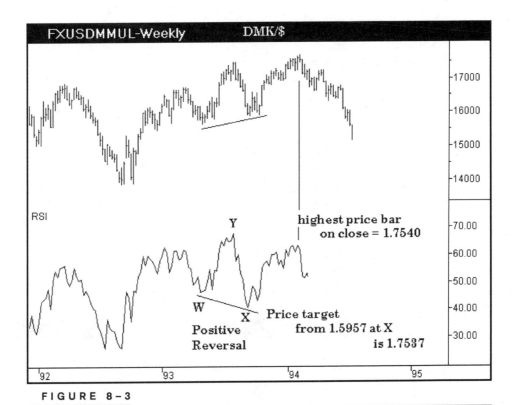

FIGURE 8-3

X, and Y, where Y is the extreme momentum low between points W and X. As described for a Positive Reversal, the momentum extreme at point Y in the RSI may not be the actual price low because divergence may be present. The oscillator will always determine the correct closing price to use.

To make a price projection from a Positive Reversal signal, use the following formula:

$$(X-W)+Y=\text{the new price target}$$

In Figure 8–3 the closing price associated with the RSI low at point W is 1.5835. The closing price associated with the RSI low at point X is 1.5957. In a Positive Reversal the closing price associated with point X must always be greater than or equal to the closing price associated with the RSI pivot at point W. It is this positive differential that defines a Positive Reversal signal in the indicator. Therefore, the price projection from near 1.5957 is $(1.5957-1.5835)=0.0122+Y$. The differential is then added to the closing price associated with the momentum extreme at point Y. The closing price that corresponds to the momentum high at Y is

1.7415. Therefore, the final target is the differential $0.0122 + 1.7415 = 1.7537$. The actual price on close February 11, 1994, was 1.7540, and it marked the end of the dollar rally at that time.

The formula to use for calculating a market decline from a Negative Reversal is as follows:

$$Y - (W - X) = \text{the new price target}$$

In a Negative Reversal the second pivot high at point X will always be less than *or equal to* the associated closing price at point W. Therefore, the points that create the differential are switched, and the result must be subtracted from the closing price associated with the RSI oscillator extreme at point Y. The signal in Figure 8–4 is actually a Negative Reversal that follows a series of price projection signals within this decline. We will look at each of these Negative Reversal signals and the price targets that develop in Figure 8–5.

There are four Negative Reversals labeled in Figure 8–5. (There are actually eight signals present. Can you locate the other four?) The three pivots that we use

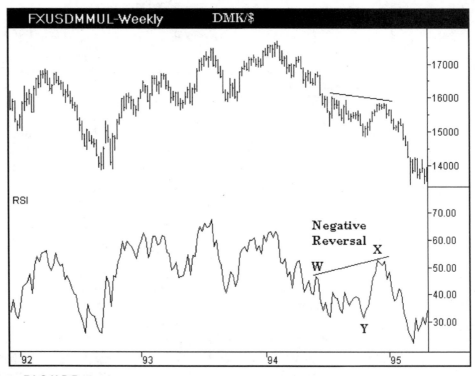

FIGURE 8 - 4

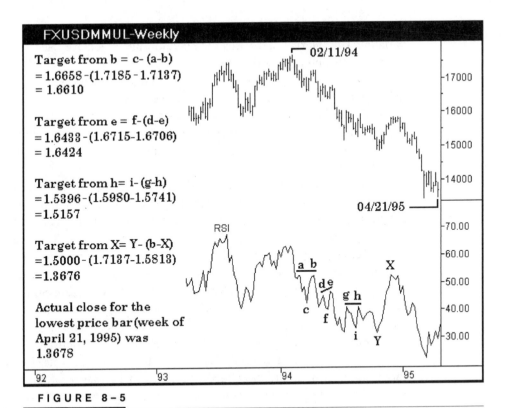

FIGURE 8-5

to make the price projection will name the signal being described. The Negative Reversals labeled in this chart are signals abc, def, ghi, and bXY. There are also signals at eXY and hXY. EXY is in fact the same signal marked in Figure 8-4 as WXY. As signal bXY is the price projection that defines the final target, we need not calculate the differentials from e−X and h−X for in this example their objectives were realized at higher levels. (There are still two additional Negative Reversals in this chart not labeled.)

The target from the RSI pivot b is calculated c−(a−b) to obtain the new price objective. Therefore, 1.6658−(1.7185−1.7137)=1.6610. The target from the RSI pivot e will equal f−(d−e), or 1.6433−(1.6715−1.6706), which equals 1.6424. The third target is from pivot h. The formula to use is i−(g−h). The results are 1.5396−(1.5980−1.5741), giving a 1.5157 objective for DMK/$. Finally, the last signal is bXY, where the price objective from X is calculated using the formula Y−(b−X). Therefore, 1.5000−(1.7137−1.5813) offers an objective at 1.3676. As mentioned in the beginning, the actual close for the price bar that ended the decline was 1.3678. Because of the price forecasting capability of the

RSI, a 14 period should always be used so that you are working from a standard variable. The interval of 14 was obtained through extensive back-testing of multiple markets and time horizons.

Often when I have given a trading seminar with Forex traders, they return home and call me to ask, "My spot prices are different from yours. Why?" Traders who have been in the business for years are unfamiliar with how their Spot market quotes are created. So I had better digress for a moment and explain why you may also see closing levels that are different from mine in your Forex spot market data.

All the major quote vendors—Reuters, Bloomberg, Telerate, FutureSource, and Bridge, to name a few—must create Forex spot market quotes by having contributing Money Center Banks and major financial institutions report their trades to the vendor. This information is gathered in several ways. There are electronic trading consoles that allow traders to enter orders directly into their system for automatic best-fill execution. These systems record the actual market levels where trades occur, and they are directly reported to a quote vendor. Some contributors have trades captured and electronically transmitted to the vendor in secondary ways. Sometimes it is the bid and ask that is reported by a contributor and not an actual market level that was traded. Regardless, the more contributors a vendor has reporting trades, the more accurate will be their market levels. Reuters has the largest number of contributors reporting Forex market levels at this time. All vendors are constantly trying to gain as many contributors as possible so that the more esoteric cross rates and secondary markets can be given fair market value indications. Naturally the most influential banks are asked to report exclusively to one vendor. So in the grand scheme of data vendor marketing plans, we will end up with differences in our Forex spot data. What this means is that if you are working with FutureSource data, we will have the same closing prices. If you work with a different data vendor, the price levels will probably be slightly different. However, the calculations that you make from your data will display the same results; all the objectives were realized from the RSI pivots labeled in Figure 8–5.

We have just taken a look at one chart, one time horizon, and one market that offered the perfect example of how a specific indicator pattern in the RSI can be used to forecast market prices. The weekly DMK/$ chart provided us with a perfect example that is essential when we are first introduced to a new method. But now there should be a lot of questions in your mind that should be asked of any indicator we use. Questions I would raise about a new method or formula are the following:

1. Does the indicator work equally well for any market in any time horizon?
2. Does the indicator have an equal probability of being correct for a rising market as it does for a declining market?

3. What is the exact character of the signal for a buy signal and a sell signal? Does the indicator have a bias and display a higher probability when buy signals form than its sell signals? Is the character of the buy signal the same as a sell signal? Many of the indicators I use display complex sell signals and develop very simple buy signal patterns.

4. Why does an indicator work? Under what conditions will the indicator fail? Few ask these questions, and we will explore ways to answer them in this chapter.

5. How can we be warned that an indicator signal is wrong? If we can detect an indicator failure, can it give us sufficient warning to take action before we lose a great deal of money?

I do not think an indicator or method should be used if the questions above have not been thoroughly researched. The DJIA and S&P 500 Index have given some well-known long-term bears a difficult time throughout the 1990s. This is not a comment directed at any one method in particular as Elliott Wave, Cycle, and Momentum Gurus have all had their turn at being squeezed into a corner by the bull market of the 1990s. Instead of ridiculing those who have stood firmly by their bearish market views, we should make every effort to learn from them as we are all vulnerable to making the same errors if we do not understand how they were misled.

Some of the people who missed the 1990 rally share the view that Global markets should be analyzed as independent entities. Internet communications have broken barriers, which has increased our need to monitor Global cash flows among international stock markets. Understanding Global leadership and recognizing that the technical signals forming in another country's charts may have greater weighting and influence than they might in one's own local market are areas where some analysts have failed to accommodate changing conditions.

Another problem is relying on indicators that perform less effectively in our changing environment. On second thought, to use the phrase "changing environment" is inaccurate. Our markets are not changing; they are rescaling. History will always repeat itself, but it is the scale and changing proportions that cause us such difficulty because we tend to use the proportions of the past to project the dimensions of our future. Yet, we have been taught by the very Gurus who now find themselves in difficult corners that markets abide by the expansion and contraction cycles dictated by the Laws of Nature that are found in all growth-decay cycles. When an analyst attempts to contradict the evidence present that an expansion phase in a market could be developing by changing the scale of the data itself from arithmetic, to semilog, to percent log, he or she is struggling, perhaps painfully, to work within the familiar proportions of the past and ignoring the natural expansion and contraction cycles of the present. If the scale of the expansion phase is larger than we have experienced in our past, so too will be the contraction phase of the cycle. No doubt the great bears of our time will look pretty good at some moments, but their livelihood has not been tied to the timing of their outlooks. Traders in general have a very different outlook. We do not really care where a market might be trading in a few years; just give us an indication it will move tomorrow and give us a chance to be on the right side.

On a much smaller scale, there is a story told in my first book *Aerodynamic Trading* about a day when my quote screens falsely reported the S&P market locked limit down as all my phone lines went down that could connect me to the Chicago Mercantile Exchange. I describe the horror of trying to make the connection to the floor when it was discovered that my quote systems were wrong and the market was, in reality, in "a ballistic rally." The story is accompanied by an intraday chart showing a 10-point rally in the S&P. All this excitement followed the market's meltdown of nearly 15 points. Today a 10-point move in the S&P market is an intraday swing of normal proportions, and I can sit through such a move while calmly eating lunch before the computer screen. The 10-point swing could just as easily reverse itself by the time my sandwich was consumed. The volatility ranges of today's market have become the normal measurement from which to make comparative judgments. No, our trading environment does not change—just the size and scale of the ranges with which we become comfortable. However, as markets expand and contract, some of our indicators may not be able to adjust to the new scale and underlying factors that contribute to the growth-decay cycle. I know in my day-to-day trading that some indicators are more suited to fast market conditions than others. It is not surprising that some of the indicators favored in the 1970s and 1980s have let some of our industry's Gurus down when they did not seek other formulas to support their primary method. The Advance-Decline line and Sentiment analysis, which are favored by analysts as secondary indicators, have missed the 1990 rally. I think the Advance-Decline line has several problems because of underlying changes, and it has no value as a timing signal. This topic always inspires a hot debate with those who favor these indicators, and I will not venture down this path much further as it is a debate that becomes a rhetorical question left unanswered. But the point that is much harder to defend is, why continue to use a supporting indicator when its interpretive value has a damaged performance record? Observing how some methods of the past have seemingly let some of our industry's Gurus down should warn us that we must continually quantify our methods on a regular basis. We therefore need to be much smarter about developing an intimate understanding of the indicators and methods we use. How can we dissect our methods so that we too do not become victims of our indicators or take their performance records of the past for granted and assume that they will work as well in the future?

Let's use this new indicator pattern in the RSI to explore the questions raised a few moments ago. We know the weekly DMK/$ chart offered a perfect scenario from which to learn how to identify future market objectives from the RSI Reversal signals. But do these signals work this well in all markets? Figure 8–6 is a weekly chart of the S&P 500 futures market. In this chart we are staying within a weekly time horizon and changing the market. The April 1997 low allowed the RSI to form a low that was below the oscillator extreme recorded in 1996. As the oscillator pivot at point X is produced from a higher price level, we have another Positive Reversal signal present. The target the signal offered at 911.35 was realized and then was significantly exceeded. Great. It worked. That's one signal, but we know today that the 1997 market low was only a correction within the context of a much larger bull market. How does this indicator perform when a monthly chart is evaluated?

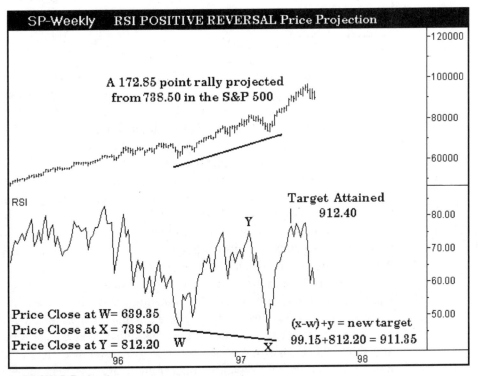

FIGURE 8-6

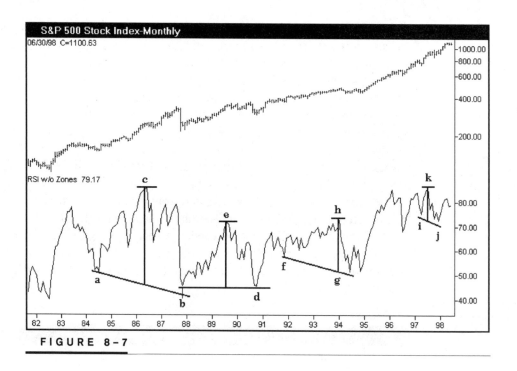

FIGURE 8–7

The monthly chart of the S&P 500 Index is displayed in Figure 8–7. The Positive Reversal signal that formed in 1997 in the weekly chart was just one signal within an entire series of Positive Reversals that had developed in the monthly chart. Signals *abc*, *bde*, *fgh*, and *ijk* have all had their price objectives realized by the market. There are numerous smaller signals not marked in this chart, but as their price projections are inconsequential now, they are not labeled. The crash of 1987 produced an enormous Positive Reversal signal in the RSI with point *b* forming a bottom above the 40 level, which we know is the support range for the RSI within the context of a bull market. Then we see that the three signals that follow develop at higher levels. The RSI pivots that form at *i* and *j* are at a higher level on the RSI *y*-axis than the pivots that form at points *f* and *g*. This is an interesting observation that would make one wonder at what point could these signals warn of an end to the expansion cycle in the market and the uptrend. Another observation is that the amplitude, or distance between the momentum highs from the RSI pivot lows, is becoming shorter. The rise from point *b* to *c* is much longer than the rise from point *d* to *e*. Each is a shorter rise than the previous signal. Now we are beginning to actually think about what makes an indicator work. Another observation is that the number of periods that separate points *i* and *j* are less than the spread between points *f* and *g*, which in turn is less than the spread between *b* and *d* or *a* and *b*. Our curiosity should prompt us to ask if these same characteristics can be observed in different markets that are experiencing major advances.

In Figure 8–8 we are looking at the S&P Stock Sector: *Oil International* in a monthly chart. In this bull market the signals that form at 1, 4, 5, and 6 are also developing at higher RSI levels. The spread between the oscillator pivot lows are variable. The signals at 3, 4, and 5 form after bearish divergence develops between the indicator and prices at the highs. In Cardwell's lectures, he will make the statement: "Bearish divergence is Bullish" and "Bullish Divergence is Bearish." Always a statement that prompts numerous puzzled faces in the audience. However, divergence is a directional signal that gives immediate guidance on a market trend reversal. If you look at Figure 8–1, you will see that a channel develops. The upper trend line of the channel is bearish divergence, and the lower channel, sometimes exactly parallel to the upper, is the Positive Reversal signal. When a Negative Reversal forms, the bottom trend line for this channel is bullish divergence. In Figure 8–8 the momentum highs that have associated prices at 282.28, 319.62, and 419.23, form channels with the signals that develop at 4 and 5. I cannot agree with the statement "Bearish Divergence is Bullish, and Bullish Divergence is Bearish," as the statement is incorrect as far as trading these signals and market timing is concerned. However, I will acknowledge that channels do form. Furthermore, Figure 8–1 clearly demonstrates

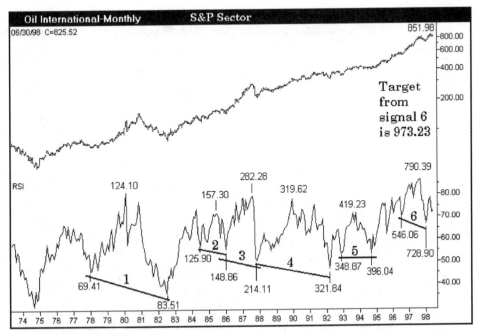

FIGURE 8-8

the channels that we may find within any time horizon that may help our analysis by warning us to be more observant about a pattern we may have overlooked. When the RSI breaks out of one of these channels, as seen in Figure 8–1, it is clearly significant, but no more so than the oscillator ranges we have discussed for bull and bear markets for all oscillators.

We were interested in the amplitude of the signals in Figure 8–7, as they were becoming noticeably shorter as the bull market aged. However, Figure 8–8 does not display amplitudes with this strong pattern emerging, and both markets are in major uptrends. We clearly need to quantify these different attributes that we are observing within these RSI signals so that we may build our confidence about the technique. We also know these signals will not work all the time. So we need to ask, "How can we tell if a price objective from a Positive or Negative Reversal pattern in the RSI will fail?"

Figure 8–9 is a daily COMEX Gold chart displaying Negative Reversals in the RSI indicator as Gold declines. In this chart are two Negative Reversals, one that realizes the price objective and a second that narrowly misses the target. A price objective is *negated* when the RSI violates the trend line that connects the two momentum pivot levels used to calculate the differential for the price objective. In this chart the two momentum highs that have corresponding closing prices

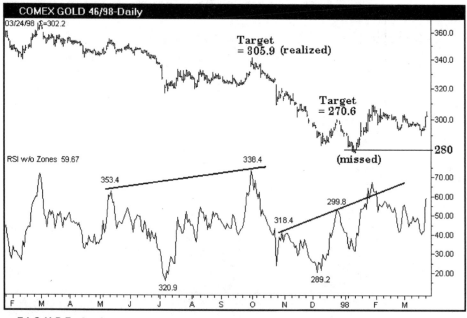

FIGURE 8–9

at 318.4 and 299.8 show that their trend line was violated and exceeded in February 1998. Therefore, the price objective that was made from this signal that pointed to 270.60 has been negated. The plus is that this signal actually has a means to define a failure. The drawback is that in these larger signals the market has traveled a considerable distance before the signal is negated.

In Cardwell's work he will add a simple 9-period moving average and exponential 45-period moving average to the 14-period RSI. We discussed how to add moving averages to indicators in a previous chapter. A Positive Reversal is viewed as confirmed when the shorter 9-period moving average is above the exponential 45-period moving average that is drawn on both the RSI and price data. If a Positive Reversal signal develops when the 9-period moving average is still below the longer moving average, he calls this chart pattern a "naked Positive Reversal" and waits for a new signal to develop that is confirmed by the averages. Negative Reversals are confirmed when the shorter moving average is below the longer period.

While this method of filtering Reversal signals works when you back-test signals in the context of historical data, it does not work well in real-time because of the tremendous displacement that occurs between the RSI indicator and averages when new data is added (please refer to Part 1, Chapter 5). You may also recall the examples that were offered to show the extreme displacement that occurs when moving averages are added on top of an indicator between the position of the indicators in a real-time bar and the changes that develop as new price data is added to the chart. There is tremendous risk in using averages on an indicator as a signal filtering technique.

However, Cardwell uses another method of filtering his signals which is of greater value that we will want to quantify through testing. The two indicator pivot levels that are marked points W and X in Figure 8–2 require a maximum limit on the number of periods or bars that separate points W and X. We saw that comparable points in the signals from Figure 8–7 were becoming more narrow. This becomes an important attribute of the signal because the spread cannot change between points W and X as new data enters the database. We have now made several observations about the attributes of these signals, and we should try to test the performance of them in as many different ways as we can.

Figure 8–10 is the exact same signal that was in Figure 8–6. I am using this signal to summarize the different attributes that need to be tested so that we may gain a stronger understanding of when this signal will have the highest probability of being correct. We want to know which attribute, if any, will have an influence on the outcome of the signal. We need to test the number of days or periods between the oscillator pivot points W and X. We saw in the monthly charts that the signal will travel upward along the y-axis. Does the RSI level these signals form at have an impact on the probability? We are interested in the amplitude of

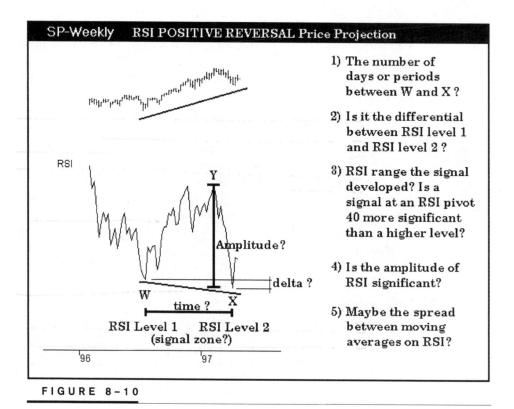

FIGURE 8-10

the signal. Does the delta between RSI points W and X have any significance? We need to test the signal as it relates to the spread of the two moving averages and recognize that the results are based on historic indicator placement. If the moving average results merit further research, we can always test the signal positions as they would have appeared in real-time. We are just beginning to dissect this indicator pattern, and the first test can use a small sampling of data in only one time horizon to see if any single attribute emerges as more significant than another.

Figure 8-11 is a Microsoft *Excel* spreadsheet that shows a sampling of test data from daily currency future charts. The data has to be entered by hand as Reversal signals cannot be automated for study. Columns C, J, K, N, and O are used to create a sort of all the data. As each column is sorted in ascending order, we are looking at the results that occur in column R: the number of days between a signal and when the market attains the target. If the signal is negated, meaning that the RSI has crossed through the trend line described in Figure 8-9 and failed, it is so marked in column Q. If the objective had not been realized but the signal had not been negated by breaking the trend line, it would mean a market position

Currency Futures

RELATIVE STRENGTH INDEX STUDY - Aerodynamic Investments Inc., Connie Brown, CTA, CMT

| | | 9 sma / 45 sma | DATE | PRICE | RSI | DATE | PRICE | RSI | RSI Delta (L1-L2) | Mean | PRICE for RSI | RSI Chart | RSI | SIGNAL Spread | PRICE | DATE OBJECTIVE | Days Between Signal & |
MARKET	SIGNAL TYPE	$SPREAD	Level 1	Level 1	Level 1	Level 2	Level 2	Level 2	(abs. val)	(L1+L2)/2	Level	Level	Amplitude	(Days)	OBJECTIVE	REALIZED	Realized Target
DM	NR	-12.18	3/13/91	63.20	28.81	4/2/91	59.56	32.85	4.04	30.83	57.98	15.18	17.67	20	54.34	Negated	failed
DM	NR	-9.54	4/2/91	59.56	32.85	4/4/91	59.52	34.15	1.30	33.50	59.25	31.37	2.78	2	59.21	4/5/91	1
JY	PR	-3.02	1/16/91	73.07	40.63	2/25/91	74.71	38.64	1.99	39.64	77.89	68.34	29.70	40	79.53	Negated	failed
SF	NR	-2.29	6/24/91	64.88	40.09	7/8/91	63.85	40.13	0.04	40.11	62.94	29.00	11.13	14	61.91	7/11/91	3
DM	NR	-1.23	6/24/91	55.70	43.03	7/8/91	54.93	43.31	0.28	43.17	54.03	31.03	12.28	14	53.26	Negated	failed
DM	NR	-0.39	4/16/91	59.58	42.85	4/30/91	58.05	44.21	1.36	43.53	56.28	26.92	17.29	14	54.75	Negated	failed
SF	NR	-0.12	4/4/91	70.87	42.55	4/9/91	70.56	44.06	1.51	43.31	69.26	34.57	9.49	5	68.95	4/29/91	20
JY	NR	0.15	4/30/91	73.05	51.87	5/15/91	72.68	52.72	0.85	52.30	71.46	42.45	10.27	15	71.09	6/10/91	26
JY	PR	0.43	7/25/91	71.80	45.95	8/19/91	72.02	47.13	1.18	46.54	73.56	63.27	16.14	25	73.78	9/23/91	35
SF	NR	0.63	8/12/91	65.91	54.50	8/22/91	65.85	55.26	0.76	54.88	63.39	39.55	15.71	10	63.93	Negated	failed
SF	PR	2.29	8/23/91	65.09	49.14	9/5/91	65.11	48.85	0.29	49.00	65.45	52.06	3.21	13	65.47	9/17/91	12
DM	PR	2.83	7/11/91	54.09	36.64	8/19/91	54.35	32.53	4.11	34.59	58.03	55.53	23.00	39	58.29	9/9/91	21
SF	PR	2.94	7/16/91	63.72	44.38	8/19/91	63.99	47.55	3.17	45.97	66.66	61.50	13.95	34	66.93	9/17/91	29
JY	PR	4.43	7/3/91	71.41	46.48	7/25/91	71.80	48.95	2.47	47.72	73.16	65.02	16.07	22	73.55	8/6/91	12
SF	NR	5.44	5/15/91	69.73	55.38	7/19/91	59.75	59.75	4.37	57.57	63.63	24.04	35.71	65	53.65	open	open
JY	PR	5.5	1/25/91	75.17	52.79	2/19/91	75.77	46.36	6.43	49.58	77.89	68.34	21.98	25	78.49	Negated	failed
JY	PR	5.68	9/18/91	74.21	61.00	9/26/91	74.49	58.11	2.89	59.56	75.21	71.29	13.18	8	75.49	10/1/91	5
SF	NR	6.04	2/21/91	78.23	43.41	5/15/91	69.73	55.38	11.97	49.40	70.23	15.98	39.40	83	61.73	open	open
DM	NR	6.39	2/21/91	66.67	45.48	5/4/91	58.86	54.75	9.27	50.12	57.98	15.18	39.57	72	50.17		open
DM	NR	6.75	5/15/91	58.56	54.75	7/19/91	56.83	61.90	7.15	58.33	54.64	26.98	34.92	65	52.91		open
DM	NR	6.75	5/28/91	58.58	53.78	7/19/91	56.83	61.90	8.12	57.84	54.64	26.98	34.92	52	52.89		open
DM	PR	9.01	9/11/91	58.47	63.58	9/19/91	58.65	59.93	3.65	61.76	59.23	67.42	7.49	8	59.41	10/3/91	14
SF	PR	9.33	7/25/91	64.84	50.83	8/1/91	64.88	50.22	0.61	50.53	65.41	54.49	4.27	7	65.45	8/6/91	5
SF	PR	10.86	9/11/91	66.99	63.74	9/19/91	67.34	60.32	3.42	62.03	68.07	79.27	18.95	8	68.42	Negated	failed

RSISTUDY

FIGURE 8-11

was still open. However, positions that have been open for a long period are viewed as opportunity costs and are just as unwanted as failures.

Column C, the spread between moving averages, is the sort criteria for Figure 8–11. The results in column R appear random. Keep in mind that this is a spreadsheet of sampling data, and Negative Reversals and Positive Reversals were tested separately in actual practice. However, the results for the moving average spread first appear to be of little value. Similar results develop when columns J, K, and O define the sort criteria. All the results for column R appears to be randomly distributed.

An entirely different result occurs when the rows are sorted by the RSI Amplitude in column N. While a small sampling of data is used for the initial test, the results in column R seem to indicate that the higher the amplitude of the signal, the longer it would take to realize a price objective and the lower the probability of the signal's success. The results in Figure 8–12 are statistically insufficient evidence as the data sampling is too small. So the next step is to laboriously plug in thousands of signals for multiple time horizons from a deep historical database and then repeat the sort criteria again. What I learned is that the initial sort in Figure 8–12 is repeatable when a statistically viable database is evaluated. The shorter the amplitude of the Reversal signal, the higher the probability that the signal will be correct and the market will attain the price objective. The amplitude for the S&P 500 must be less than 24 in a daily chart. To those who may have attended one of my lectures, you will know the amplitude I use to reference was 18. A change has occurred in the test results because of the higher volatility we now experience in the S&P 500 and shows how critical attributes for an indicator may change over time. The testing phase of the indicators and methods we use should never be viewed as complete and final.

What are the amplitude limits for other markets? What about intraday versus longer-horizon time intervals? I will lead you in the direction that I know is the right course, but I will not hand the research over on a silver platter. That is for you to undertake, and it is an extremely important step. It is through this testing phase that the indicator you use and its character will become intuitive. All the indicators I use and blend into a trading system must undergo this elaborate phase of testing so that I know what the limitations and capabilities are of each indicator or method.

I once had a trading model stolen by an employer and later heard through the grapevine that the organization lost a fortune using the model in the currency markets. I knew the model would be very costly for anyone who did not understand that I have components that are used only in certain market conditions, and some signals that develop are always used to fade the market. As an example, the method of monitoring the Stochastics Default Club was described in earlier chapters. The methods described for reverse-engineering are used only in extreme market conditions. A fast market condition during very short horizon trading charts

RELATIVE STRENGTH INDEX STUDY - Aerodynamic Investments Inc., Connie Brown, CTA, CMT

Currency Futures

(Sorted by: RSI Amplitude - Column N)

MARKET	SIGNAL TYPE	9 sma/ 45 sma SPREAD	DATE Level 1	PRICE Level 1	RSI Level 1	DATE Level 2	PRICE Level 2	RSI Level 2	RSI Delta(L1-L2) (abs. val)	RSI Mean [L1+L2]/2	PRICE for RSI Level	RSI Chart Level	RSI Amplitude	SIGNAL Spread (Days)	PRICE OBJECTIVE	DATE OBJECTIVE REALIZED	Days Between Signal & Realized Target
DM	NR	-9.54	4/2/91	59.56	32.85	4/4/91	59.52	34.15	1.30	33.50	59.25	31.37	2.78	2	59.21	4/5/91	1
SF	PR	2.29	8/23/91	65.09	49.14	9/5/91	65.11	48.85	0.29	49.00	65.45	52.06	3.21	13	65.47	9/17/91	12
SF	PR	9.33	7/25/91	64.84	50.83	8/1/91	64.88	50.22	0.61	50.53	65.41	54.49	4.27	7	65.45	8/6/91	5
DM	PR	9.01	9/11/91	58.47	63.58	9/19/91	58.65	59.93	3.65	61.76	59.23	67.42	7.49	8	59.41	10/3/91	14
SF	NR	-0.12	4/4/91	70.87	42.55	4/9/91	70.56	44.06	1.51	43.31	69.26	34.57	9.49	5	68.95	4/29/91	20
JY	NR	0.15	4/30/91	73.05	51.87	5/15/91	72.68	52.72	0.85	52.30	71.46	42.45	10.27	15	71.09	6/10/91	26
SF	NR	-2.29	6/24/91	64.88	40.09	7/8/91	63.85	40.13	0.04	40.11	62.94	29.00	11.13	14	61.91	7/11/91	3
DM	NR	-1.23	6/24/91	55.70	43.03	7/8/91	54.93	43.31	0.28	43.17	54.03	31.03	12.28	14	53.26	Negated	failed
JY	PR	5.68	9/18/91	74.21	61.00	3/26/91	74.49	58.11	2.89	59.56	75.21	71.29	13.18	8	75.49	10/1/91	5
SF	PR	2.94	7/16/91	63.72	44.38	8/19/91	63.99	47.55	3.17	45.97	66.66	61.50	13.95	34	66.93	9/17/91	29
SF	NR	0.63	8/12/91	65.91	54.50	8/22/91	65.85	55.26	0.76	54.88	63.99	39.55	15.71	10	63.93	Negated	failed
JY	PR	4.43	7/3/91	71.41	46.48	7/25/91	71.80	48.95	2.47	47.72	73.16	65.02	16.07	22	73.55	8/6/91	12
JY	PR	0.43	7/25/91	71.80	45.95	8/19/91	72.02	47.13	1.18	46.54	73.56	63.27	16.14	25	73.78	9/23/91	35
DM	NR	-0.39	4/16/91	59.58	42.85	4/30/91	58.05	44.21	1.36	43.53	56.28	26.92	17.29	14	54.75	Negated	failed
DM	NR	-12.18	3/13/91	63.20	28.81	4/2/91	59.56	32.85	4.04	30.83	57.98	15.18	17.67	20	54.34	Negated	failed
SF	PR	10.86	9/11/91	66.99	63.74	9/19/91	67.34	60.32	3.42	62.03	68.07	79.27	18.95	8	68.42	Negated	failed
JY	PR	5.5	1/25/91	75.17	52.79	2/19/91	75.77	46.36	6.43	49.58	77.89	68.34	21.98	25	78.49	Negated	failed
DM	PR	2.83	7/11/91	54.09	36.64	8/19/91	54.35	32.53	4.11	34.59	58.03	55.53	23.00	39	58.29	9/9/91	21
JY	PR	-3.02	1/16/91	73.07	40.63	2/25/91	74.71	38.64	1.99	39.64	77.89	68.34	29.70	40	79.53	Negated	failed
DM	NR	6.75	5/15/91	58.56	54.75	7/19/91	56.83	61.90	7.15	58.33	54.64	26.98	34.92	65	52.91		open
DM	NR	6.75	5/28/91	58.58	53.78	7/19/91	56.83	61.90	8.12	57.84	54.64	26.98	34.92	52	52.89		open
SF	NR	5.44	5/15/91	69.73	55.38	7/19/91	59.75	59.75	4.37	57.57	63.63	24.04	35.71	65	53.65		open
SF	NR	6.04	2/21/91	78.23	43.41	5/15/91	69.73	55.38	11.97	49.40	70.23	15.98	39.40	83	61.73		open
DM	NR	6.39	2/21/91	66.67	45.48	5/4/91	58.86	54.75	9.27	50.12	57.98	15.18	39.57	72	50.17		open

RSISTUDY

FIGURE 8-12

139

requires oscillators that are not normalized; yet I might ignore them entirely when a time-consuming contracting triangle is unfolding. We test our indicators to identify high-probability outcomes for a signal and to identify the conditions in which they will perform well. *If a signal develops that is predictably wrong over 90 percent of the time, I do not care that it is right or wrong, as long as the outcome is consistent and predictable.* Therefore, some tools I use are interpreted as countersignals. When a firm went to great lengths to liberate a particular model from me, I assure you an instruction manual on how to use each component of the model was not offered. Indicators that can be used as countersignals are not discussed in this book so that I do not unnecessarily complicate the progression of building blocks that are consciously being developed within each new chapter. However, if in your own testing, you find an attribute that is highly predictable, don't discard the indicator just because it is always wrong.

We need to discuss the RSI amplitude attribute in greater detail now that it has been identified. Figures 8–5 through 8–8 all display weekly and monthly charts. The Reversal signals marked in these charts all have fairly large amplitudes. Andrew Cardwell for years has calculated the basic RSI formula by hand because he has a better feel where the indicator is heading and does not warmly embrace computers. But he has known intuitively that the amplitude of his signals is important, and he was not at all surprised by the results of my RSI study. (No more surprised than when I was insistent we had to test the RSI period 14 that is used as a fixed interval for all markets and time horizons. We set up an elaborate test and left the computer on its own to crunch numbers for over three hours. The final interval that the computer declared optimal? 14! He just shrugged his shoulders and laughed. "Computers, humph.") Cardwell's lectures will put emphasis on the number of periods between the oscillator points W and X (Figure 8–2). He considers signals to be very strong when there are fewer than 9 periods between points W and X. A 3-period signal is viewed as an outright gift to a trader (meaning that there is only one bar that separates the RSI pivots at points W and X). However, there is a very high correlation between the amplitude of a signal and the spread between points W and X. As the amplitude shortens, so too will the spread narrow, but computer back-testing does show that a higher probability will occur if greater emphasis is placed on the amplitude rather than the spread between points W and X.

Finally, we need to return to the domino effect that was described in prior chapters as signals appear first in monthly charts, then weekly, daily, and on down into the shorter-horizon time intervals. In all of the weekly and monthly charts used in this chapter, know that the signal first appears in the longer time horizon, *but it is not the trading signal.* The numerous Reversal signals that realize their price objectives in the chart examples for this chapter do not occur only in that one time horizon. A trend reversal will first be detected in the monthly chart; then the signal must develop in the weekly, daily, 120-minute, and 60-minute chart if that is the final time horizon in which you enter a trade. Frequently the repetition of signals in each successive bar chart of a shorter time interval will display a signal with a shorter amplitude. This is an extremely important feature of these signals and perhaps the hardest to monitor as it requires tremendous patience to wait for the signals to develop in the various charts. Once the trend reversal has occurred, the signals will repeat often as the trend accelerates. This was demonstrated in Figure 8–5 for DMK/$ in which the price objectives are detailed for the entire dollar decline.

While the information that Cardwell extracts from the RSI extends far beyond the price projection techniques that I have introduced to you in this chapter, there is a valid underlying concern when so much information is drawn from a single study. What if the indicator itself fails? At times the market will develop a trend reversal that was not preceded by bullish or bearish divergence in the RSI or display Positive or Negative Reversal signals in a chart. In my experience the principal weakness is the absence of signals when they should have developed prior to a major market move. It is for this reason that I had to develop an indicator that could warn when the RSI was going to be caught off guard. The Composite Index that was introduced to you in earlier chapters is the solution to this problem and becomes a valuable addition for other methods. We will examine the Composite Index in great detail when we look at custom indicators and discuss modifying formulas for personal preferences in Part 3.

We have now looked at two methods I rely upon to determine a market objective: Fibonacci and RSI Reversal signals. Only one method remains of the three that I have strongly endorsed. The time has come to look at the methods of W. D. Gann. It is not going to be as painful as you might think, but now would be a good time to grab a fresh cup of coffee before we tackle the next topic.

CHAPTER 9

Calculating Price and Time Objectives from a Gann Wheel

In earlier chapters I made frequent references to the fact that I heavily rely upon the analytic methods of W. D. Gann. This is true to such a degree, no pun intended, that I would abandon all other methods before relinquishing my Gann Wheel. Well, maybe I have to put the Composite Index at the same level of dependency. However, I would abandon Elliott Wave, all other momentum analysis formulas, and even Fibonacci analysis, though reluctantly, before giving up Gann. That is a very strong opinion. It has also been stated that this is the one method I would not divulge to anyone. So what is a chapter about Gann analysis doing in this body of work?

The problem is that I have made a very strong endorsement for the methods of W. D. Gann by stating that his method is my most valuable tool, and I may have ignited a motivational spark in some of you to seek out the ways of Gann. In response, you might go forth and spend a lot of money on the limited number of books published on the subject. Then, after possibly devoting years of dedicated research to the subject, you may come to the realization that something is missing. You will not know what is missing, just that after spending much time and money, you will find yourself face-to-face with an invisible wall. The wall will be the last elusive piece of the puzzle that makes Gann usable in all markets. Like so many before you who have traveled the same road, you will abandon the work of Gann, frustrated that you had been misled. As I may have been the person who inspired you to explore Gann in the first place, it will be me to whom your frustration will turn. So you see, I am obligated now to give you a solid introduction to Gann analysis, and then, more importantly, give you an up-front explanation of why so many people leave this method frustrated and bewildered. The reason is that they lack one small piece of information that they never knew existed.

No, we will not dive into a discussion about price squares and labor over stacks of charts that display so many lines drawn that the price data itself has become obscure. Why? Because Gann isn't that difficult. *It can be made to look that difficult,* but in fact it is quite rational. If I introduced Fibonacci retracements to you by showing only multiple overlays of numerous calculations, Fibonacci could be made to look as mystifying as Gann. A really coherent and comprehensive book about Gann analysis has yet to be written. Perhaps the book does not exist for the same reasons I will not go beyond the basics with you now; it works so incredibly well we do not want to give it away.

What is Figure 9–1? A floor plan for the Great Pyramid of Khufu in Gizeh? (Bill Gates's software will spell it "Giza." However, don't trust a computer company with the only surviving Wonder of the Seven Wonders of the Ancient World.)

GANN WHEEL ANALYSIS

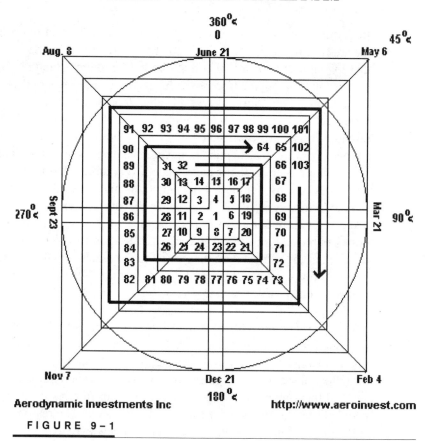

Aerodynamic Investments Inc   http://www.aeroinvest.com

FIGURE 9–1

While this diagram is not the floor plan of a pyramid, it could be since a *pyramid* is defined as "a solid figure with a polygonal base and triangular faces that meet at a common point." The external slant edge of the pyramid is nearly an exact 0.618 Fibonacci ratio. The rise just described is the only thing the diagram in Figure 9–1 has omitted. This first illustration is a Gann Wheel, this square of nine calculator is one of five tools Gann utilized, and my flippant referral to a pyramid is not as light-hearted as it may sound. The rising slope has not been omitted from Gann's work as the rise will become the time axis.

There are many times when Gann calculations and Fibonacci ratios will trip over one another. The market levels at which these two methods converge are just downright phenomenal. There is no other way for me to describe the market reactions that occur when these two methods intersect at the same price levels. The Gann Wheel and the Fibonacci number series are different. (Let's not venture into the square aspect of his time calculations at this moment as it will not clarify the common price objectives that occur.) It is possible that the pyramid structure is the best model to demonstrate why these two methods offer mathematical confluence points.

Let me back up a step and share with you how I was introduced to Gann analysis. Like many readers, whenever I used to view a Gann chart, I would think to myself, "Of course you realized a market's objective—there are so many lines and targets on that chart you were bound to hit one of them." Then one day, Dennis Meyers who had been a client of mine for about three years stated, "I have to know more about your S&P price projection methods. Now!" Meyers was a brilliant intraday off-floor S&P trader in Chicago and an assertive bull dog when he wanted information. He was primarily a Gann trader, and after three years of observing my Fibonacci tables derived from using the multiple overlay techniques that I described for you, he was convinced Gann and Fibonacci had some sort of common foundation that extended beyond the obvious and that could be discovered when you knew both methods. He did not know my method of using Fibonacci and his Elliott Wave had several major weaknesses. I, on the other hand, did not know anything about the work of W. D. Gann. So began the melting of two minds and methodologies.

We soon became inseparable during the trading day as we could read a three-minute chart and know which of us had stepped on the other in the S&P futures market. We began to combine our research findings and knew we had something much larger than either of us would have stumbled upon alone. We found that Gann vibration points that coincide with Fibonacci cluster zones can stop a market to the tick, even in meltdown or ballistic fast market conditions. This remains true in the S&P even though the index has tripled since the research was started. Meyers passed away before we could complete all our research, and it will take years to finish the work we started together alone. One hypothesis is that the shape and proportions found within a pyramid had more information than just ratios as the Fibonacci Sequence and Gann Wheel are both demonstrated within this structure. This structure also has a fourth dimension that I will discuss well into the body of this chapter.

The chapter on Fibonacci explained that the name the ancient Greeks gave to the 0.618 ratio—the Golden Section—went back in history much farther than the accountings from ancient Greece. The Great Pyramid of Khufu in Gizeh was built around 4700 B.C., and there is a record from about 2000 B.C. that describes the pyramid as having the proportions of the Golden Section, or "sacred ratio." Measurements from modern-day analysis show that the ratio of the distance from the center point at ground level to the base edge, to the external slant edge of the pyramid is nearly an exact 0.618 ratio. The proportion of the slope's rise to the base is the only missing projection in a Gann Wheel—at least, at first appearance the rise seems to be missing. But Gann time projections utilize Fibonacci ratios so the common bond between these two methods becomes more interesting. Now let's go back to Figure 9–1.

The outside border is a square, and there are several squares that progressively become smaller in Figure 9–1. If each square were in fact a typographical feature for a pyramid, it would be much easier to visualize this illustration. The number 1 in the center would be the peak of the structure. However, the Gann Wheel is flat and not three dimensional. It is estimated that the Great Pyramid of Gizeh contains 2.3 million blocks of stone. Did you know the individual stones arranged in this manner create a calculator? Let me explain.

Instead of putting the first stone for a pyramid on an outside perimeter corner, start by counting the stones from the peak and work down toward the base and outer perimeter. In Figure 9–1 the peak is labeled 1, and then a clockwise movement is followed as the number series is incremented by 1 unit. The tricky part is the bottom left corner for each square as the next number must move out one square and then the numbers will continue to increase by one unit until the next outer square is filled again. The numbers 81 and 82 clearly illustrate this movement from one square out to the next. The center of the diagram is always 1, and the incremental numbers always move in a clockwise rotation. Here is how the numbers relate to one another and how this pattern becomes a calculator.

Draw a circle that touches all four sides of the largest square. Pretend you are cutting a round pie into six equal pieces. I have drawn these proportions within the circle in Figure 9–1. The horizontal and vertical cross sections display a double line so that I can later rotate all the pieces in the pie, so to speak, and you will still know where the top slice originated. All right, so far so good I hope. The circle has six equal sections, and we know a circle has 360 degrees to complete a full rotation. The top of the circle can be viewed as our starting point, or "ground zero." As we move clockwise to the right corner, we would cross the 45 degree angle of our circle. Right angles would be 90 degrees, and directly across from the top is 180 degrees at the bottom of Figure 9–1. We continue moving clockwise until we return to the start and complete the journey around the circle at 360 degrees. Therefore, zero and 360 degrees mark both the start and ending point of our circle.

Here's how this structure becomes a calculator. Find the number 15 on the Gann Wheel. If a stock were trading at a price of $15, what would the price objectives be using a Gann Wheel? The number 15 is perfectly aligned under the zero and 360 degree angle marked on the top of the Wheel. Because the number 15 is aligned with zero, we need make no further adjustments; just read the Gann targets straight off the Wheel. The 45 degree price objective from 15 is 17. It is the next number that aligns with the 45 degree line that travels toward the top right corner. The number 19 crosses where the 90 degree line was drawn. We would use the phrase "$19 is 90 degrees up from $15." Now skip over to 180 degrees, and find that $23 is directly opposite $15. (We would still say, "$23 is 180 degrees up from $15" even though 180 degrees appears below the zero line or starting point. As long as you are obtaining higher price objectives from the Wheel, the results of the angles are always "up" from the starting level.) At 270 degrees, $28 is the price objective. A full 360 degrees up from 15 is $34. (You will have to add two numbers from 32 to fill in the blanks and complete the Wheel in this diagram.) That is how a Gann Wheel is used.

Why did we skip the bottom right corner angle, which would be 135 degrees? Because, like Fibonacci, some calculations are more important than others. The Fibonacci ratios 0.382, 0.500, 0.618, 1.000, and 1.618 are relationships we know are the critical ratios to identify. There are other Fibonacci ratios, and sometimes we become aware of them as well, but they rarely define a major target; perhaps just a minor consolidation prior to the larger trend continuing. This is also how the various Gann angles are interpreted. We have a circle that is divided into quarters and sixths, but we also need to divide 360 degrees into thirds because 120 degrees and 240 are extremely important. The angles of greatest interest in financial markets are 45, 90, 120, 180, 240, 270, 315, and 360. Are all these angles important? No. Not in all markets. Equities define major support and resistance levels at 45 degrees, 90, 180, 270, and very major support and resistance for any market is a full 360 degrees up or down. Bonds will view 90 degrees, 120, 180, 240, and 360 degree angles as major targets. Spot currencies tend to react in a significant manner to 90 degrees, 120, 144, 216, 270, and 360. What about commodity markets? I honestly cannot say as I do not trade any market associated with

"roots" or "hooves," only financial markets, so I have not done the research needed to answer this question.

The angles of greatest interest for a financial market in a rally are the same
angles for a market decline. Let's see if we can identify the major support levels
from a price level of $15 using the Wheel. Instead of moving clockwise as we did
to find resistance levels, we will move counterclockwise to find support because
the numbers decrease as you move counterclockwise. The first target will be 45
degrees down and is located at $13 where the 45 degree line crosses the top left
diagonal. The $11 level would define 90 degrees down. A full 180 degrees down
is at $8. We will skip directly to the 360 degree target, which is at $4, the number
just below $15. If you can follow the Wheel to identify these price targets, you
now know how to obtain price objectives using Gann Angles. True, there is much
more. But you just managed to learn how to calculate Gann price objectives without running into a host of nasty terms that serve only to muddle and complicate an
otherwise simple calculator.

We have just calculated objectives from a single price level. By now you are
likely aware of a common theme in this book: After we have discussed how to do
a method one time, we then repeat the method multiple times. We discussed using
multiple cycles in Chapter 2. We used different time horizons in various charts to
obtain confirming oscillator signals and filter out low-probability signals. We also
applied multiple Fibonacci retracements in Chapter 6 to identify the more significant target zones. So it should come as little surprise that we will now need to
identify the confluence points where major angles overlap when *multiple* Gann
projections are derived from *different* price levels. As an example, when a 180
degree price objective overlaps the exact same price level that marks a 360 degree
projection from a different pivot, there is a higher probability that the market will
respect that objective.

The final step is to observe where the confluence Gann price objectives
overlap the confluence Fibonacci target zones and RSI Reversal targets. When
the three methods define a major objective at identical price levels, it will
reveal a *precise* target. On occasion after all this work you will experience a
day when the market completely ignores one of these major confluence points
you identified from monthly, weekly, and shorter-horizon charts that you had
been watching with great anticipation for some time. It is rare, but when the
market does ignore important confluence objectives defined from multiple
techniques, *it immediately tells you your market is rescaling and the growth-
decay cycle described earlier in this book that contributes to the expansion-
contraction cycle for any market has shifted to a new mathematical grid.* It is
similar to Continental Plate tectonics. As one plate grinds past or under the
next causing an earthquake, new geologic measurements are always taken to

ascertain the true displacement and new typographical features after the event. (I knew my elective course on Geomorphology would be used some day! Just made an old professor at the University of Toronto really proud to see this analogy squeezed into a financial book.)

When the market makes the next pivot *beyond* the major target it just ignored, it will mark a pivot that is within the new larger framework that you must now identify. To do so, repeat all the calculations from different pivot levels to find the originating pivot levels that the market is now using as milestones for the latest move. This is not a comment addressing intraday data; it is when your long-horizon projections seem to be run over. *You were not wrong.* Accept that something very significant has just changed and you can work backward to find the new mathematical grid from which to construct a new road map for the bigger picture in your market. There is a lot of work required to achieve the precision necessary to reduce capital exposure and create higher gains. The point is that it can be done.

I continued to offer institutions my evening market reports on the Internet after my investment pool was established because I found that being accountable to other professionals gave me the discipline I needed to ensure all these calculations were revised every single night. This is the silent grunt work that takes place when everyone else has long since returned home or headed off to the neighborhood pub when the markets close. When the trading day ends, we would all rather take off and have some time to unwind. However, I found that having to revise my tables and put my market views on paper that others might follow motivated me to return to the office and ensure I too was properly prepared for the next day. When you use methods that require multiples in everything that you use, it is very time-consuming. I am never concerned about giving my major targets to other institutions because they do not have my methods to revise these numbers for fine-tuning purposes throughout the trading day.

As multiple price objectives need to be made from a Gann Wheel, let's look at making a price projection when the starting price is not perfectly aligned under the zero/360 degree line as was present in the first example when we calculated the objectives from $15. In this example I need to calculate the Gann price objectives for a market that made a price low at the number 65. You will find that the number 65 is located on the right corner axis of Figure 9–2. The Gann Wheel itself is actually two or three different pieces. The bottom is generally a white opaque Plexiglas or plastic material. It will have the squares and number series printed on the surface. The circle that is added to Figures 9–1 and 9–2 is actually on a clear acetate film that can be rotated. On this separate overlay is the circle divided into sixths. It is attached by a pin to the center so you will never see the number 1 on a physical Wheel. Sometimes a second clear acetate film is added that divides a circle into thirds. It is not essential to have a separate overlay as some wheels combine cycle division of sixths and thirds on the same acetate film. To calculate the targets from 65, move the zero and 360 degree axis to the right so that it is aligned with your starting value of 65. Now you can just read the targets from the wheel. Figure 9–2 shows a starting price that was shifted 45 degrees to the right from the orientation drawn in Figure 9–1. Clearly the zero/360 degree angle can be rotated to any number within the wheel and the divisions within the circle will retain their relative distances from the zero line. The price objectives for a rally from 65 are 69 (45 degrees up), 73 (90 degrees up), 81 (180 degrees up), and 91 (270 degrees up) and a full 360 degrees up from 65 is at 101.

There is a catch, as you have not been given a critical aspect of the Gann Wheel. If you want to calculate an American stock price from a Gann Wheel, you are *nearly* armed and ready to go. All you need is a Gann Wheel and a stock

GANN WHEEL ANALYSIS

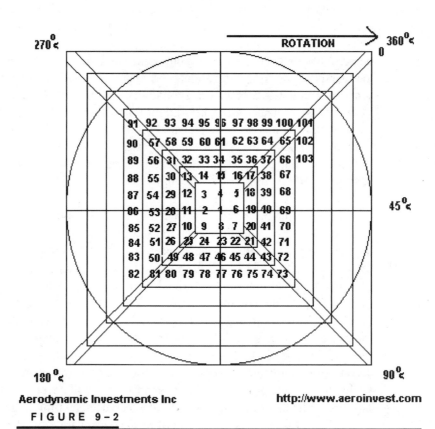

Aerodynamic Investments Inc   http://www.aeroinvest.com

FIGURE 9–2

that trades over $150 dollars. Tilt? The Gann Wheel increments demonstrated in Figures 9–1 and 9–2 have incremental values of $1 dollar. That will suffice only for a stock that is trading over $150. A stock that trades between $20 to $90 is better calculated using a $\frac{1}{2}$-point incremental scale. These scaling differences apply to futures markets as well (except currency future price objectives can be calculated directly from a 1-point incremental Wheel without difficulty).

So what is the catch? Too much work and extremely labor intensive? That would be true, but, in addition, many traders abandon Gann analysis because they find it does not work in *their* market. As an example, if you trade bonds or the S&P, *you have to know that there is also a conversion to apply to the Wheel.* Unlike stocks were you can change the scale to define a more fitting range, futures markets actually require a conversion factor. If you did not know that a conversion factor was required and you just read levels straight off the Wheel for bonds or the S&P, there would be no chance of identifying the correct price objectives. Those of us who know the conversions for these major financial markets are not going to share them with the general public. This may explain why most published books about Gann use stocks in their chart examples. Stocks do not require conversions.

Some people have the original letters and works of Gann, and the conversion factors are apparently described in those more obscure articles. I do not own any of these documents and fear the ones I saw that Denny Meyers possessed were destroyed when his estate was sold by family members who did not know the value of the original Gann letters in his files. All my attempts to acquire them or to have them preserved failed. However, knowing how the conversion factors are created is the key, and it does explain why some people can have exceptional success utilizing the methods of Gann, and others are left penniless thinking it must have been voodoo.

While the revelation that a conversion factor is used will understandably discourage some of you from going any further and tempt you to skip the remainder of this chapter, please know that the best is still ahead and you can use Gann's time projections without conversions. There are also several other aspects to be aware of concerning Gann's work even if you elect not to pursue his analytic method any further. So hang in there as this discussion has only scratched the surface. Besides, aren't you curious about the fourth dimension within the pyramid that I passed over so quickly in the beginning of this chapter? Good. Thought that might work. Onward.

Gann's most important finding was that equality between time and price will mark extremely important junctures for any market. His concept of how he calculated time projections can be used by anyone who grasps the underlying foundation of his work. Therefore, we are about to discuss how the Wheel is used to calculate time objectives, which is one of the most significant aspects of his work.

Time objectives not only mark potential pivot points for market turns but time objectives also provide us information about the duration of a major trend. Gann kept Monthly, Weekly, and Daily charts. His long-horizon work was Yearly and Quarterly. If you are an intraday trader, is there any value in a Yearly chart? Tremendous value as Gann's work can identify high-risk days for a trend change that were projected from at least 15 years of data. How?

The Gann Wheel is a cycle calculator, and Gann's focus of study was in the use of cycles in both time and price. His work also references cycles based on planetary movement, *but he was not referring to esoteric Astrology.* Gann's calculations are strictly mathematical geometric relationships based on planetary movement along measurable distances that form elliptic orbits relative to the Earth. Gann's work is better described as the study of seasonality and cyclical confluence points in time.

Today we accept that markets have seasonal probabilities for trend biases throughout a year. We also know when the moon completes its 28-day cycle forming a full moon that we may see exaggerated market action. We discussed using multiple Fibonacci projections to identify higher-probability objectives from overlapping confluence price levels. Gann was simply making multiple projections to increase the probability of his time objectives. He would calculate the time it takes for each planet to travel 360 degrees and then determine their confluence points when their cycles would overlap. When planets displayed geometric cycles that where aligned, he knew a higher probability existed that a market might experience a change in trend. That makes a lot of sense if you accept that a full moon just might exaggerate a market's movement. A logical step is to then ask, "If the distance traveled by the moon and resulting seasonal cycle is of any consequence to a market, might not the seasonality of multiple planets that travel a full 360 degrees not have greater influence when they align on a similar day?" In concept it is not different from using multiple Fibonacci calculations to find a higher-probability price objective or making multiple Gann calculations from different market levels to find overlapping targets. If multiple projections can increase the probability for price objectives, why not apply this method to time projections? Is that not what we attempt to do when we plot multiple symmetrical time cycles within a chart? Gann was just ahead of us all by using time projections from different planetary calendars.

To grasp this concept of calculating time objectives, we need to first discuss how dates are derived from a 360 degree circle and Gann Wheel using our 365-day Julian calendar. Then we can look at how to calculate the cycles of other planets and define confluence points in time. This topic can be made to sound incredibly complex because Gann had to convert everything to two-dimensional conventions used in his era for map making. The text that was written does not translate well when we are in a society that can handle three-dimensional video games and virtual-reality simulations. Gann sounds so complex because of its reliance on squares. In reality, his squares are not square roots but just a map maker's tool of repeating squares to define a fixed charting dimension. As soon as the conversation starts to discuss the "Square of Nine and 52," most people understandably escape through a back door really fast. So we will not head in that direction. Like the price calculations we just covered, time projections are not that difficult either.

In Figure 9–1 you will find the date June 21 at the top of the Wheel where the zero and 360 degree angle was drawn and December 21 is located on the opposite side at the 180 degree angle. There are dates also marked at 90 degrees and 270 degrees as well as at the 45 degree corners. As Gann was a student of seasonality, it is no surprise to find the dates of the summer and winter solstices and spring and fall equinoxes at the 90 degree angles of the circle. (I know, I forgot too and had to look it up. So if you are curious, the points at which the sun crosses the equator are the equinoxes, when day and night are most nearly equal and the only time we are at right angles to the axis of the Earth. The points at which the sun is at a maximum distance from the equator are the solstices. That would be when the days and nights are most unequal. The earth's axis is tilted 23 degrees and 27 minutes away from the perpendicular, in case your next trivia game should ask and a free beer depends on the correct answer.)

These dates are like the incremental numbers in the middle of the Wheel that we used to calculate price objectives. They are in fixed locations and are printed on the bottom portion of the Wheel. In reality, the Wheel will display an outer circle not shown in Figure 9–1. The diameter of the outer circle is the diagonal of the largest square. So a circle is drawn to connect each corner. This outer circle then divides 360 degrees into equal proportions so that 364 days or a full year equals 360 degrees. The top of the fixed circle is always June 21.

The targets are very easy to read as 180 degrees from June 21 would be December 21. Ninety degrees from June 21 is March 21. If your start date for an extreme price high or low is a number other than June 21 which is aligned directly under the zero/360 degree line, just move the acetate overlay so that the zero/360 degree line crosses the date you want to start from and then read off the dates. If I want to know 180 degrees from May 6 on the top right corner, I move the acetate overlay that has the zero/360 degree line at the top of the Wheel over to the right so that the zero/360 line crosses May 6. The date directly opposite May 6 at 180 degrees is November 7. That's it—not so hard.

It is very important to know that if you are calculating from a price low, the date objective does not necessarily imply a price high. It denotes only a change of trend, and if you decline into a time objective like November 7, you could end up with market lows on both dates of November 7 and May 6. A single time projection within a single calendar year in my experience is of little significance. What is of greater value is very long time horizon objectives. Keep in mind the time horizons Gann analyzed were Yearly, Monthly, and Weekly charts. So how does one divide weeks and months into 360 degrees? Actually, it is very easy to do.

We have just defined how 1 calendar year equals 360 degrees. We know 1 year has 52 weeks. The 52 weeks can be equally distributed around the circle. In Figure 9-3 the top is zero. Then we would place 13 weeks at 90 degrees, 26 weeks at 180 degrees, 39 weeks would fall on 270 degrees, and 52 weeks completes the full 360 degree cycle by marking the top again. That was easy. How about months

GANN WHEEL ANALYSIS

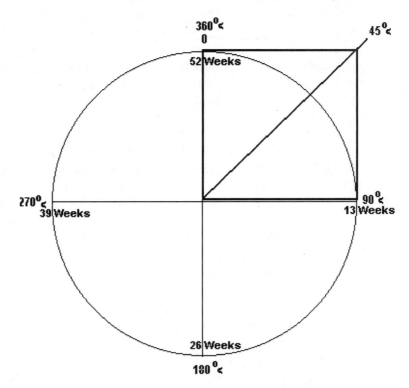

Aerodynamic Investments Inc   http://www.aeroinvest.com

FIGURE 9-3

or years? Thirty years would be 360 months, and $7^1/_2$ years or 90 months aligns with the 90 degree angle; 15 years is 180 months, etc., etc., etc. You got it!

Now let's tackle the concept that usually wipes out the majority when they pick up a book about Gann analysis. The 90 degree angle is the basic angle of the square. (Yes, the squares are approaching, but they are easy too.) To turn the weeks 0, 13, 26, 39, and 52 from looking like a circle as we have in Figure 9–3 into a straight line, you need to imagine grasping a hoop. Place your hands at the zero and 360 degree mark on the top of the hoop. Now cut the hoop at the top and open your hands so the circle becomes a straight line.

Voilà! Squares. Figure 9–4 is "The Square of 52," and Gann calls it "The Master Calculator"—very fancy name for a basic square that can be used on a weekly chart. But this square has some pretty interesting characteristics. (It actually represents 364 calendar days, and at the end of every seventh year there is a gain of 7 days.) The Square of 52 is composed of 7-day periods, and a larger "calculator" could be 104 weeks wide which equals 2 years.

Figure 9–5 displays a chart showing the Square of 52 plotted with the Weekly Cash S&P 500 Index. I am grateful to Peter Pich who used his *Ganntrader 3.0*[1] software to create this chart for us on July 22, 1998. It is important for you to see that Gann does not create charts with excessive meaningless lines when the vibration point for a specific market is understood. The reason the Square of 52 was selected is that you can see that the S&P market has been respecting this confluence projection. The January 1998 low coincides with the $^1/_2$ square of 52, and the August 1997 high corresponds to the prior square of 52. We are again at an important juncture, and only time will tell if this market will again respect this objective or not. The Square of 52 is not the only Gann calculator you will learn about if you venture further into this field of study. As an example, the Square of 144 will be important for currencies. I suspect you now have a better idea about some of the more rudimentary concepts within Gann analysis. In no way can one chart demonstrate all that Gann analysis has to offer.

We must start to head back toward the start of our discussion, which stated that Gann and Fibonacci will trip over one another and that a pyramid could be an interesting model for both. The days of a full year when distributed around a circle fall at key angles at 45 days, 90 to 92 days, 120 days, 135 to 138 days, 180 days, 225 days, 240 days, 270 days, and finally 315 to 318 days. In terms of weeks these specific days are $6^1/_2$ weeks, 13 weeks, 17 weeks, $19^1/_2$ weeks, 26 weeks, $32^1/_2$

[1] Peter A. Pich, e-mail address: gann@>plix.com. Gannsoft Publishing Company, 806A Gillette Road, Colville, WA 99114-9647 USA.

GANN WHEEL ANALYSIS

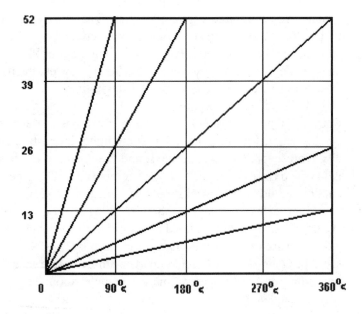

Aerodynamic Investments Inc   **http://www.aeroinvest.com**

FIGURE 9–4

weeks, 35 weeks, 39 weeks, $45\frac{1}{2}$ weeks, finally 52 weeks. These divisions divide a year equally into $\frac{1}{8}$, $\frac{1}{4}$, $\frac{1}{3}$, $\frac{3}{8}$, $\frac{1}{2}$, $\frac{5}{8}$, $\frac{2}{3}$, $\frac{3}{4}$, $\frac{7}{8}$, and 1 year. Recognize those ratios? They are 0.125, 0.250, 0.333, 0.50, 0.625, 0.75, 0.875, and 1.00. No wonder Gann and Fibonacci cross paths. The slant rise of the Great Pyramid which has a 0.618 ratio to the base line from the center is Gann's time calculator. There are three dimensions in the Pyramid, which encompasses the triangle, square, and circle. The three dimensions represent height, width, and length. But there is a fourth dimension. It is Gann's Master Calculator or Square of 52, which encompasses time periods. Seven times 52 equals 364, or 7 years. (I'm skipping how to deal with a Leap year as it is just a conversion.) Through the study of the relationships between the circle, the triangle, and the square, the fourth dimension can be identified, and that is about where I will leave you in this introduction to Gann analysis. Appropriately we have come full circle in our discussion and have returned to where we began by looking at the shape of a pyramid as a model.

I have left a few loose ends that should be put in their place before we move on to the next chapter. I mentioned that Gann used multiple calendars. Our discussion about time has only touched upon 364 days, which is approximately a full rotation for Earth to complete one orbit around the sun. It takes the moon 28 days to orbit the Earth, so 28 would be 360 degrees and 14 becomes 180 degrees for that cycle, and so forth. Gann created 360 degree orbital calculators for all the planets, and one has to know the time it takes each planet to move 360 degrees to duplicate his work:

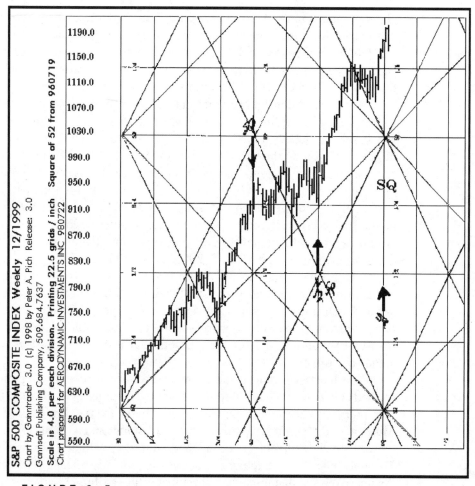

FIGURE 9-5

Planet	In Terms of Years	Number of Days to Travel a Full 360 Degrees
Mercury	Less than a year	88.97
Venus	Less than a year	224.70
Earth	One year	365.25
Mars	1.88	686.98
Jupiter	11.86	4331.98
Saturn	29.46	10,760.60
Uranus	84 years	30,685.50
Neptune	167.79	61,285.25
Pluto	247.69	90,465.38

Gann produced multiple time projections and identified where confluence points overlapped from these independent calendar cycles. As you see, there are also a few Fibonacci numbers in this list (as an example, 88.97 days), and it would seem we could be coming to similar conclusions by approaching the problem from different angles. (Ouch. That was a terrible pun.)

A planetary confluence point in time relative to earth's orbit would suggest to Gann a high-risk time objective had been identified for a market trend reversal. *It does not imply a market top or bottom.* Just a change in direction. I also have no opinion on the validity of this theorem as I have insufficient results and experience in real-time to comment on its merit. However, if there was ever an opportunity to test the validity of Gann's planetary alignment work, the solar system alignment we are approaching May 5, 2000, in Figure 9-6 can be viewed as the single greatest confluence point to test his theorem within our lifetime. All the inner orbital planets of our solar system will align May 5, 2000, with key dates occurring through May 28, 2000. This will not occur again for nearly 6000 years! Is this an event I would use to trade a market? No. Because how do you test the impact of such an alignment that has never been seen by a financial market and will not occur again for another 6000 years! So statistic viability and determination of market probability is not possible. Market probability has to be measurable for me to jeopardize assets, but this certainly does warrant conscious curiosity.

The Internet certainly makes our task easier to identify alignments than the methods Gann would have used in his work. The orbit representation in Figure 9-6 was prepared using the orbit predictor offered by the National Air and Space Museum of the Smithsonian Institution in Washington, DC. You can use their model directly on the Internet at the address: http://www.fourmilab.ch/solar/solar.html. To apply Gann's research methodology be sure to select *equal orbit* analysis. Another Web site that might be convenient is the Griffith Observatory in California. You can read all about the May 5, 2000, alignment at the following Internet

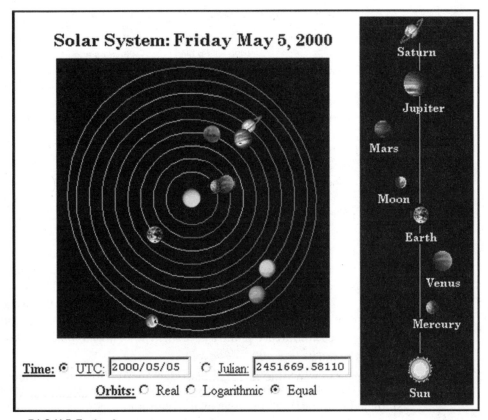

FIGURE 9–6

address if you want to know more: http://www.griffithobs.org/SkyAlignments.html. Personally I will rely entirely on technical chart signals from which to trade. This information is utilized the same way I would view a cycle bottom approaching in a monthly chart. Of interest, but certainly not a reason to pull the trigger to initiate or close a trade.

If I return to using only our Julian calendar, I can illustrate further for you how angles within a time calculator can become important confluence points. Keep in mind that Gann would then overlap these confluence points from Earth's orbital calendar around the sun with the confluence points that were identified for the individual planets. Gann's multiple overlays simply identified higher-probability time objectives. Here are few examples: The date June 2, 1998, marked the 180 degree target from the December 5 low in the S&P 500 Index. The same date was also 90 degrees up from the March 5 low and 144 degrees from the November low.

Dow Jones Industrial Average for the Month of June 1998

June 2nd	1992 was a high	6 years ago
June 5th	1990 was a high	8 years ago
June 14th	1949 was a low	49 years ago
June 17th	1983 was a high	15 years ago
June 22nd	1988 was a high	10 years ago*
June 22nd	1992 was a low	6 years ago* (confluence date)
June 25th	1962 was a low	36 years ago*
June 28th	1991 was a low	7 years ago
June 27th	1994 was a low	4 years ago
June 30th	1989 was a low	8 years ago

(36-year target falling within 3 days of a 10-year and 6-year target is a time window to be monitored.)

There were no planetary confluence points identified for the month of June 1998.

A market top occurred July 20, 1998, near a time confluence objective and there has been a decline from a high of 9367.8 to a current low as this is written to 8855.7. A 512.1-point decline in the DJIA from the high is only a 5.5 percent decline. But you might agree that this is still a fairly respectable reaction to a Gann time and price confluence point, *and we will soon turn to other methods that warn the current correction may not be over.*

That actually covers a lot of ground about Gann analysis, and if you want to explore this field further, you likely have a better head start now than if you had stumbled into this field on your own from scratch. So I can now leave this topic with a clear conscience, which after all, was my original objective when I opened this chapter.

CHAPTER 10

Using Oscillators with the Elliott Wave Principle

OBJECTIONS AND MISUNDERSTANDINGS

Perhaps the most hotly debated and controversial analytic method in our industry today is R. N. Elliott's Wave Principle. Some of the common arguments used to build a case against the Elliott Wave Principle are the following:

"It is too subjective."

"Analysts have been caught on the wrong side of the market or with diametrically opposing views about the Dow Jones Industrial Average."

"Too many alternative market scenarios can be suggested by the same analyst."

"Different analysts can interpret the exact same pattern in different ways."

"If you scan different time horizons, for the same market, you can find any pattern you want to prove your market opinion."

Did I leave any out? Probably, but I have certainly listed the most common points often raised as objections toward this methodology. I can take these issues further by addressing each separately.

Let's start with the first objection: "It is too subjective." Yes, it is. Did an Elliott Wave practitioner just cross the line to stand beside the "nay" voters? Don't jump to that conclusion so quickly. I contend that there are several causes contributing to the subjectivity issue. The first problem is that there are a vast number of wave interpretations demonstrated in countless newsletters and published services that violate the basic tenets of the Wave Principle. This problem can be resolved by specifically highlighting some very apparent and common misunderstandings within our industry.

However, these misunderstandings are not the only cause contributing to the subjectivity argument. I will show you in a few pages a wave interpretation that meets every rule and guideline for this methodology. However, when this chart was labeled in a real-time context, I knew the interpretation would most likely be proven wrong by the market. The chart in question will offer an interpretation that most Elliott Wave practitioners would have used. The difference is that the skill level required to label the current data versus developing a wave interpretation that will provide a map for the market's future path will require a higher level of skill. An analogy can be offered to illustrate the difference. While many people can learn how to press the correct keys on a piano to reproduce a sonata written by Beethoven, few will develop their skills sufficiently to learn how to turn these same notes into music that others would pay to hear played. There is a rhythm and harmony in the movement of the markets, and some people are "wave deaf" as others might be tone deaf or musically challenged. Some people can hit all the right notes, but it still comes out wrong.

If not outright wave deaf, one can be "wave handicapped" to the character or frequency of a market's action for a variety of reasons. As an example, I currently rely on Gann analysis for U.S. T-Bonds and then consider wave counts only if they are very distinctive. However, I know why intraday bond charts are complex and choppy at this time as it fits the wave character of the larger picture for this market and actually adds weight to the longer-horizon outlook. Therefore, my current intraday problem in bonds is only a temporary situation. Unfortunately, some people cannot see wave structure at any time because they are unable to see proportional balances within that market's price chart. In equity indices, I know that I can pick up wave frequencies and structure very quickly. That gives me the confidence to listen to my gut feeling when price structure suggests overriding another technical method. The hardest aspect of the Wave Principle is to tell people they are technically right, but to then state in the same breath that they will likely be wrong because there is no balance or proportion in their interpretation.

Might you be wave deaf? It really comes down to a left-brain/right-brain issue. You already know if you have an artistic ability or not. I do not mean that you have an ability to paint or draw. Find a stick from a tree that is at least 2 feet in length. Don't look at your pen or pencil and think you will improvise. That will be too easy as a pencil is too short. Live in a big city? Find an object like a fireplace tool that is used to poke logs or shovel ashes. Even a broom would do. Put the object on the floor by only grabbing the extreme top so all you gain by moving the object is information about its weight. Now before you pick the object up, study it closely. You must pick up the object at its fulcrum point by using no more than three fingers. That is the point where the object will be balanced and the left or right side will not suddenly take a dive back toward the ground when you pick it up. If you need to make only a minor adjustment of no more than one figure's width to find the perfect fulcrum point, then you likely have a sense of proportion and balance in your mind's-eye.

Another easy test. Are you the one in your family that gets to proclaim a picture is straight when it is hung on the wall? Or do you have to run for a level to rely on scientific fact? Good luck in an old Victorian home where the corners, floor, and ceiling are rarely perpendicular or parallel. A picture in such an environment will not look straight if you use a level as you have to balance the picture to offset the multiple parallax errors within the room. My father would have been wave deaf as he measured every picture to perfection from the floor or ceiling. Scientifically he knew the picture was perfect. However, my mother, an interior designer, would quietly "fix" his final calculations that my eye also required so that the picture would look straight to anyone else who could tell the difference. He could not see the adjustments, and one day we had him measure a picture to prove we had made a change. He was horrified to learn he couldn't see that a large painting had been shifted nearly 7 centimeters between its top corners from the base boards. The change was needed because the ceiling caused a parallax distortion, and the shift made the picture appear straight within its environment.

Anyway, if you think about it, you already know if you are graphically handicapped or not. You can still learn to label charts and understand other people's wave interpretations, but your own interpretations as a real-time trading tool might be weaker. In my opinion this is the most important area of study once someone knows the basic building blocks of the Elliott Wave Principle. There are a few methods that can help you find higher-probability scenarios. *As an example, start your wave count in the middle of the market's move instead of from its origin or extreme high or low.* You will see a few different methods used in this chapter to develop a wave count.

We are not quite done with the subjectivity argument. A strong point people make is that "analysts have been caught on the wrong side of the market or with diametrically opposing views about the Dow Jones Industrial Average." That is true. I worked for Robert Prechter a few years prior to the Centennial Olympic Games in Atlanta. I was accountable for the day-to-day analysis of the S&P 500 Index. In addition to an evening report, I transmitted frequent intraday real-time wave counts with market objectives for institutional traders to consider with their own analysis. These traders monitored the live updates throughout the day on their Bloomberg, Reuters, Telerate/Bridge, and DTN quote systems.

During the time I worked for Bob Prechter, I was extremely bullish on the U.S. stock market. I will show you why later. While that particular outlook was correct, there have been other occasions when the market has proven my opinion to be dead wrong. The institutional traders that used to monitor my live wave counts from their quote screens know I had to eat humble pie for dinner on several occasions.

The S&P 500 is my specialty, and you will fully understand how two people can utilize the Elliott Wave Principle differently and derive different opinions by the end of this chapter. In a capsule summary, you will see that I *construct* wave interpretations from technical indicators. The final results will look the same to you, as a labeled chart will be defined, but the underlying considerations that went into that wave interpretation will be entirely different than using price structure alone. This is a very unorthodox method of applying the Elliott Wave Principle.

Therefore, the technical indicators one uses in conjunction with the Wave Principle and how they are used will contribute to the subjectivity of our wave interpretations. The balancing act between indicator direction and price structure will be demonstrated. Find the right balance, and it is possible to move in perfect synchronization with most of the twists and turns the market will develop. However, overlook an important piece of information from either the Wave Principle or an indicator and the synchronized dance will assuredly step off track. Of course, we can step off track using indicators alone. *However, use the Elliott Wave Principle alone and you will be out of sync more often than if you used just indicators.*

I can see how that last sentence may be used out of context. But before you jump to the conclusion that I have implied the Elliott Wave Principle is of little value, let me point out the flaw in that hasty assumption. Indicators have a very

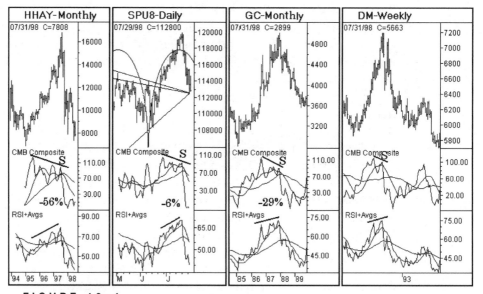

FIGURE 10-1

serious inherent weakness that cannot be corrected by just adding another indicator or developing a new formula.

Figure 10-1 displays similar sell signals when the Composite Index and RSI diverge in four different markets. How do you know just how large a correction will unfold from these identical signals? Oh sure, we have calculated targets, lots of targets, *but which one will be the likely bottom?* The monthly Hang Seng signal preceded a 56 percent decline. A daily S&P signal has *so far* produced a 6 percent decline. Gold fell 29 percent before the Composite Index found its first pivot. The weekly DMark futures chart fell 20 percent, and it had not bottomed. These identical bearish diverging sell signals leave us with the same question: "Just how far down will this market go?" You can see that the markets are oversold and that a countermove up can be expected, but will the next sell signal lead only to an even stronger leg down in these markets? So the Elliott Wave Principle becomes the much-needed tool we can use to obtain information about the size of the reaction we can expect from any given indicator signal. Elliott is hard to live with, much harder to live without. Just don't live with it alone!

Another common objection is that there are "too many alternative market scenarios that can be suggested by the same analyst." We can also fold into this same argument: "Different analysts can interpret the exact same pattern in different ways." An intellectually honest Elliott Wave practitioner will admit that there are times when there are no discernible wave structures from which to build a highly probable interpretation. It is better to openly admit that sometimes the Elliott Wave Principle has little more to offer than the development of a slew of scenarios. Every analytic method will have periods when it is not decisive. Sometimes we just have to wait, and we would be better off keeping the ideas being considered to ourselves until the market becomes more defined. Elliott takes numerous hard knocks in this regard. In an effort to pick up a lost trial, we may openly discuss all that we might think or hypothesize from little more than muddled, congested price bars that form wandering data tracks on our screens. Guilty as accused. But recognize that one who "sees" waves in market data will lose his or her own center of inner balance when he or she has lost the pattern of the primary markets.

My whole day goes out of whack just because my world has lost its quiet knowing that "my" S&Ps are tracking and are at a certain position within a larger framework. All is right in my small world when the market's footprints have again been identified. So the inner struggle that goes on when you "lose it" is to watch an addict go into withdrawal convulsions. Our whole world seems to fall into turmoil. Not a pleasant sight, and all the alternatives that spew out are the symptoms of inner anguish to regain our own sense of balance.

Sometimes the Elliott Wave Principle is a curse. Once you begin to see waves, you cannot turn them off. I look at a graph in Microsoft *Money* displaying my own bank account and see an "Expanded Flat" pattern and think to myself, "Good, it is time for a third wave rally." Then I panic when I see five waves up! One firm I worked for in Boston had their much-respected Harvard Economics Graduate present an in-depth case to the firm's Asian principles as to why the future for the Pacific Rim markets looked so bullish. When I was asked why I looked so pensive at the end of the presentation, I had only one comment: "Just one problem—all your charts display completed five wave rallies." It marked the start of a war between the two of us.

In hindsight, neither of us was correct. While a decline did unfold from the five wave patterns that were present in those earlier charts, the markets then extended. Only after the extension was satisfied did the much larger declines unfold that we are all more familiar with now. But that one meeting marked a more important milestone for me as it was this presentation that first awakened me to the need of tracking the Globalization factor that had entered the North American equity markets. Ever since that meeting, I have analyzed Asian, European, and U.S. equity indices in an effort to understand who is leading whom and what the Global ramifications are of varying expansion-contraction cycles. You can turn to Appendix B to see examples, but just be aware that an analyst that tries to juggle a Global set of wave interpretations will likely develop different wave interpretations than the analyst that may focus on just one market. The issue concerning different wave interpretations for similar markets is a complex one.

Just one last addition to the too-many-alternatives argument before we move on: Some people will not tolerate seeing the word *alternative* at all. If you fall into this group, you might be among those who do not understand why there should be an alternative market scenario. It can be strongly stated that there is no doubt in your mind that the market will move in a certain way to a certain target level. That outlook should always be stated with a market level that identifies where you believe you are wrong. Should the market exceed or penetrate the marker you have defined as proof that you have stepped off track, then there should be a scenario prepared in advance to explain what might be developing that you had first considered to be *a much lower probability.*

The problem with the alternative view is when you are not given a do-or-die level to show where the analyst believes their favored outlook will be wrong. The analyst that does not have an obligation to state where he or she is wrong is not trading that market. *The accuracy that a trader must have about where he or she may be wrong is more important to his or her longevity than will be the accuracy of his or her market forecasts.* Knowing where we are wrong will dictate where our stop placement should be and further defines our risk-to-reward ratio. I would much prefer to be wrong on the reward aspect of the ratio than to have made an error on the risk portion of the equation. The reward might be more or less, but risk exposure to capital must be very precise.

Placing stops near market levels that negate a favored wave interpretation is poor money management. As an example, never place a stop below the third swing in a triangle that we call "wave *c*." The slippage exposure will be horrendous. Therefore, you must devote as much effort to defining the levels where you might be wrong as you do to calculating where you believe the market might go if you are right. Within this framework the alternative game plan is not a hedge to a favored opinion. Preparing an alternative scenario simply shows we are trying to think ahead, knowing that when in battle, it is hard to be objective about a new market direction once the better view has been proven wrong.

If analysts ever use their alternative market scenario to state "You see, I was right all along because we said the market might would do *xyz*, then they are not being intellectually honest with you or themselves as their higher-probability scenario was wrong. Just step back. Reassess your position. Then move forward again. But if there is no favored outlook to begin with, that is an entirely different problem. Far too often analytic services read "If not this, then that," and they use this sentence construction all the time. It warns me that something is lacking in the methodology being applied.

The last common objection mentioned at the start of the chapter was, "If you scan different time horizons for the same market, you can find any pattern you want to prove your market opinion." Sigh. This objection about picking the best time horizon to support your wave count is usually expressed by traders who are wave deaf. We will go through how larger patterns subdivide. Short time horizons are just the smallest building blocks of the whole *and must fit the whole*. However, the shorter the time horizon, the faster you can see when a market is beginning to develop a move not within your larger game plan. Traders who focus on the smallest building blocks within a larger pattern will be able to react faster than traders who focus only on the larger pattern. The latter group often gets caught in an updraft or downdraft because they tend to force the short horizon to fit their longer horizon opinion. Traders and analysts focused on the long-term pattern will be caught more often. Before we can address this topic fairly, we need to discuss the basic patterns of the Elliott Wave Principle.

Impulsive Waves

Let's try something different. We will not be discussing stick charts or line-on-close charts because many people find it hard to translate a straight-line illustration into a High-Low-Close (HLC) bar chart in a real market environment. It is also more important to realize that it is the market action above and below the close that can kill a trader! So no line charts this time.

In addition, it is really boring for the reader to have to wade through pattern after pattern when there is no real context in which to see how all these patterns may flow together. You do not want to read a descriptive list about Elliott patterns, and I certainly do not want to spend the time to write one. *So let's do this in real-time.* I have a chance of being dead wrong in a book that is expected to have Global distribution. Is that any different than a market report transmitted live around the world? Not really. But be assured that I have used every single method outlined in this book in order to try and find the starting point for a real-time scenario that will give me the best chance possible to start off on the right side of the market.

We will apply all the techniques previously described as they are needed. This will help you understand how they can be used in a real market environment that will become a time sequenced event. Keep in mind that I have to still maintain my normal job and trade from the ideas described. So please permit me to switch to a journal format so that I can try to keep up with the extra workload that is now deadline oriented. We are going to have to make wave count adjustments along the way. I am constantly making minor adjustments in short-horizon charts. So that will be helpful as it is nearly impossible to discuss this aspect within a static chart. If I step off track, it will be extremely informative to show you how to reassess your original game plan and understand when to pick the new count up for a trade. So right or wrong, we should end up with much more information than a cataloged listing of 13 Elliott Wave patterns when the chapter concludes.

Some readers will have already picked up on the time sequence of all the charts in this book. The RSI chapter was the only one that needed a chart with a best-fit example when Positive and Negative Reversal patterns were introduced to you. That was a fairly complex concept, and a clear example was needed to show how the calculations are made for future price projections. The Derivative Oscillator chapter was the first written, and then the rest of the book shows charts in their chronological order from June 1, 1998, toward an August deadline. There was no need to reference an extensive record of carefully preserved examples as all the methods described in this book are techniques I rely upon every day. Without knowing it, you have been witnessing examples of real-time chart analysis.

Chapter 1, Figure 1–4, showed Hong Kong's Hang Seng Index on June 3, 1998, and the comment was made at that time when the chapter was written that the Hang Seng market did not have a bottom in the daily chart. Looking back now on July 24, the market low in that chart was 8351 on June 2. The market has since declined to 7351, which is a major Fibonacci support cluster and Gann confluence zone. It was such a major confluence support zone utilizing both Gann and Fibonacci that it was a very high probability target. It can be said that 7350 is not only a major confluence zone of support but is now akin to being a cliff as there is an absence of support levels directly beneath this level. Figure 6–11 in the Fibonacci chapter illustrates what I mean when I refer to a "cliff" at a support level or a gap forming under a support zone. So there have actually been numerous real-time examples throughout all these charts that have not been brought to your attention.

So here's what we will do together. I tried frantically to complete the Gann chapter by a certain date because I knew the Gann time objective that was approaching would be my best target window to start the Elliott Wave chapter. I missed my target date by a couple days, but I recorded the following at the end of the Gann chapter:

> A market top occurred July 20, 1998, near a time confluence objective, and there has been a decline from a high of 9367.8 to a current low as this is written to 8855.7. A 512.1 point decline in the DJIA from the high is only a 5.5 percent decline. But you might agree that this is still a fairly respectable reaction to a Gann time and price confluence point, *and we will soon turn to other methods that warn the current correction may not be over.*

So that's the market we will track, and Appendix C records the market reports that were written leading into this market pivot for clients. The opinions have recorded dates so they cannot be changed now.

The S&P traders might be frustrated that I will use the DJIA to track a real-time scenario rather than our futures market. I chose the DIJA because I am concerned that traders unfamiliar with the Elliott Wave Principle would become completely lost if they were to see the Globex night session data that we have to contend with now in the S&P 500 futures market. It would make a difficult topic more complex than it should be for someone less experienced. I promise to spend extensive time on the S&P itself at some point within this chapter. Actually, I dread using the DJIA because it will add to my workload. The targets for the DJIA are usually of little interest to me except for longer-horizon curiosity. But the DJIA always creates a cleaner wave pattern.

In addition, I had created a problem for myself in a public broadcast. While daily reports for a market correction have been copied for you in Appendix C, the general public had only the DJIA target on record as I would not release the S&P objectives. On Friday, April 17, 1998, I was in the Los Angeles television studio KWHY-TV being interviewed by Richard Saxton. The following excerpt is from that live interview:

> *Richard:* Are you looking toward Dow 10,000, as most analysts are, now that the 9000 level is behind us?
>
> *Connie:* No, 9000 is of no particular significance in the methods I use. What will be far more important is how the DJIA reacts to 9339. Both Gann and Fibonacci work suggest this is a critical area. If we can pass through 9339 without a hitch, we will reach 10,000 fairly easily. But I do not think the market will be able to break through 9339 without some sort of [a] reaction.

Richard: What sort of "reaction" are you expecting, and what is your target for the S&P?

Connie: I'm sorry, the S&P objectives cannot be discussed today, but a 10 percent correction could develop if the DJIA stalls near 9339. [The three S&P targets were 1176, then 1199, and if exceeded 1207. The last two did not imply a range.] That's a very rough guess as I need to see what the market actually looks like when we reach that level.

So, unwittingly on my part, DJIA 9339 became public record and was given much more attention by some than was ever intended. I am now in a bind as the DJIA closed four days ago at 9337.9. I did not even know that was the close until e-mail messages flooded my inbox. In truth, I think the target was missed as the high in place is 9367.8. The September S&P target is right on with a high at 1199.40 and shows a better pattern to use as a start. However, let's stick with the DJIA and avoid the S&P Globex problem that will distort even the simplest pattern. First, we need to discuss the most basic building block within the Elliott Wave Principle: a five wave pattern. Then we can begin the real-time journal.

The world of R. N. Elliott, and your lifetime sentence to count waves forever more (at least I warned you!), begins with a simple five wave pattern. Figure 10-2

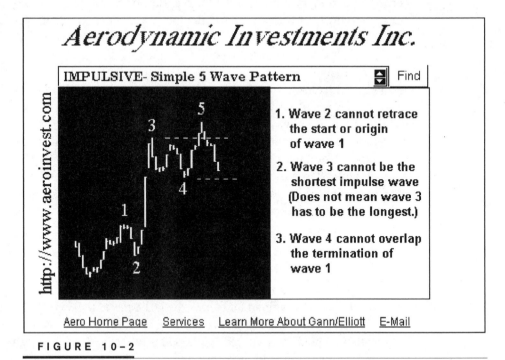

FIGURE 10-2

is a 1-minute bar chart of the Cash S&P 500 Index so it cannot be subdivided any further into a smaller bar chart. As mentioned earlier, don't use tick charts for wave pattern purposes. In my opinion if you cannot use tick charts for wave patterns, then you should not apply them to technical indicators either. Tick charts are bars where a fixed number of trades define a bar. As an example, a 25-tick bar chart *will have no time axis.* While using tick charts is not recommended, using Point-and-Figure charts is recommended as diagnostic tools. We'll have to come back to this later so that we don't stray too far off our present discussion.

The expansion cycle of a market unfolds in a pattern of five waves. A new trend begins with a few well-informed or lucky traders that move the market in what will later be seen as the start of a larger move. The first leg is called "wave 1." The rest of the crowd assumes the prior trend is still the dominant market direction, and this causes the first correction we call "wave 2":

Rule 1: Wave 2 may not break below the origin of wave 1.

In Figure 10-2, wave 2 down retraces part of wave 1. Some markets, such as currency markets, characteristically retrace most of the first wave. That comes from knowing the personality of your market after years of sitting before a computer screen. Whatever is the normal character for a market in a very short horizon chart will someday be seen in that market's longer-horizon charts.

From the end of wave 2 a strong rally then develops because the sleepy traders who assumed the former trend was still in force are now squeezed out, and they have to unwind their positions at the same time the majority are trying to establish a position when they realize a new trend is unfolding. Everyone is entering orders on the same side of the market for one reason or another so the third wave is most often the strongest:

Rule 2: Wave 3 cannot be the shortest. This rule actually leads to a common misunderstanding. *Wave 3 does not have to be the longest*; it just cannot be the shortest when compared to waves 1 and 5.

Then you have traders who want to take some profits, and this action forms the second correction that becomes the fourth wave:

Rule 3: Wave 4 cannot overlap the end or termination of wave 1.

The Wave Principle only has three rules. Easy. Everything else is a guideline. Meanwhile the traders that missed the strong rally that developed in the third wave position have been sitting on the sidelines of the market waiting for a chance to participate in the next move. So, sure enough, after some profit taking, they step into the market and buy in unison, forming a fifth wave up in the direction of the larger trend now in force. In a very short horizon, who's left to buy? Right. The retail traders who just discovered something is happening in this market and their orders press the trend just a little more. Now the whole pattern is ready to be corrected with a three wave movement down. The five wave cycle can then repeat itself once again.

Waves 1, 3, and 5 are called *impulsive waves* as they are clearly dominant and define the direction of the trend being studied. Waves 2 and 4 are the corrective phases of the five wave cycle. People get so fanatical about the internal construction of these waves and how they are built upon blocks of fives and threes. It is far more important to understand and feel the rhythm unfolding in a market before diving into the construction of the different patterns. Even then you have to know only which leg in the pattern is the most critical. You do not need to memorize the internal components of a Swiss watch by reciting 3-3-5s or 5-3-5s. Because all we really care about is how to tell the time, not build the watch. Some quote systems allow you to compress the *x*-axis. *By compressing the scale, you force yourself to study the rhythm and proportions unfolding in the market because you cannot see the finer details.* This is something I will frequently do within any time horizon as it is too easy to get caught up counting every little squiggle wiggle in the chart.

Figure 10-3 displays three markets with a compressed *x*-axis; the weekly Hang Seng Index, the weekly NASDAQ Index, and a 40-minute DMK/$ chart on

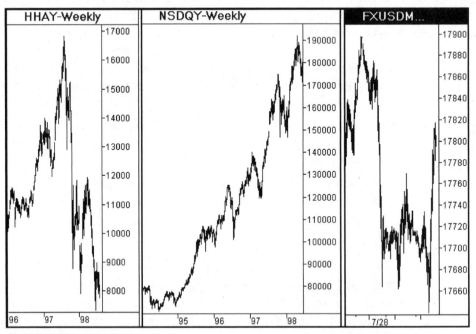

FIGURE 10-3

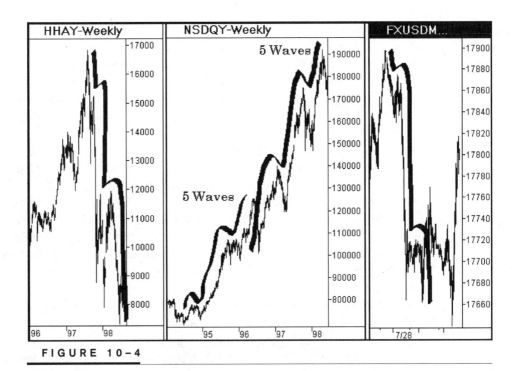

FIGURE 10-4

the far right. Your first task is to please mark each chart so that balanced five wave patterns emerge.

Let's look at the Hang Seng chart first on the left. Did you mark five waves down from the top to the very bottom? Or did you feel five waves down ended at the low in early 1998? Guess what—it does not matter which one you prefer because if you thought a five wave structure ended at the low in early 1998, you would be on the right side of the market because a large rally then followed. You had the right rhythm. Your indicators would have warned you that the rally into the 1200 level in late March was another major sell signal. We have guidelines to help us determine balance and proportions, but you didn't need them as you were on the right side of the market.

Next, let's review the weekly NASDAQ chart in the middle of Figure 10-4. I deliberately had to scroll this chart back so that you could not see the present data. The real chart is a five wave advance. However, if you found a five wave pattern from bottom to top in the NASDAQ chart in Figure 10-3, you have a problem. You need to be able to see that some of these waves should be grouped together as they have similar character. As a group, they also have balanced proportions within their relationships. There are two pairs of five wave structures in this chart. The second five wave pattern into the high is much more forceful than the first.

Textbook Elliott Wave practitioners may become troubled with the fifth wave in the first five wave pattern in this chart. You'll immediately start to subdivide it as we cannot stop ourselves from doing so. The data has been compressed precisely for this reason so that you are unable to see clearly if any structure has internals that subdivide into 5s or 3s. Who cares about the internals in this chart? When the first five wave pattern concluded, the market declined right to the previous fourth wave target zone and then produced a major rally. So stick with a view of the total picture. (If you are new, note that I'll explain the "previous fourth" comment in a moment as I know I jumped ahead of you. Stay with me.) But this is why some of the strongest textbook Elliotticians get themselves into trouble toiling over every little squiggle with an objective to catalog and connect perfect patterns endlessly together. The point is that *you did not need that level of expertise to make money from the pattern.* So don't lose sight that our mission is to drain the swamp around the bank, not count the alligators! A trader that can feel the harmony and rhythms of the market will end up being right far more often than the expert analyst who strives to catalog and label every squiggle correctly.

I know I just lost someone trying to use this chapter as an introduction when I had to jump ahead, so let's back up and fill in the gap. Once we have a five wave pattern in place, there is going to be a move in the opposite direction to correct the entire five wave cycle. After staring at these redundant patterns so often in all time frames, we know to anticipate where the next target will be located when the market corrects a completed five wave cycle. We call this target zone *the vicinity of the previous fourth wave.* Take a look at Figure 10-2. Where wave 3 topped and wave 4 bottomed, there is a dotted line marking the start and end of wave 4. The target following a five wave pattern will be to this zone, which is *anywhere* within the range of the previous fourth wave. That is extremely helpful to know in long-horizon charts as we now have a sense of the size of the correction that will follow from any indicator signal that coincides with the end of a five wave pattern. If my Gann time projections are correct and we now have a five wave pattern visible in a weekly DJIA chart, our real-time scenario could get pretty interesting.

In Figure 10-1 we were unable to determine the magnitude of those market corrections from just observing the sell signals in the diverging indicators. It is only after we have added new information obtained from the Elliott Wave Principle that we gain a sense that there is a larger road map that we can turn to as a guide. It is as if someone were giving us directions by stating, "Turn left at the next corner and go straight until you reach California" as opposed to stating, "Turn left at the next corner and go straight until you reach the next McDonald's restaurant." The scale is entirely different though both directions correctly begin with an immediate left turn at the next corner.

The last market in Figure 10-4 is a 40-minute DMK/$ chart on the far right. If you are just learning, you will likely mark the entire data in this chart as a five wave pattern from top to bottom. That's OK for the information you have been given so far. The more advanced Elliott Wave analyst will recognize that the last leg down is part of another pattern that the novice will easily recognize by the end of this chapter. However, both the novice and the advanced Elliott Wave practitioner will be on the right side of the market as both would have been looking for a rally in the dollar from the price low in this chart. (The more experienced wave counter would be scrambling to again reverse or step aside where this chart data ends. The novice will soon understand why.)

Let's go back to the NASDAQ chart in the middle of Figure 10-4. We said markets move in five wave patterns in the direction of a larger trend. This chart shows two five wave advances in a clearly defined bullish trend. The total picture is not a complete five wave pattern, and the second pattern of five waves is clearly stronger than the first. What is happening? This market is extending, which means that once *another* five wave pattern forms over the first two in this chart, we will then have a larger five wave pattern. The reason is that the impulsive waves in positions 1, 3, and 5 are themselves constructed from smaller five wave units. So three sets of five wave patterns that still abide by the three rules stated for the simplest five wave pattern in Figure 10-2 will become a larger five wave pattern. Let's take a closer look at an extending five wave pattern in Figure 10-5, and then we can start our day-to-day tracking of the DJIA.

Take a look at the last five wave cycle in Figure 10-5. Each wave is labeled 1 through 5 into the price bottom. The start of the last five wave cycle is marked wave (4) at the top and the bottom is marked wave (5). As you look up the data and then study the whole structure, you can see that this last move down is the fifth wave within a larger five wave cycle. Wave (3) in the middle is so forceful that it is nearly a straight line, and it is hard to see that it can be subdivided into five distinct waves from the top of wave (2) to the completion of wave (3). That is why we drop down to the next shorter time horizon so that we can confirm that a five wave structure is present as more price bars become available for study. The price decline is so strong, however, that we already know that it is a third wave decline. The assertion that you should look at different time horizons to pick a pattern that best fits your view is wrong through ignorance. *Regardless of the time horizon we use to view this third wave down, it must have internal building blocks that form smaller five wave patterns that are complete.*

If you play Blackjack and know how to count cards for a single deck, you also know it is much harder to count six decks of cards. A trader that has a wave count in a weekly chart will then subdivide the data in a daily chart so that it compliments the longer time horizon. If you then view 60-minute, 15-minute, 5-minute, and 1-minute

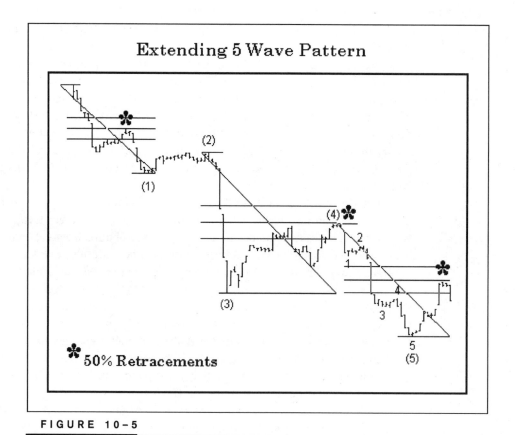

FIGURE 10-5

charts, it is like adding another deck to the dealer's shoe. You have to count them all and continually adjust the balance and proportions as dictated by the new data. The reason it can be done easily, however, is that there will always be the recurring theme of the five wave pattern subdividing into more detailed five wave patterns. In reality, I do not have to count down six decks of cards all at the same time as one would have to do before a Blackjack dealer. (Then you cannot let the pit boss catch on to what you are doing! Counting wave structure is much easier.)

A market that is extending is much easier to count if you start in the middle of the chart. Tilt? I know, this one sounds screwy at first. Put the backs of your thumb nails together; then put them on the 50 percent line that defines the Fibonacci ratios for wave (3) down in Figure 10-5. By putting your thumbs back to back on the chart, you have marked the midpoint of the strongest part of the market's move. Now move your thumb nails apart diagonally so that they touch the start and end of wave (3). They should now be on the high marked (2) and the low marked (3). Now comes the important part. Move your thumbs to positions "(1)" and "(4)." Next, move your left thumb diagonally upward past a full set of *five waves.* Now move your right thumb down diagonally until the right hand has passed over five waves. The left and right hand should move across a set of five waves that has similar proportions. In markets developing very large extending patterns, I would then move my left thumb upward across another five wave unit and follow that action by finding a counterbalanced move with my right. When you have as many sets of fives on the left hand as you do on the right, it is a completed five wave pattern that has subdivided several times to create one larger unit.

Why am I using such a scientific tool as my thumb nails? Because my hands will cover everything else up, and I cannot see the chart until I separate my hands. This eliminates any bias. I can always find where the strongest part of the market's move is on the chart. Then start from that midpoint and work out. Some extending waves are like the EverReady pink rabbit; they just keep going, and going, and going.

What if the next five wave pattern that the market forms is even stronger than the first that defined our midpoint? We would then have to make an adjustment and use the stronger move as the new midpoint. Our DJIA scenario could create a lengthy extending pattern, and we may have to use this technique at some point. It is always balance, rhythm, and proportion that should be given the greatest thought for any chart.

There are three asterisks marked at 50 percent Fibonacci retracement levels in Figure 10-5. The first asterisk is the fourth wave up within the first five wave pattern down that completes wave (1). The second asterisk marks a 50 percent retracement for all of wave (3) and becomes the area of resistance for wave (4) up. Once the entire extending five wave pattern is complete, the first bounce up is to a 50 percent retracement relative to the last five wave cycle in the sequence or the fifth wave. You would now want to know the Fibonacci retracement ratios relative to the entire decline as well. These repeating ratios show the market is extending, *but not expanding, its scale.* Proportions remain about the same. If the decline were accelerating, the corrective rallies would begin to fall short of the 50 percent retracement levels marked in this chart. We covered this topic in great detail within the Fibonacci chapter so we'll not venture down that same road twice. But the internal Fibonacci ratios and resulting math grids on the screen are extremely important. Figure 10-5 gives us an overall picture that has symmetry and balance.

Let's begin to study the DJIA real-time and track it through the remainder of this chapter. The challenge will be to continue building our knowledge about the basic building blocks that we use within the Wave Principle so that we can keep up with the real-time market patterns that develop. Permit me to switch to a journal writing style in an effort to make my task a little easier.

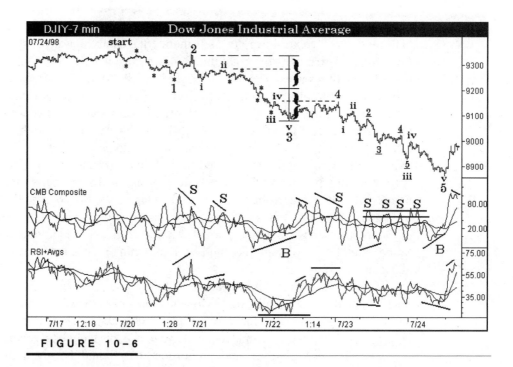

FIGURE 10-6

It is now July 24, 1998.[1] In Figure 10-6 we have a 7-minute chart of the Dow Jones Industrial Average. The chart was labeled so that it could be used in my evening market report. However, it is not the best interpretation when balance and proportion are considered so a new chart had to be constructed.

In Figure 10-5 we saw how a larger five wave pattern can be subdivided into three individual sets of complete, though smaller, five wave patterns that follow one after another. It takes three sets of complete five wave cycles to construct a larger five wave pattern, and they cannot break the first three rules that were defined for Figure 10-2. However, it is not enough to simply find five waves that meet *minimum* requirements and sit back, content with the knowledge that the market has reached an important pivot. This is true even when our supporting indicators offer major signals to compliment our view that the five wave cycle is now complete.

In Figure 10-6 the five wave pattern labeled will meet all the rules and guidelines of the Elliott Wave Principle. First locate the pivot levels labeled 1, 2, 3, 4, and 5 in Figure 10-6. As we have not discussed how to label subdivided waves, we can take this opportunity to do so now. The high in this DJIA chart at

---

[1] Figure 10–1 was added July 29 when I realized an important point had been overlooked in the original arguments. The journal entries for Figures 10–6 to 10–10 had already been written.

9367.8 was made on July 20, 1998, and the chart shows the correction into the close of July 24. Start from the price high in this chart and follow the first five wave decline that forms wave 1 down. The individual subdivisions within wave 1 are marked with only an asterisk. They need to be labeled with something other than numbers 1 through 5 to avoid confusion with the larger structure unfolding. So the smaller subset that we refer to as *one lesser degree* should be marked i, ii, iii, iv, and v. Beneath wave v we put the number 1 to show where we think the first five wave cycle ended. Then there is a correction marked wave 2 up that leads to wave (3) down. Within wave (3) we again run out of labels, as wave iii itself subdivides further into another small five wave pattern. The small five wave cycle that is marked with asterisks between the end of wave ii (better said, the start of wave iii) and the end of wave iii is what we call the *third-of-third* wave because it is wave iii within 3. This wave position is always the strongest part of any market move. We will use an underlined number when we run out of ways to differentiate additional subdivisions in the chart next time.

As the patterns subdivide into smaller portions, we refer to each as one lesser *degree*. Bob Prechter's labels make more sense than R. N. Elliott's, though we keep running out of ways to subdivide intraday data. The following labels are described in more detail in the book *Elliott Wave Principle: Key To Market Behavior*[2]; (I) to (V) is reserved for Supercycle Degree, I to V denotes Cycle Degree, and then numbers 1 to 5 within circles are used for Primary Degree. The degrees which follow are the more common ones you will see; Intermediate Degree uses (1) to (5), Minor Degree uses the numbers 1 to 5, then i to v for Minute, and finally 1 to 5 for Minuette.

When you subdivide wave structure all the way down to a very short time horizon, it is very easy to run out of conventional characters. I will use 1' to 5', then 1" to 5" as the primes easily fit electronic word processing. But others have used .1 to .5 and then ..1 to ..5. The dots are very hard to read, particularly if the chart is faxed, but the method I have been using is not a whole lot better. Just know you have to be consistent so that others might be able to follow your interpretations. The numbers contained within a circle denoting Primary degree are hard to use with modern-day computer keyboards. *TradeStation* will not permit an underlined text character. So many of us become a little sloppy about strictly adhering to the correct degree symbols. You will find the symbol (1) is frequently used in a very short time horizon and does not imply Intermediate Degree because we do not have enough variations to easily label intraday data. So please do not make any long-horizon assumptions from an intraday chart. I will not go further into explaining *degrees* as you can refer to them in Robert Prechter and A. J. Frost's

---

[2]Robert Prechter and A. J. Frost, *Elliott Wave Principle: Key To Market Behavior,* 7th ed. (Gainesville, Georgia: New Classics Library, 1995).

book[2] or access my Web site to see a table of the common degree notations. Recognize that the variations just offered for the numbers 1 through 5 that denote wave degrees are used only with five wave patterns. We have not discussed corrections against the trend that use the letters A, B, and C and other appropriate variations for their specific degrees.

We left off where wave 3 down was complete in Figure 10-6. We then see a correction unfold *back to the previous fourth wave.* We covered this phrase earlier, and you may want to turn to Figure 10-2 if you need a quick recap. The correction becomes wave 4 up, and then we have an extending pattern that creates wave 5 down into the price low. That's it. We have just labeled every twist and turn in an extending five wave pattern that is now complete. Or is it complete? That is how most analysts will end their wave interpretation *as most people try to find the best fit for only the data that is present on their screen or chart.* This interpretation would be the best fit. However, I do not think that this chart represents a completed five wave cycle even though there is a buy signal at the price low where the Composite Index is diverging with RSI.

We must now take the chart in Figure 10-6 past the point where others will view their analytic task to be complete. The first problem is that the distance traveled in wave 5 is greater than the total distance of the price decline that unfolded in waves 1 and 3 combined. Did I make an error in my identification of wave 3 itself? No, I do not believe so. The reason is that wave 3 is clearly a complete structure with really beautiful proportions and ratios within this unit. I have added some visual guides on the chart so that you can see the tremendous symmetry within the segment defined as wave 3 down. There must be something else going on within this market's data. I then need to study the complimentary buy and sell signals within my indicators to see if they align with the significant pivots that mark the end of waves 1, 2, 3, 4, and 5. There is divergence between the RSI and Composite Index to warn us of these market turns.

The buy signal that forms into the bottom of wave 3 appears early. It is not. Look more closely. Both the Composite Index and the RSI are developing Negative Reversal price projection signals with each new oscillator peak that develops. The divergence near the July 22 date correctly warns that the market will attempt to bounce each time the Composite Index tests the trend line for that indicator. However, the Composite Index advances while prices are only moving a relatively small distance upward. The bounces are very weak. We had charts in prior chapters to highlight this important relationship between oscillator versus price movement. *You are on the wrong side of the market if the oscillators can move without prices following.*

We then see the Composite Index forms a Negative Reversal where the oscillator makes a new high at a lower price level compared to prior oscillator peaks.

This signal marks the end of wave iv up within wave 3 down. There is also a Negative Reversal signal in the RSI that meets the amplitude requirements we defined for the RSI. (If you skipped the RSI price projection chapter, you will find the RSI signals that I am referring to very difficult. You might want to go back to pick this information up first as the RSI Reversals offer invaluable technical information for constructing wave counts.)

Finally, the buy signal of greatest significance produces wave 4 up. We previously demonstrated that the most significant oscillator pattern relative to the moving averages is a signal that coincides near the intersection where the short moving average crosses above or below the longer moving average on the oscillator. In this chart the crossover in the Composite Index that occurs earlier has been deliberately set up as an early warning. The crossover in the RSI is the true timing signal.

At the top of wave 4 in Figure 10-6 we have a sell signal that leads to a series of four S labels denoting sell signals that align within a horizontal channel of resistance. This is the significant piece of evidence that we have been trying to find. "It is?" you may ask. What did we just find? The channel that you see developing in the Composite Index is a characteristic pattern found within a third wave position or a market coiling in preparation for an expansion eruption to a larger mathematical grid for future internal structure. When this indicator pattern develops, I know to adjust all my future Fibonacci price projections. In Figure 10-5 the five wave pattern extended, but it did not rescale its symmetrical proportions. The retracements all challenged a 50 percent ratio of a portion of its larger movement, and the decline was orderly. In Figure 10-6 we have a five wave pattern that will likely develop into a larger five wave structure. This indicator pattern of consecutive sell signals that form a horizontal channel in the Composite Index is the same as a seismograph recording of a minor tremor before a larger earthquake occurs. Now follow the indicators past this channel where the buy signal leads to an indicator pop into the last bar on the right of this chart. The term "an indicator pop" was coined by George Lane. The indicator screams SELL.

The oscillators are overbought, and the two indicators have diverging peaks within a close proximity to one another. *This is exceedingly bearish.* The chapter on the RSI revealed that peaks that form divergences within a spread less than 9 periods apart should be considered very strong signals. In this chart both indicators display this strong signal. However, this is not the only technical information available from the final indicator positions aligned with the most recent data. Both the RSI and Composite Index are overbought at oscillator highs that form at lower price levels compared to other oscillator peaks which we now know is a *Negative Reversal* signal. Reversal signals develop only in bear markets.

All right then, we know the chart is clearly telling us that the market will decline further. *But it is also giving us more subtle information warning us not to "bet the farm"* immediately. The market will not make a major decline from the market levels in the last few bars of Figure 10-6. How do we know this? Look closely at the Composite Index peaking in the most current data of Figure 10-6. It is making a peak at a level (compared to the indicator's *y*-axis) that is higher than any other peak that this indicator created within this chart. Recall a prior discussion that stated, when an oscillator successfully creates a new high or low by breaking through a former horizontal range of resistance support for that indicator, the market will have sufficient punch to come back and test the former indicator range after the new indicator extreme has been alleviated. In my experience the oscillator nearly always returns to test the former range of resistance support for that indicator. That is why I use the Composite Index because it has not been normalized and can travel any displacement above or below zero that it may want to go. So we now know the market is going down further after it attempts a back-and-fill pattern from nearby levels. *The next step is that we have to think of a wave count that fits this additional evidence.*

We also have to factor in the Negative Reversal signal present in the oscillators and work with the information we gained from the series of horizontal sell signals that warn us the market will rescale to a new proportion with the next move. Here is how I go about finding a revised wave count that might compliment all the pieces of technical evidence within our current puzzle.

The chart in Figure 10-7 is the exact same chart we saw in Figure 10-6, except that I have made a copy of the first part of the decline from the high, rotated that segment of data 180 degrees, and then pasted the copied segment onto the back end of our existing data. Why? We know markets create symmetrical patterns. When I copied the beginning cycles within our five wave pattern and pasted them to the last bar in Figure 10-6, it was very easy to see that the

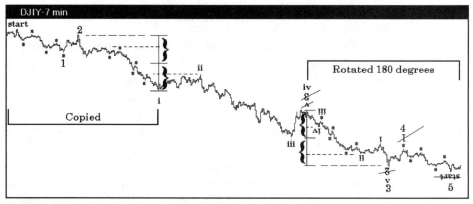

FIGURE 10–7

market had not formed a completed five wave pattern that displayed symmetry because it in fact was still trying to extend into a larger structure. We knew that from the oscillator signals. If you look at the pasted segment added to the right side of Figure 10-7, you will see that the original labels from Figure 10-6 are still present, though upside down, because the data has been rotated. Use the thumb nail method if you have difficulties seeing this. What had been labeled wave v of 5 down is now marked wave iii within wave 3 down. The graphically manipulated interpretation in Figure 10-7 helps us see an extending pattern, but do not forget that the oscillator position into a new high is telling us there will not be an immediate breakdown. A down up and then down pattern is what we need. OK, so the pattern in Figure 10-7 is helpful but not the exact puzzle piece that we need.

Take a closer look at wave iv up in Figure 10-7. What if wave iv is incomplete? A more complex correction would incorporate the down up pattern the oscillator wants, and then we can break down into a fifth wave. I like that idea especially when we consider that the Wave Principle has a guideline for alternating the character of patterns that form within wave positions 2 and 4. If you look at Figure 10-2 again, you will see that waves 2 and 4 alternate in the amount of time each takes to complete their corrections. If you have a simple wave 2, you can expect a tricky wave 4 and vice versa. So the guideline of alternation fits our present scenario really nicely.

There are no cycle lows on the horizon to challenge the back-and-fill scenario, so let's go with the following game plan. The current fourth wave is incomplete, and then we can expect a decline to a new low, and then we can see what else the market will give us. To determine the target for the price low, I will combine the Negative Reversal signal we have in place in Figure 10-6, Fibonacci swing projections, and Gann. Gann will have the highest weighting.

One last note about the graphic cut-and-paste technique demonstrated in Figure 10-7 before we move on. This is something you will be able to do in your mind very quickly after you start to utilize the Wave Principle. Knowing that proportional balances may occur between the first part of a market's move and the latter will enable you to identify price targets and also what the character of the move will look like as it nears a resolution. In other words, a slow choppy start might be how the market's move ends by repeating a slow choppy pattern into its conclusion. We cannot make that assumption now because of the series of horizontal sell signals in the chart warning us that an expansion may form.

It is important to know for price projection purposes that wave 5 is frequently equal in size to the first wave or will develop a Fibonacci relationship such as 1.618 relative to the first wave. I will not spend a lot of time on price projections for Elliott Waves because you already know how to calculate every Fibonacci relationship by applying the techniques we discussed at great length in the Fibonacci chapter. So there are very few new relationships you need to learn as the prior techniques in the Fibonacci chapter will produce the correct objectives. What we have yet to discuss are price projections within corrective patterns and from triangles, which we will cover later in this chapter.

Someone might think it would have been much easier to just remove some of our subdivisions in the 7-minute chart by moving up to a longer time horizon, rather than going to the trouble of graphing a future path as shown in Figure 10-7. Someone else might see us change our time horizon and think we are looking for a pattern that best fits our market view. Ha! Let's see what the longer time horizons would do for us now.

Figure 10-8 is the exact data that was displayed in the 7-minute chart now plotted in a 15-minute bar chart. The labels in this chart are those we used in Figure 10-6. When you change time horizons in *TradeStation*, that system will try to keep

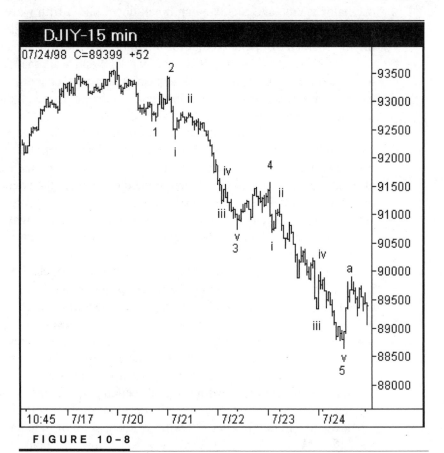

FIGURE 10-8

the labels in place that were added to the 7-minute chart. I have not touched this chart other than to change the time period used to plot the *x*-axis. The wave structure that unfolds within wave 3 down in this interpretation still appears to be the strongest because it is the most direct and displays fewer back-and-fill retracements. However, you might notice the pattern of sharp breaks throughout wave 5 in this interpretation and the increasing volatility. These visual clues in Figure 10-8 are harder to read than the indicator signals that we discussed in Figure 10-6, but the wave count is clearly intact and defines a five wave structure in this time horizon.

If an extending five wave pattern can hold together when compressed into a 15-minute chart, will it continue to look like five waves in a 60-minute chart? The labels applied to the 7-minute bar chart in Figure 10-6 remain visible in the 60-minute chart offered in Figure 10-9. While we can still see that a five wave pattern might have been made from the price high to the current low in this longer time frame, we must consider with much greater interest what has just come into view. The rally that developed into the high still has the old labels displayed from the analysis when the market was advancing. This prior work shows that we were working toward the completion of a five wave pattern and the decline unfolding now has already exceeded the previous fourth wave. The previous fourth wave would have been the most likely target for a minor pullback. So we now have to step back and look at an even longer time horizon as it is becoming clear we must know how this current five wave rally in Figure 10-9 fits into an even bigger picture for this market.

What you are seeing demonstrated is one of the ways I apply the Elliott Wave Principle differently from the way Bob Prechter applies it. While I work from the smallest building blocks possible and work upward into a longer time horizon, he starts with an extremely long horizon interpretation and then looks for substructure within progressively shorter time frames to compliment his longer-horizon view. I take the approach of building from the small and working upward because my risk management dictates accuracy in the very short time horizons. I can be less accurate in the really big picture because I am always revising the underlying components within a market as they develop. I have little interest in the really big picture just as long as I'm trading from the right side over the next few hours or days. Prechter, on the other hand, cannot change his view every few minutes or days because his greater interest in the really big picture that may define major pivots within terms of decades. So this is one way that we apply the Wave Principle differently.

I spend extensive time reviewing the bigger picture when my short-horizon building blocks begin to step off track or they are out of sync and challenge the longer-horizon view. But what if the short horizon does not warn you that a change is brewing? Yes, this can also happen. If you get too complacent in the shortest time horizons and *do not review the Global picture* to see what might be brewing

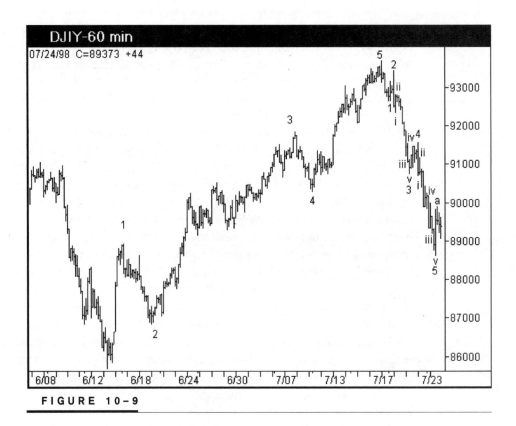

FIGURE 10-9

beyond the boundaries of your own market, you may be clobbered some day by an unexpected surprise.

Now that we have a completed five wave rally present in Figure 10-9, we want to see how this latest five wave structure fits into a rally that has been forming an extending pattern. The top right chart within Figure 10-10 shows the current decline relative to the completed five wave rally displayed in the 60-minute chart. On the bottom right, using a compressed *x*-axis, is the weekly DJIA chart. The second arrow to the right in this weekly chart marks the low that corresponds to the five wave rally highlighted in a box in the daily data. The weekly chart, bottom right, has a Fibonacci grid added, and what is being tested is to see if the current high and major low that formed in October 1997 would meet the internal relationship test that we discussed in the Fibonacci chapter. It does pass this test as the remaining arrows bring to your attention prior pivot levels where the market showed respect to this same mathematical grid derived from the present high. No wonder our 7-minute chart is warning us that an expansion to its present scale could develop. Now look at the window displaying the daily S&P 500 futures data in Figure 10-10. You will see that all the former signals and wave interpretations that were used in the past are still present. This pattern was the subject of a great debate. The debate concerned a triangle pattern, and we will come back to this chart if the DJIA makes its own triangle. We will discuss corrective patterns later.

The price high in this chart may in fact be the resolution of a large five wave pattern that began in October 1997. The guideline that the Wave Principle provides us is that a five wave pattern will target "the vicinity of the previous fourth wave." Hello. We have arrived already within this target zone. But the range of the fourth wave is admittedly very large. The sell signal present in the Composite Index when it diverged dramatically with the RSI is going to lead to a fairly healthy correction with all the evidence building against the DJIA. The indicators in the daily S&P chart show that a bottom is not in place in this time horizon either, and we therefore know the long-term trend lines marked by moving averages in this chart will be violated. Also what about that additional five wave pattern marked from the October 1997 low into the high? That interpretation from the October 1997 low may, or may not, be correct. *All I really care about is that a possible Elliott Wave pattern is present that developed into a major Gann price and time target.* I do not care what this current Elliott Wave pattern is on my screen. I do not need all the

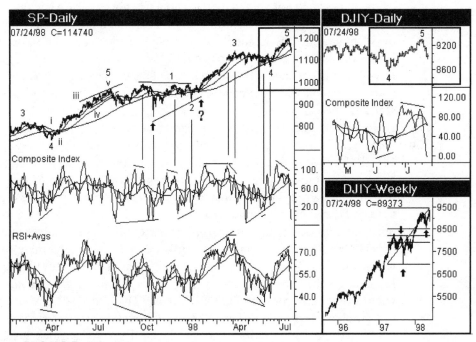

FIGURE 10-10

answers to trade tomorrow. I've seen enough to know this could get ugly. To go further, I will need to show you how I analyze long-horizon charts as that would be the next step to study our weekly and monthly bar charts for these indices and the underlying S&P 500 Sectors themselves. So I will walk through the approach I use for longer-horizon work, but not tonight. It is now 4 A.M. on July 25, and the Globex session has been slipping nicely within our down up scenario that was developed several pages ago in Figure 10-6. Let's see what pattern the market ultimately develops. Good night.

Corrective Waves

The down up market action our indicators warned us could occur in Figure 10-6 is what has developed in the DJIA and S&P 500 futures market. But to discuss these down up patterns in terms more useful than letter shapes and direction, we need to build our Elliott Wave vocabulary to include the corrective patterns that serve to bind five wave cycles together.

While most people will develop an ability to see a five wave structure within price data fairly rapidly, some people may find it difficult to see the patterns that correct a completed five wave cycle. It is clear what a textbook line drawing representation of these patterns should look like, but it is not as clear what the patterns should look like in a real market environment. In addition, more than one individual building block is generally required to complete a market correction, and there is some confusion about the connector between these individual patterns, the dreaded *X wave*. I can understand why the confusion exists because I too had to struggle with corrections until Dave Allman taught me how to feel the pattern for an individual structure. Feel a pattern? Yes. Allman walks you through hundreds of sequential charts to help you gain a feel of a particular pattern in his Advanced Workshops. Although I cannot do that here, I can provide some analogies that may help you.

Before we look at our first corrective pattern, you need to know the level of aptitude you presently have for working with graphic patterns that change their orientation. I am dyslexic in that tables of numbers and letters are difficult for me to read. Tabular characters tend to transpose their positions in my mind's-eye. I am not an options trader for that reason because the strike price tables and calculations for delta, gamma, and theta in tabular form are a visual nightmare for me. I work with them only on rare occasion and with great anguish. But the flip side of this limitation is that I have a photographic memory and a graphic aptitude that more than compensates for the tabular weakness. The point is that you may not know that graphic puzzles are difficult for you. Corrective patterns are just puzzles once you know their underlying building blocks. Let's try a quick visual test to see where your starting point might be located.

▶**1**. If the following shape is folded into a cube shape, which picture best represents the result?

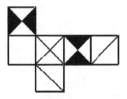

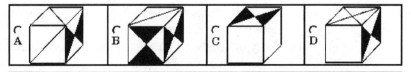

▶**2**. Which of the designs best completes the following sequence?

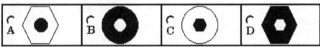

▶ **3** . Which of the figures below the line of drawings best completes the series?

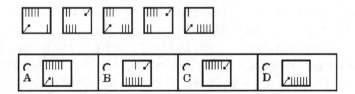

▶ **4** . Which of the figures below the drawings best completes the series?

MENSA International   http://www.mensa.org

FIGURE 10-11

There are four graphic puzzles in Figure 10-11. You should give yourself no more than four minutes to select your answer based on the original guidelines for these questions. These four questions are from an introductory sample quiz, considered elementary, by MENSA International. Their Web site can be found at http://www.mensa.org, and these questions are from their *Mensa Workout* page. I'll explain why these questions have the solutions they do and why each is very similar to a market problem. Elliott Wave corrective wave patterns are like graphic puzzles, and markets frequently ask us to "complete the series." The difference is that our quizzes are more fun because when we "complete the series" correctly, we put money in our trading accounts. That's the fun part!

If you had any trouble with the first question in this quiz, you will be applying R. N. Elliott's wave patterns in a real-time market environment about as comfortably as I work with options tables. The reason such a bold analogy can be offered is that the first question is the type of puzzle an Elliott Wave trader is solving all day long and the first question in the quiz is far easier than the puzzles the markets will create for us. The correct answer is B.

The second question in the quiz shows how you might be thrown off balance by different market character that serves as interference or noise. Market character can impact corrective patterns. For example, the up-down-up or N pattern referred to earlier may not be a distinct N when you look at it in the data for Euros versus a stock index. Nonetheless, it is the same pattern. In question 2 when the outer shape is a hexagon, the center is a circle and vice versa. The correct answer is A. Two outer circles with internal hexagons would be followed by two exterior hexagons with inner circles. The black and white colors simply alternate. This is an easy question. A harder question would have been, "What would be the next pair of shapes that follow within this series after solving for the missing fourth shape?" That would be closer to what you would be asked in an actual Mensa test. The mathematical relationships have already been defined to extend the series. No, I'm not giving you the answer to this revised question. Maybe in a seminar or conference.

Question 3 is one I really like as you frequently have to change the orientation of a pattern to correctly identify the mathematical relationship that is developing within a market's price structure. Figure 10-7 showed one example where I copied the first portion of a decline, rotated it 180 degrees, then pasted it to the back of the actual data in that chart. Question 3 is the same type of puzzle. While this problem is harder than the first, it is very much like an Elliott Wave application when adding indicator signals. While the number of lines on the side with the stick will increase by 1, the side opposite the stick decreases by one. The correct answer is C. The stick simply shows that the orientation of the entire graphic is rotated 180 degrees with each new frame as the stick is alternating sides. The correct answer requires a final rotation.

Question 4 is another graphic puzzle asking you to "complete the series." Did you notice that the first column had six petals, while the second only had five? The first row is solid. The second row has lines radiating into the center. The correct answer is E as it is the only solution offered that fits in the series.

How did you do? If these questions were easy for you, we are ready to charge ahead into any corrective pattern at full speed and you will likely have little trouble. At the other extreme, if you struggled with all of these questions, please accept that with work you will learn the mechanics of how to press the correct keys on the Elliott piano, but most likely you will never learn to play the music using this particular instrument. I bet you are the options wizard in your firm who can manipulate delta, gamma, theta tables all day long without effort. Even duration and convexity calculations in bonds are a breeze (Ugh). It is a left-brain/right-brain development issue again, and it is no reflection on one's intellect. Please accept that this next section may be harder for you, but stick with it as the indicators from prior chapters will be applied in a real-time scenario.

Our indicators told us to look for a price movement that would look like the letter N. This pattern fits into the family of corrective patterns called "Flats." They are illustrated in Figure 10-12. Have you ever watched a springboard diving competition? Think back to the Summer Olympic Games. Even if you saw only an advertisement on television and never watched any of the televised events themselves, you saw divers launch themselves from a springboard into the air. *The Flat pattern is the exact same feel.* The Flat on the left of Figure 10-12 is the diver taking off from the platform, which is a solid structure. You jump up, land with both your feet on the edge of the platform, then jump as high as possible. You do not get much higher than the start of your first leap because there is no give under

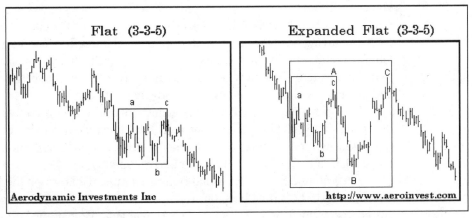

FIGURE 10-12

your feet before your final jump from the edge. On the other hand, the Expanded Flat pattern is the diver on a springboard. The diver takes the same approach by taking a step to the edge of the diving board, but then his weight presses the diving board down below the board's horizontal level. The resulting displacement will be lower than it was with the approaching step toward the edge. The spring displacement of the diving board then projects the diver higher than would have been possible from a solid surface. All divers must then abide by the force of gravity.

The only difference between the diving analogy and the market pattern is that the "diver" can bounce on either side of the diving board or platform in a weightless environment. Hence, the same pattern can develop in an upward trending market as can develop for a declining market as demonstrated in Figure 10-12. The three movements of the "dive," or correction, are labeled a-b-c to identify that the market action is counter to the five wave pattern preceding it. Here is the key to this entire pattern: Forget the 3-3-5 references for a moment at the top of Figure 10-12. *What is important to know is that the final move to the edge of the platform or springboard will always be hard to count.* The process of elimination makes our task much easier. The market action will get choppy, and what will frequently be obvious is that the b-wave portion of the move, which can be in the direction of the larger trend, will not be easily subdivided into a five wave cycle.

If it is not a five wave structure, it has to be a three. It doesn't matter what kind of three wave pattern it is. The middle leg within Flat corrections will be choppy because there is a lot going on. A diver will lift only one knee before planting both feet on the edge of the board. Why? *Because he or she is about to change his or her direction of trend and he or she needs to stabilize his or her prior movement before he or she can be projected in a new direction.* That is exactly what the market is doing. Don't get hung up on categorizing all the internal squiggles. If you can sniff out a b wave, you have it made. The point I am trying to make is that it doesn't matter if the first leg looks like a five because the choppy pattern to the edge of a diving board is far more important. Feel them first in your gut. The problem with representative line charts for these patterns is that you never get a chance to feel the pattern's action within a market. In my opinion that is why Elliott Wave patterns used without the aid of other indicators are deadly.

Look what happens when we add an oscillator to the corrective Flat patterns in Figure 10-13. The indicators contribute the same type of tension or inner expectation that we might have when we know how a springboard should ultimately move when it is overextended from a horizontal position.

A 20-minute September Bond futures chart is displayed on the left in Figure 10-13. A very short time horizon was selected to show what is meant by "different character for a market." Once the Expanded Flat pattern is completed, the Bond market is slow to resume the former trend. The character in this 20-minute

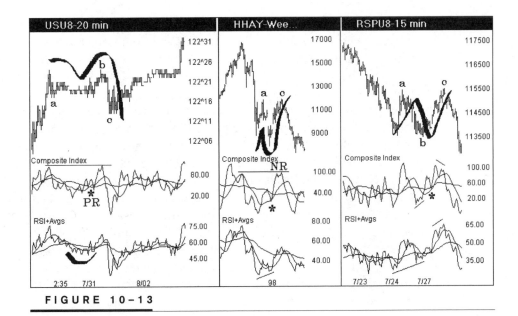

FIGURE 10-13

chart is exactly what Bond traders are accustomed to viewing in longer time frames as Bonds frequently take time to make a trend change. The Expanded Flat pattern itself for the correction is not different from the market illustrated in Figure 10-12 except that Bonds are forming the corrective pattern under the springboard. Can't see it? Flip your book over, look at this page from the next page while holding the page in front of a light source. (I do this all the time: Print a chart and take it to a window or lamp. Flip it. Look at it from the back. Have a bias to sell everything in sight? Next time you are not sure of a buy signal, print it out and look at the chart from the back of the page upside down. Then ask yourself if you would sell it. Bias problem solved.)

In the September Bond chart in Figure 10-13 notice the Positive Reversal marked in the Composite Index that forms in the oscillator lows on either side of the asterisk. At the top of wave b the Composite Index forms a double top. Notice that wave b in this example does not move much past the origin of wave a. Did anyone ever say it had to move well past the start of wave a? No. So don't look for the perfect textbook pattern in the real world.

The middle chart in Figure 10-13 is the Weekly Hang Seng. Now you know why the first decline in early 1998 was not the end of a five wave pattern in Figure 10-4. The top of wave c of (4) in Figure 10-13 was accompanied by a Negative Reversal signal in the Composite Index. (The acceptable amplitude of the signal in the Composite Index is much larger than what was defined for the RSI.) Notice that wave b down (the decline from wave a to the next low that leads to wave c up) coincides with a buy signal in both the RSI and Composite Index. An asterisk adjacent to the Composite Index when it is testing support marks a very strong signal.

Turn back to the DMK/$ chart in Figure 10-4. Earlier I mentioned that you would soon know why the new low in the dollar within this chart was not part of the original five wave pattern. The chart displays a five wave decline (into a double bottom) followed by a perfect Expanded Flat. We are able to make a price projection for the distance wave c may travel by first measuring the distance of wave a. (from the end of the marked five wave decline up to the level near 1.7770 in Figure 10-4). Now flip your Precision Ratio Compass over so that you project a 1.618 relationship from the bottom of wave b from the price low in this chart for the dollar relative to wave a. The rally that follows is in fact exactly to the 1.618 relationship. Do not exceed this measurement; if you do, your probability will be significantly reduced that your Expanded Flat pattern will be the correct interpretation.

Let's return to Figure 10-13. Wave c up in the Hang Seng is well below the 1.618 relationship with wave a. I did not suggest that wave c had to form a 1.618 relationship, just that it is a frequent target and should be known as it also marks where you may be wrong if it is exceeded. In the Hang Seng chart there is a Negative Reversal in the Composite Index, divergence peaks in close proximity between the Composite and RSI, and the market is overbought into wave C. The final clincher is that wave C up has a completed five wave pattern. *Wave C's in Flat patterns will always be five wave patterns.* You are not going to wait any longer to see if the present five wave advance will extend so that a perfect 1.618 relationship develops with wave a to form a textbook scenario. The Hang Seng chart clearly fits the springboard diver analogy, and we can also see at the top of wave c that the diver is losing momentum.

The last example on the right in Figure 10-13 is a 15-minute view of the September S&P 500 futures market. Nice looking Flat. Also look at the date of this chart. This is our down up pattern that our indicators warned us about in Figure 10-6 on July 24. The S&P correction became a Flat forming the letter N we referenced before we knew what the pattern was called. This pattern and chart allow me to emphasize the point stated earlier that the key in these patterns are the b waves. Wave b down in the September S&P chart is choppy, and we cannot see a distinct five wave structure with all the internal overlaps that develop. Remember wave four cannot overlap a first wave, so this decline into the low is not a five wave structure. *It must therefore be a three wave decline, and that spells "flat."* I know, wave a looks like a five wave pattern, and the textbook line-on-close descriptions all state that wave a must be three waves. Nonetheless, wave b is producing buy signals at several points in the oscillators. The information you want to focus on is if wave b within this pattern will break the origin of wave a. Are you diving from a platform tower or a springboard? Actually you want a springboard because the wave c's that follow can be serious money-making patterns as they have such strong or five wave patterns that develop out of the b wave. However, in this case the S&P futures do not get the aid of a spring bounce, so they retraced only the distance of wave a. That is a Flat. The best advice I can offer you for these patterns is that once you identify the chop that forms the internals of the wave b segment within a Flat, stop trying to categorize it. Trade it.

Beware that b waves can get very emotional in bigger pictures. Straight-line capitulation drops can be b waves as well. The key is that they will always be a three wave pattern.

Our real-time tracking of the DJIA in a 15-minute chart is updated now in Figure 10-14. While the September S&P developed a Flat pattern, the DJIA

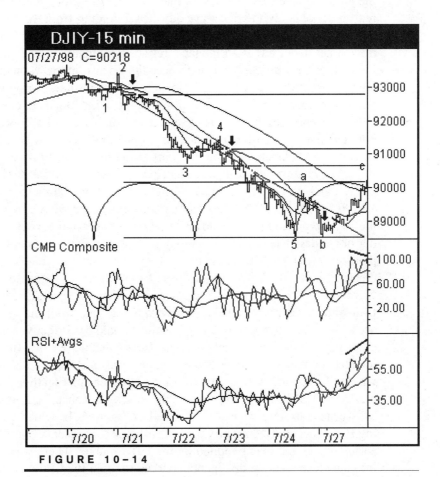

FIGURE 10-14

produced an Expanded Flat. Notice that wave b down in both the S&P and DJIA retrace back only to the start of wave a. I didn't say that Expanded Flats must penetrate the origin of wave a. Yes, in a perfect Elliott world, that is true. Not in the real world. However, we know an Expanded Flat is forming in the DJIA because it must form five waves up from the end of wave b in either pattern: a Flat or Expanded Flat. The pattern to the end of wave a is only three waves, so to finish five waves, we know the end of wave a will be exceeded. Where will the target be? The 1.618 relationship with wave a, which is higher than the current market high near toward the close for July 27. Now we need to determine the market path for tomorrow.

In Figure 10-14 we have divergence between the Composite Index and the RSI. The RSI is abiding the range rules defined for a bear market by topping near the 60 to 65 level. Do we have a market top now? No, I do not think so for one reason. If we study the five wave advance unfolding from the end of wave b, it is missing a couple of bars to form the final fifth wave up. Figure 10-14 also shows the market under a 0.382 Fibonacci retracement that many people will be able to identify. Expect an early advance near the open tomorrow, and we will use the advance from the end of wave b down to the small black arrow in this chart as a tentative measure to define tomorrow's target. Why? Balance. I am a fanatic about balance because the market is obsessed with balance and proportion. Also waves one and five are frequently equal. If we should surpass a small "pop" to form equality and balance with the first part of the move, we will have to look toward the 1.618 relationship with wave a. That will also mark the level where we view our Expanded Flat pattern to be wrong. Let's see what tomorrow brings.

It is July 28, 1998, after the market's close, and we see in Figure 10-15 that the DJIA produced a minor advance on open today and headed south the remainder of the day. The decline into today's low was a five wave pattern, which means that we were right to be on the lookout for an extending five wave pattern when we created Figure 10-7. The DJIA doesn't look like 10-7 because one leg down is wave b within the Expanded Flat correction. Then the second leg down became the fifth-wave to complete our larger five wave decline from the high. Figure 10-15 shows how the extending five wave decline would be correctly labeled if you wanted to mark all the internal subdivisions. Notice that wave c of 4 (the high this morning that completes the Expanded Flat pattern) advanced to a 1.382 relationship with wave a. The reason for falling short of the 1.618 calculation (horizontal black arrow marks the 1.618 relationship) is that there was a Fibonacci cluster at 1.382.

This is exactly what we discussed in Figure 6–10, when we were considering Fibonacci confluence points in the Fibonacci chapter. We are now finding that earlier discussion being applied by the DJIA market. There was a strong rebound into the close, and the divergence marked on both the Composite Index and RSI,

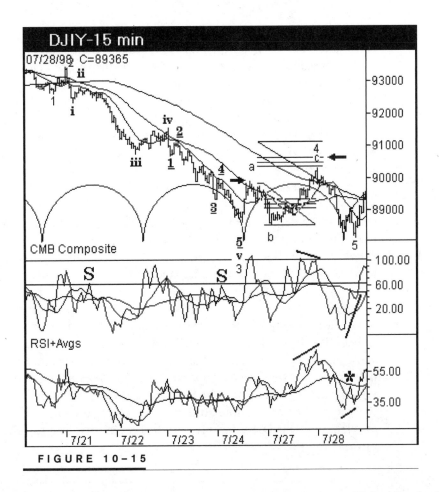

FIGURE 10-15

compared to the price low, warns that the near-term advance will develop further gains. The fastest way for a market to develop a countertrend move is to connect two five wave patterns together and then resume the larger trend. This is not a Flat pattern as the market does not retrace all of the first leg we called wave a. Chances are fairly good that we will see only a minor pullback followed by further gains tomorrow, so we need to look at another corrective building block that will fit this scenario. We have all the earmarks in place for what we call a *Zigzag* pattern to develop, so let's move on to discuss this pattern.

If you currently utilize the Wave Principle, may I have your attention just a moment longer regarding Expanded Flats before we move on to Zigzags? I really need to try and resolve a point about which the industry is clearly confused and downright befuddled. There is no such pattern as an "Irregular B." There has never been an "Irregular B." Prechter used to call the Expanded Flat pattern an "Irregular

Flat." The name referred to the entire pattern, and wave b in this pattern was never irregular. The name was wisely changed because there is nothing *irregular* about it. You will see these patterns far more often than the simple Flat, which is just the letter N. The expanded variation of the Flat is so common that it makes a lot of sense to call it what it really is: Expanded Flat. So please, no more Irregular B's. OK?

The next pattern we need to discuss is a Zigzag. I cannot think of an analogy for this pattern because if you miss this one, it is more like a hit-and-run accident and all you want to do is get the license plate number of the truck that just ran over both you and your trading account. You can sense these aggressive corrections on the horizon before they appear on your screen. That is why I am very suspicious tonight of the chart pattern in Figure 10-15. We know a larger correction is due in the DJIA as the entire five wave cycle could be complete from the high. We also have a five wave advance into the close that forms from a five wave decline, so we know the market rebound is incomplete. I do not know if the current five wave advance into the close will just turn into a three wave pattern. But should the market keep five waves clearly in place, and then try a minor pullback, we should consider the Zigzag further. Watch for cycle lows, indicator signals that seem stronger than prior signals, and other similar indices like the Cash S&P and OEX all positioned for a larger rebound. This will warn that a Zigzag could be near because these corrections are very common patterns in a strong trending market because *they take the least amount of time for the market to develop.* The market tries to get the correction over and out of the way as fast as possible so that it can return the larger trend that is usually accelerating. Our DJIA chart has been accelerating. You can see that supporting information fits.

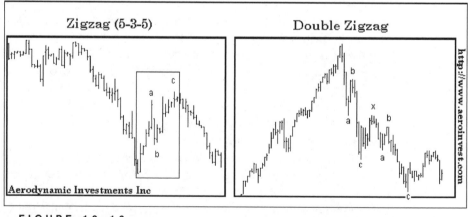

FIGURE 10-16

A Zigzag as displayed in Figure 10-16 is made up of two sets of five wave cycles back to back. That is all there is to a Zigzag pattern. If a minor pullback develops in the DJIA tomorrow, we know to expect this sharp correction as wave b down *cannot retrace all of the first five wave structure.* Why? Because then we would have a Flat, and our first five wave unit would not have been a five wave structure at all. Remember, I do not care what wave a looks like, though five waves will make me think of a Zigzag immediately. However, if a wave b choppy price pattern appears *after the five wave move that cannot retrace the first leg we called wave* a, get out of the way immediately or reverse. You know a Flat is not developing.

The second five wave pattern usually travels a *minimum* distance equal to the first five wave pattern that formed wave a. It is common to see a 1.618 relationship in the second five wave pattern relative to the first. They are sharp. Take few prisoners along the way. Then reverse just as quickly about the time you begin to question if you are wrong about the prior trend returning. You are not wrong — just a victim of the Zigzag.

Zigzags sometimes travel in pairs. Figure 10-16 shows a Double Zigzag, and we encounter our first x wave. It is also one of the most abused x waves in the business because it is not used. As soon as many analysts see a Zigzag pattern develop and they have an opinion that the larger correction is incomplete, they hastily label the a-b-c internals of their first Zigzag as "wave A within a larger correction." Wrong. Wrong. Wrong. If your Zigzag internals are then called "wave A within a larger correction," *you MUST be stating that the market will retrace the entire distance traveled by waves a-b-c of your Zigzag or greater.* Why? Because an a-b-c that is labeled "wave A in a larger pattern" must develop as a Flat or Expanded Flat. Period. No other option. Flats always retrace all of wave A, and Expanded Flats should attempt to exceed the origin of wave A. So if you don't think the entire distance will be retraced, the next move must be called "an x wave."

An x wave is simply a wildcard that allows you to take one recognized corrective building block and use it to link an other corrective pattern together. The different building blocks should have some sense of balance and proportion between the individual puzzle pieces. You get two wildcards per corrective pattern, or two x's. We will look at these more complex patterns at another time. More likely we will not need them for our DJIA chart now. The Double Zigzag in Figure 10-16 is the monthly chart of the Nikkei. Frequently the first Zigzag and the second Zigzag will also have a Fibonacci relationship between them.

Zigzags all look similar regardless of the market in which they develop. In Figure 10-17 the weekly Gold (futures GC) chart and the 60-minute data of the September London FTSE futures look similar. Two back-to-back five wave patterns. Fast. Direct. Sharp. Then the larger trend resumes. The London FTSE futures

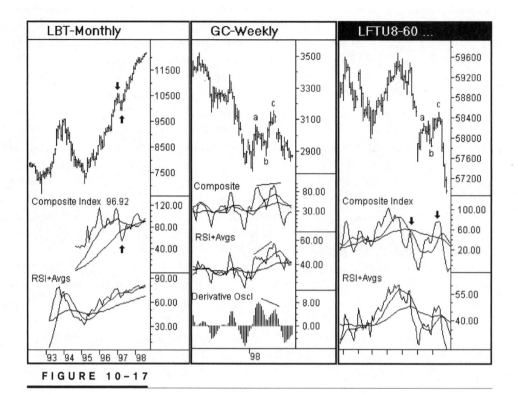

FIGURE 10-17

on the far right shows a Negative Reversal signal forming in the Composite Index with the tops of waves a and c black arrows. This is very common. Gold displays an indicator divergence as does LBT. The LBT chart on the left is the monthly chart of Italian Government Bonds. I do not have data in a shorter time horizon to check the substructure of the decline marked between the arrows on prices, but this sure fits the character of a Zigzag. I'll bet it is, and it likely caused a lot of Lira to change hands along the way for some traders.

When the market on July 29 produced a three wave decline, marked wave b in Figure 10-18, that lead to a Zigzag pattern, I started to jump up and down with excitement. Why? A profitable trade? True, but that was not the only reason. I was excited because the market was forming a Zigzag right on cue for the book! So I can now wipe the perspiration from my brow and continue right where we left off two days ago. Violà! La Zigzag. While the first five wave advance extended to complete wave a up, there is a clean three wave decline to complete wave b down that did not retrace all of the first bounce from the low. In today's session for July 30, 1998, we completed the second five wave advance to end a perfect textbook Zigzag. No major accomplishment to encounter one in real-time as most Zigzags are that distinctive and clean. Wave c in our Zigzag has not traveled a distance equal to wave a as measured from the bottom of wave b. I do not think it will this time because just one minor push over today's high will complete Elliott Wave patterns developing in the S&P. The S&P will top at a major Gann target. The indicators in Figure 10-18 are at the same levels that marked the top of wave 4 up. We know Zigzags frequently form in markets that want to get the correction completed as soon as possible, so we have all the right ingredients for a sharp trend reversal. Do not hang around to look for a perfect Fibonacci target between waves a and c. Instead, calculate the next larger move, which should be down.

I have removed the prior label at the low suggesting wave 5 and replaced it with an *f* to make a strong point about this market low. In the DJIA we have five waves down into that price low in Figure 10-18. The Expanded Flat that formed wave 4 up in the DJIA becomes wave A up in the S&P futures. Then wave B into the low and a

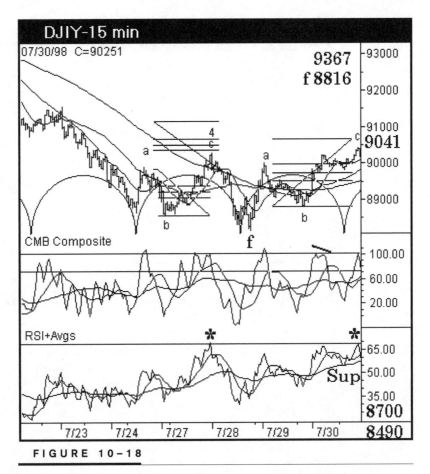

FIGURE 10-18

clean five wave advance expected to end tonight in the Globex night session will complete a large Expanded Flat. We will look at the S&P futures closer toward the end as the Globex data will be more difficult. However, it means I have two Indices tracking and indicators that suggest further market weakness.

Orthodox Elliott Wave practitioners will calculate the next market objectives by measuring the distance of the first five wave decline and then projecting Fibonacci swings from the end of the correction. The 0.618, 1.00, and 1.618 relationships will be identified. However, traders who want a more accurate price objective should measure the entire distance traveled in the first part of the move. That means the five wave pattern in the DJIA or the five wave pattern and *wave* B *down to the new low as occurs in the S&P.* Use wave B's that exceed five wave patterns always for Fibonacci swing projections.

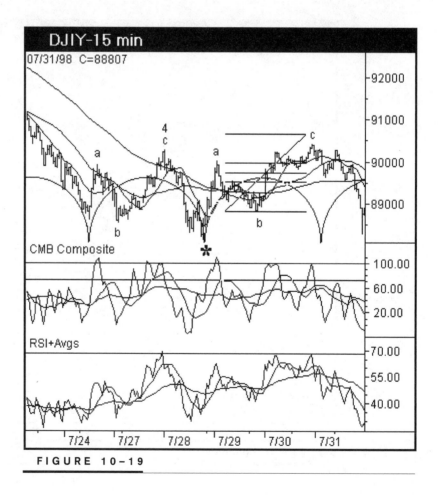

FIGURE 10-19

In Figure 10-18 the DJIA high was 9367, the price low at f was 8816, and the market high for wave c up is 9041. The 0.618 and 1.00 price projections are 8700 and 8490. The first target is a high-confidence target. The 8490 level from 9040 seems extreme. There is also a Gann objective at 9038, but we need to see how the market reacts to the first objective and what wave structure and indicator action forms prior to thinking about the second target. We are set for the next trading session.

July 31, 1998, brought a decline from our Zigzag pattern. The first target we calculated of 8700 has not been realized. However, with this new session we can see that our technical indicators do not display a price bottom. Both indicators have declined to prior oscillator extreme lows, and we know to expect a bounce in the next trading session followed by further selling as these indicators will not produce bottoms in their current positions. Wave structure appears to be accelerating as the market is moving in a direct pattern to each new low made throughout the day. The 8700 objective should not be revised at this time. Notice an asterisk at the price low. I have changed the cycle position in Figure 10-19 from what we had been using in Figure 10-18. Why? We know cycles are not symmetrical, so keep the cycles in view on your chart current. This new period aligns the cycle to the actual price low and captures the early decline from today's action. An adjustment was indicated.

August 3, 1998: In a startling development, we see that the U.S. market is in serious trouble in Figure 10-20 as we view the chart from today's session. We have a sharp decline followed by a three wave corrective rally. The market then declines to new lows and closes into the lows of the session. A more serious problem is that the daily S&P chart has a major cycle low due to bottom tomorrow in the daily time horizon. In the short time horizon the indicators in Figure 10-20 have every bearish signal present that we have discussed in this book to date. I could not have constructed a better summary than this if I had tried. Indicator divergence, a Negative Reversal in both the Composite and RSI, price structure acceleration, and the price low today is 8785, which has still not realized our first objective at 8700. The second target at 8490 that looked crazy when first calculated on July 30 is being confirmed in the chart displayed in Figure 10-20. It is not clear how long it will take us to reach the second target. Time predictions are always a problem.

We will calculate a new Fibonacci swing in Figure 10-20. Measure from the top of the Zigzag pattern to the price low prior to today's three wave corrective rally. We find that the 1.00 and 1.618 Fibonacci objectives are 8642 and 8491. The 8491 target duplicates the Fibonacci target at 8490 that we identified from Figure 10-18. A Gann target also resides at this level. *Confirmation.* Today's 8785 low has still not realized the 8700 target. While the market spent time producing a back-and-fill correction prior to the sell-off into the close, this consolidation into the close is not a fourth wave near the end of a five wave pattern from the end of the Zigzag.

How do we know this? Not from Elliott Wave structure. The RSI has a Negative Reversal in place, and the two peaks forming the signal are marked *N* and *R* in Figure

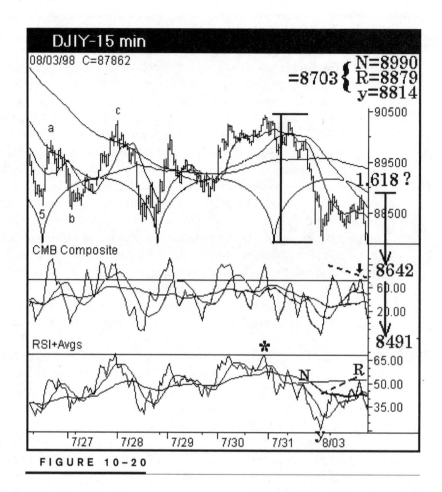

FIGURE 10-20

10-20. All the price-on-close levels that you need to make a price projection are recorded in the top right corner. The formula is in the RSI chapter if you need to turn back. The price projection from this Negative Reversal is 8703. The first target at 8700 is now confirmed, but so too is the second at 8490. The amplitude for the RSI is greater than the guidelines I gave you. But we also have a cycle low approaching in the daily data, accelerating wave structure, and strong confirmation of a target much lower than 8700, which is 8490. If the market breaks 8700, there will be a problem. The amplitude in the RSI is not a contradiction. It would be if it were the only evidence present.

I mentioned earlier that wave b's are choppy in short-horizon data, but they may form capitulation lows in longer-horizon data. The only way to tell is the position of your indicators. As a cycle low is approaching, it is less likely that the current decline will be wave b down from the Zigzag pattern within a larger Expanded Flat. Only time will tell.

August 4, 1998: The second target was 8491 from yesterday's price action that confirmed the 8490 objective from July 30. Figure 10-21 shows what has transpired in today's session. The market did not bat an eye at 8700. Look at the closing print in the top left corner of Figure 10-21. Target 8490–91; actual close was 8490.9. We got here much faster than I expected, however. Here is the bigger problem: Use the thumb nail method from the midpoint of the decline from the high in Figure 10-21. You should have defined the midpoint to be near the point where the second backward S crosses the price data. The backward S marks only the 1.618 projection that was made from the decline that developed yesterday on August 3. The current decline is not a complete five wave pattern, and the indicators do not display buy signals.

I'll suggest a minor rebound upwards on open as the last decline into the close still needs a small fourth wave up and then a drop to a new low. The Gann

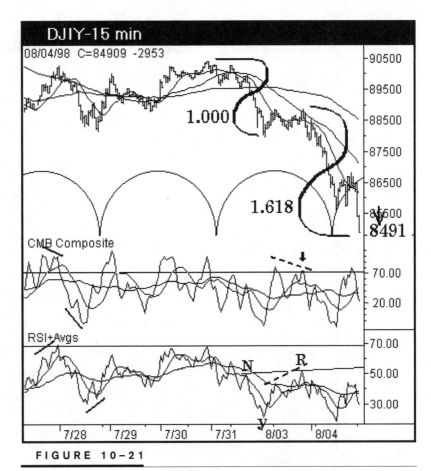

FIGURE 10-21

target at 8410 is the objective I would rely upon as the Fibonacci projections below 8490 cannot be confirmed at this time.

Figure 10-22 now shows the DJIA on August 5, 1998, after the market has closed. The last chart suggested a minor bounce with a decline toward 8410. This was not quite right as a bounce or consolidation did not develop until the market realized the Gann objective providing followthrough from the prior day's melt-down. The market bottomed at 8411.3. I'll take that since the target was 8410, and then a rebound was attempted, which is labeled "wave a of 4" in Figure 10-22.

This may raise the question, how do you know which price projection method to use in which situation? I use all the methods described and try to think which level makes the most sense. The method I lean on more than any other is Gann. If Gann had little to offer, I would switch to whatever method offered information. The 8410 level was a major confluence zone or cluster of Gann targets that actually fell

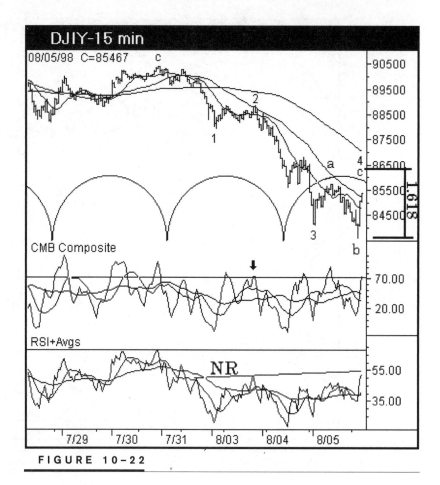

FIGURE 10-22

within a narrow range between 8409.4 and 8411.7. I elected to round off the cluster and give you 8410. The market actually rebounded from the top of the target zone.

The advance to the high now marked wave a of 4 is a Zigzag pattern that is clearly a three wave advance. The decline that followed into the low has wave structure internals that could fit either a three wave or five wave decline. That is a problem. However, the advance that follows into the close is clearly a developing five wave advance, so the last leg down into the low will be viewed as a b wave. Prior to the rally into the close, we thought that we might see an Expanded Flat pattern develop. We know wave c up within an Expanded Flat can target the 1.618 relationship relative to the distance traveled by wave a. This objective has been marked in Figure 10-22. So we know if the market should exceed the 1.618 target and trade near 8650, we may have to reconsider the final decline, which is now marked wave b of 4 as it is hard to tell what it is.

You will notice that the Composite Index broke above a prior momentum peak and that wave c up has allowed this indicator to return to a horizontal line defining resistance for this indicator. The same horizontal line of resistance is where wave 2 up ended (black arrow in Figure 10-22). Further weakness to a new low could develop tomorrow, and the target would allow balance to occur from the early stages of the decline from the price high in this chart. Measure the distance traveled by wave 1 down, and use that relationship to measure a 1.00 and 1.618 relationship from current highs.

The decline as labeled from the high in Figure 10-22 needs a fifth wave down to complete the larger decline. However, we have our first real conflict beginning to develop. It is not clear if the last leg down called "wave b of 4" is a five or three wave structure. Extending patterns in real-time are always tricky. It is possible that the last leg down is a fifth wave to end wave 3 in the 15-minute chart. There is also conflict present between the S&P futures chart and the DJIA tonight, and the two indices have to be watched.

In Figure 10-22 notice that a trend line extends from the RSI Negative Reversal signal that gave us the 8703 price objective in Figure 10-20. The RSI indicator is now approaching this same trend line. If the market produces an immediate reaction to this resistance trend line, we can be more confident about a fifth wave decline developing. However, if the market is capable of moving the RSI through this trend line, it will be a warning that a more complex pattern could be developing. We need to watch the market closely tomorrow as it is extremely oversold in a 120-minute time horizon now.

It is August 6, 1998. We have finally stepped off track as the market did not decline from the simple Expanded Flat pattern we suggested yesterday. Figure 10-23 shows today's trading session. We may have correctly identified an Expanded Flat pattern, but this is just one pattern within a larger puzzle, and there are several factors that must be balanced.

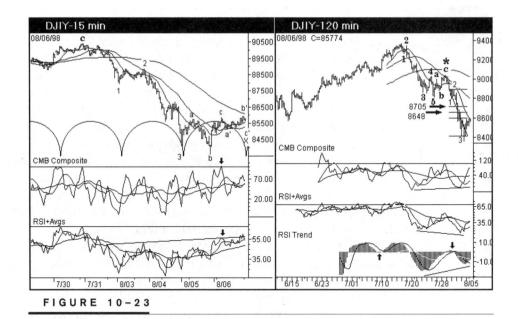

FIGURE 10-23

In Figure 10-23 you will see that the Composite Index challenged the horizontal trend line drawn to define the maximum displacement in the 15-minute chart of the DJIA. The test during today's session is marked with a black arrow. The last time the Composite Index challenged this extreme was at the price high that completed the Zigzag corrective pattern marked wave c up at the high of our 15-minute chart. It is a major top. Never do we want to see this oscillator break above this extreme range defined by the maximum oscillator peaks, because it would mean that underlying strength is building within the market for a larger advance. From the black arrow the Composite Index then declines rapidly while the price action produces an insignificant choppy pullback that fights the sell signal the entire way down. The decline being described is called wave a′ down in Figure 10-23. This is a warning because we know if our indicators move a distance much greater than prices are able to move, we are most likely on the wrong side of the market.

A rally is then attempted, and it is a very distorted looking advance that leads into a high near the close marked wave b′ up. The advance toward the close is what I would call a "choppy mess," and it is very well suited to be the character of a wave b advance in a short time horizon chart. Either the market is fighting the advance, though that is unlikely as it fought the decline as well into wave a′ down, *or the market action within waves a′ and b′ is screaming at us to look for a cycle low approaching that we have not defined in Figure 10-22.*

We have witnessed the corrective patterns called "Flats" and "Zigzags" develop in this decline. However, the market has three puzzle pieces that it may use to create a corrective pattern. The third pattern is the triangle, which occurs when a market becomes range bound and moves sideways. Markets tend to allocate corrective puzzle pieces in a balanced manner. Maybe we are due. Triangles are very common in small corrections when the market is waiting for a cycle low to pass.

The cycle in the 15-minute chart of Figure 10-23 has now been adjusted from where it was positioned in Figure 10-22. The new position selected offers an alignment with three prior price lows. It now suggests that the market will experience a cycle low on open tomorrow. The price data marked wave a′ and wave b′ are what motivated us to look more closely at our cycle placement. We did not discuss price character into cycle bottoms when we discussed cycles in Part 1. But now you are ready for this discussion as we are face-to-face with a real-life example. Markets will either decline into cycle lows, *or they will do all they can to waste time until the cycle low is in place.* In a long-term chart, markets may form extensive corrective patterns that aggressively go nowhere until a cluster of cycles has bottomed.

In Figure 10-23 the price action that forms from the low marked wave a′ into the high marked wave b′ is undeniably choppy and distorted price structure. There is not going to be a five wave structure within that mess. However, this choppy action has been incredibly informative for us already by highlighting the cycle we have now identified. The same choppy price action is also telling us what the market will do tomorrow. All this information from just the two small moves labeled waves a′ and b′? Yes. The technical indicators would not be much help to us right now. The market will either complete a small Expanded Flat pattern that it started today by forming wave c′ down into the cycle low that should bottom early in tomorrow's session, or the market is simply wasting time until the cycle low is in place, after which it will advance sharply without further delay. As I do not think the market will make a new low from this price structure, we have now been politely introduced to our first complex correction.

We now have to use the dreaded x wave because it takes three corrective patterns to satisfy one complex correction. We first encountered the use of an x wave in Figure 10-16 when a Double Zigzag was introduced. People in the industry clearly hate to use the letter x. I suspect there is confusion about how to use the letter x. If the waves marked a′-b′-c′ in Figure 10-23 form a very small Expanded Flat, we would then have only two corrective patterns. The first is an Expanded Flat pattern with internals marked a-b-c, and the second corrective pattern would be a smaller Expanded Flat with internals called a′-b′- c′. The price action into the price pivots called a′ and b′ are very small moves in both time and movement relative to the structure we called a-b-c. For these proportions it would be wrong to imply a′ and b′ were the same degree as waves a-b-c in the first pattern. Therefore I know to immediately drop the wave count down by one lesser degree because of the balance consideration. I should use a and b with an underline to be formally correct. But

TradeStation does not offer an underlined text feature, and in the heat of battle I do not care. Just know it is one lesser degree. When the second corrective pattern is complete by forming wave c′ down, we will then have two back-to-back corrective patterns. This is a problem. Markets always require at least three patterns to satisfy a larger correction. So the second pattern with internals called a′-b′-c′ is just a connector, and we call it "wave x." Our complex pattern will not be satisfied until the market completes a structure we can define as waves a-b-c-x-a-b-c.

Knowing that we must always develop at least three corrective patterns back-to-back is of tremendous value now. If the market can produce a wave c′ decline that just breaks below the start of wave a′ into tomorrow's cycle low, that would be ideal. Then the market could continue upward to develop the advance we need to produce waves a-b-c. That would mean a fairly decent rally to develop another a-b-c advance in the DJIA chart. Instead of a wave c′ decline, the market may stall and go nowhere until the cycle low is in place. But that would imply the market will develop an a-b-c advance from nearby market levels. Either way, the market should go up tomorrow.

While the small price action marked wave a′ and wave b′ is offering us a wealth of information, there is another reason to anticipate that further gains are a high probability. There are conflicting indicator signals present in Figure 10-23. The 15-minute DJIA chart is displayed along with a 120-minute bar chart of the DJIA. The Composite Index and RSI are diverging in the 120-minute chart suggesting that an advance could be near. Another indicator has been added called the *RSI Trend*. We have not had an opportunity to discuss this indicator, but it is needed right now. I am looking at the RSI Trend oscillator to see when an overbought or oversold condition has been alleviated by watching to see when this oscillator crosses back through its zero midline. This is one of the main signals I am looking for in this indicator. You will find a black arrow pointing down toward the RSI Trend oscillator that coincides with wave 2 up. That juxtaposition in wave count and oscillator position is a confirmation signal. There is also an upward pointing arrow that has developed a signal in conjunction with a fourth wave during the rally into the high. We can see this oscillator has much more room to advance before it will cross the zero line again. That means the idea we are developing of a complex correction that will produce another a-b-c advance will fit the technical picture within this 120-minute DJIA chart. There is tremendous divergence between the RSI Trend oscillator and our price data. We have just seen an example of how this oscillator is used, and we will give it more attention when we discuss using oscillators on oscillators. The RSI Trend is an indicator derived from another oscillator, and it is used only as a lead signal. It is leading. We will follow it into tomorrow.

In contrast, the 15-minute chart is once again overbought. Our previous overbought signals have been aligned with declining oscillators in the 120-minute chart. If you study the two time horizons in Figure 10-23, you will see that there is a directional conflict. It is this indicator conflict that will create complex corrective patterns. I'm not sure how we will end up.

I knew this conflict was developing yesterday. But the key is not to jump ahead of the facts present within our data. We can think ahead, but we must not trade ahead of the facts. Patterns actually take *much* longer to develop in the market than they do in our minds. This timing difference is probably the primary source of most of my own trading errors. I trade from the ideas constructed within my head sometimes rather than from what is on the screen. Trading too far ahead of the market's structure and its corresponding technical evidence will cost you money.

On the other hand, we have to be ahead of the market in order to trade. I struggle with this fine line constantly, and it is only strict money management that keeps me in the P/L race. Being able to read small pieces of the market's puzzle, as we have done for waves a′ and b′, can be a fault as well. I do not trade the S&P well from a 1-minute chart in an effort to reduce capital exposure because I continually have a stream of ideas developing through the trading day as the market action unfolds. *The fault is losing sight of your original game plan.* So the evening reports are as much to keep me in control and focused within the next trading session as they are to inform clients about what I may be thinking. A larger capital base allows me to move up to an 88-minute chart, which slows the rapid spin of ideas that develops in a 1-minute chart. Once the new data starts streaming into the charts, I need my evening report to serve as an anchor so I don't steer off course.

Tonight we can see that the DJIA has advanced to a level directly under a Fibonacci 0.382 retracement in the 120-minute bar chart and to a Gann target that aligns with the moving average. This is a wait-and-see juncture at a critical market level. If the market declines immediately from this area of resistance, wave c′ of x down will be favored. Even a stall into the cycle low will lead to another a-b-c advance, so we should be able to read the innuendoes that the market is transmitting fairly easily tomorrow. If the market *unexpectedly* reacts more strongly to the cycle in Figure 10-23, then expect wave 5 down as this will be against the longer-horizon chart, and a key reversal swing back up could follow in the same trading session tomorrow. No damage has been done financially in either of these views that tracks with the cycle low.

Did I just suggest three wave interpretations from the same price data? Yes. The favored opinion is that a minor decline on open will then lead to a three wave advance toward 8705. The target is marked in the 120-minute chart and is the 0.618 relationship of the measured move. The market is currently at the 0.382 retracement in this same chart. A variation is that the market will ignore the cycle entirely and just advance. Is that an alternative? No. It is allowing some room for the market to take control of the timing on how it will advance toward the *same target,* and the data must still develop a three wave structure into that price objective. A weak open or not does not change the favored view that the market will advance. That is where people get so confused.

The alternative wave count is a market decline to a new price low. That is what is unexpected. We know it would be wave 5 down. But we must have a price objective that defines where our favored scenario may be proven wrong. We know wave c' down should not really exceed a 1.618 relationship with wave a'. We now have a target to monitor if wave c' down gets too zealous. A break below that relationship would mean that we are in trouble as the market would then challenge the current low in the chart for Figure 10-23 and we would then be trading from the alternate scenario. A decline to a new low is a much lower probability because the 120-minute DJIA indicators are clearly attempting to advance.

The chart prepared for Figure 10-23 is in fact the chart used in tonight's client report to show the risk now present from conflicting time horizon signals. Predicting the market open is not as easy, but the view that a rally will then develop is a high confident outlook. While the target for the DJIA is 8705, the target for the September S&P is 1107 derived from a Gann Wheel, which is an important objective from the current price low.

There is an asterisk in the 120-minute chart that marks the high where the Zigzag pattern is completed. The convention is to mark the first five waves down with the number (1) below wave 5. The a-b-c Zigzag pattern would then be wave (2) up. I am not sure that the larger picture is going to become an extending pattern that will end at wave (5) down, so I'll just label two back-to-back five wave units together and then see where we are at that time. I tend not to give much attention to larger-degree labels until forced to confront them. These charts are not perfect cataloged illustrations but rather day-to-day charts of working battle plans within a larger war in progress.

The DJIA market action for August 7, 1998, is displayed in Figure 10-24. We are doing very well today as the DJIA has rallied to a market high of 8710.0 and the September S&P has realized a high of 1108.50. Our original targets were 8705 and 1107.

Just one problem: *Right market direction, right targets; wrong pattern.* We needed a three wave advance into these objectives and did not get one. The cycle identified yesterday has not produced a wave c' decline to complete a small Expanded Flat pattern. Instead, the market has elected to stall into that cycle low. It was an option we had considered as we knew the cycle was present that would allow the market to react in this manner to the cycle. Therefore, wave x has become a triangle. A rally then unfolds throughout the remainder of the day toward our objectives. Here is the problem. The advance that develops out of the triangle is not a three wave structure. It is a five wave pattern. So that means we have a Zigzag in

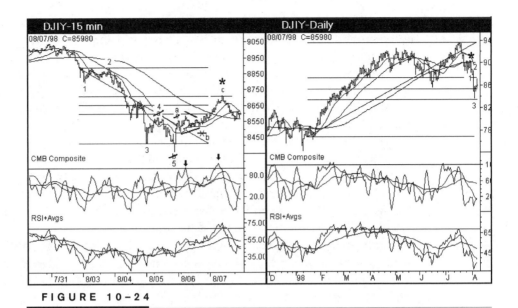

FIGURE 10-24

place from the market low into a major price target. The current rebound to a 0.618 ratio in the 15-minute chart from the price low means that we must look at a much bigger picture now to consider our options. In addition, we are now forced to accept that the final leg down is not wave b of 4, but a fifth wave. We are making a wave count adjustment based on facts, not based on trying to fit structure into our analysis. Big difference, and the change can be seen in Figure 10-24.

Figure 10-24 also displays the current chart for the daily DJIA. The daily chart shows that the current price low at 8361.9 is nearly an exact 0.618 retracement. The current advance that has developed today to 8710 is to the 0.382 ratio within this same mathematical grid marked on the daily chart. The reasons that these specific pivot levels have been used in both these charts to calculate Fibonacci ratios are fully described in the Fibonacci chapter. Why the price spike in the daily chart has not been used to calculate the Fibonacci retracement targets is also explained in the Fibonacci chapter in great detail. This offers a real-time example of why spikes should not be used to create Fibonacci retracements.

We have a new problem. We can see from the daily DJIA chart in Figure 10-24 that the entire decline is not a completed five wave structure from the high marked with an asterisk. We have just labeled this same decline as a five wave structure in the 15-minute chart. Is the current price low wave 5 down or wave 3 down in an extending pattern? To try and answer this question, I sometimes use Point-and-Figure charts. Use the dimensions 100×3 and 50×3 for intraday decisions in the S&P. That is the answer to the primary setup question you will have after you learn what a Point-and-

Figure chart is. I'm afraid we do not have time to go into this chart methodology prior to tomorrow's session. We need to be addressing if the second five wave unit is extending further or is complete. The question developing in the short-horizon data is, "Where will wave 4 up become too proportionally large to still be within wave (3) down?" The asterisk in Figure 10-24 would be wave (2) up having followed our first five wave decline. The current bounce in our daily chart that we know is a Zigzag from the price low is not too large yet to still be considered wave 4 up within wave (3) down. I just painted myself into a corner, and I am now forced to label the charts with the higher degrees. OK, I'll give in and add them to our next chart.

The time frame or corrective price structure that constitutes "too large" and out of proportion relative to the whole structure developing is an important issue. As a general guide, if a correction has taken over twice as much time to develop as a more simple pattern within the same "unit" or cycle, it is less likely a correction within the same degree. In other words, we do not know if the rally that developed right to our target today is wave 4 up in an extending wave (3) decline, or wave a up within a developing wave (4) correction. Wave (4) is a larger degree and might develop more than just a simple Zigzag from the bottom. That is why the idea wave a of (4) is suggested. But is today's simple Zigzag rally sufficient to satisfy an entire correction?

It has been so long since we first discussed Figure 10-2 that I suspect you may have forgotten a point or two from that chart. So, a quick recap: The Elliott Wave Principle provides us with a guideline to anticipate alternating corrective patterns between waves 2 and 4. We need to know that now. The guideline implies that if we have a simple pattern develop within wave 2, there will be a higher probability that a more complex pattern will form in position 4. Easy.

When we look at the daily chart in Figure 10-24, we see a sharp quick rebound characteristic of a Zigzag correction. We also know Zigzags frequently develop when the market wants to get the correction over with so that it may resume the larger trend. The current advance is about half the time the market required to rally into the asterisk. It fits the guideline between waves (2) and (4). Now look at the rebound relative to the decline from the high. Wave 2 up is choppy, and this bounce is clean and simple. The rally into the 0.618 retracement objective does not overlap wave 1 down. We can go either way still, so we are not getting anywhere fast from just looking at structure in these charts.

We are forced to look at the bigger picture before we can do any further work in the shorter-horizon charts. But what is the current market opinion? No opinion. The point is that no opinion should be attempted until additional analysis is considered. We are tapped out you might say in the short-horizon charts.

Won't we miss a trading day if an opinion is not offered? Yes. However, we have been tracking a 1006-point decline in the DJIA from a pivot level most people never suspected would become a significant top. We haven't missed a beat throughout the 10.7 percent decline now in place. Our indicators even warned us about the sharp rally that developed today that became the strongest retracement since the entire decline began. We can afford to take a day off now to evaluate where we stand in the bigger picture. Let the short-horizon price action go where it will without us on Monday. Today's session for August 7 is a Friday, and we have a weekend ahead. I'm tired because describing the evening analysis in this format has meant a workload that frequently takes until 3 A.M. to finish. Monday will be reserved for longer-horizon work, and then we can continue. It is called *pacing*. Take a mental "time-out" after a big move, and then come back to the short-horizon price structure. We can pick it up from there.

It is now Monday, August 10, and the DJIA and S&P are drifting nowhere in particular. We have not missed anything in the market so far. It would appear that the market is taking a day off as well. Until now we have focused only on the DJIA. The September S&P futures contract must use the Globex night session for both wave structure and price projections. As I've mentioned a couple of times, this will make the wave structure far more difficult for someone just learning how to apply the Elliott Wave Principle. However, your time has come to view the S&P chart because there is an important indicator signal in this chart.

In Figure 10-25 is the 240-minute chart for the September S&P 500 futures market that was captured today about 2 P.M. on August 10. The structure labeled in this chart suggests that the decline from wave (2) is not a complete five wave pattern. Waves (1) and (2) have been added to make this discussion easier to follow. But I still resist implying that this entire decline will develop into a five wave pattern because in the very big picture this will become a fourth wave down. It will likely end after a very large Zigzag pattern from the high is in place. (Why? This is the fastest way for the market to get the correction over with as the larger trend will return to record new price highs.) The proportions developing fit nicely. We would then label the entire decline waves A-B-C. So do not assume I am a bear for much longer.

Wave 4 up, to my sense of balance, is on the verge of being too large to proportionally fit the decline from the top of wave (2). However, it has not exceeded twice the time consumed to develop wave 2 of (3) so we are still within acceptable boundaries. If this advance is wave 4 up, it should be satisfied now at the 1108.50 high that was made on Friday.

My sense of balance needs wave 4 up to end right now, and this view is given some confidence by Stochastics. This indicator is telling me what the next market move will be. How would you interpret this indicator? The Stochastics indicator in Figure 10-25 has declined from the last peak (double asterisk) to a support level created by placing moving averages on the indicator (single asterisk). Meanwhile

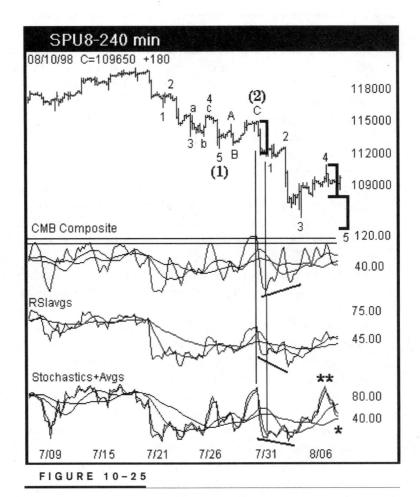

FIGURE 10-25

prices have held their ground. Why, that is exactly what we have used to suggest we would be on the wrong side of the market if we were short. The market is not following the indicator. Therefore, the market should advance provided that the indicator holds the support average. So why am I comfortable with the idea that wave 4 up has a top in place now?

Because viewing Stochastics as a buy signal right now is not a correct interpretation for this indicator. I am very relieved that this signal developed now because it would have caused a lot of people to step off track at this juncture and I did not think to discuss it earlier. I do not trade from Stochastics as you are seeing, but I watch it for two reasons: to monitor the Stochastics Default Club discussed in the beginning of the book and to monitor this formula when it is correctly set up for one specific signal. The first interpretation to suggest a rally tomorrow considers only the indicator travel from the double asterisk down to the single asterisk. *It does not consider the character of this indicator and how Stochastics responds within a trending market.*

Wait. This is not fair because we have not been tracking the S&P, and we have not spent a lot of time discussing Stochastics. Fair? This is war! Grab anything you know works in war. I use the Composite Index and RSI with moving averages as the basic palette from which to analyze a market. I know there are specific signals that must be watched for in other indicators. The signal in Stochastics that is present now is one of those I must be on the lookout for at all times. The methods we covered for reverse-engineering, other indicator formulas, and various price projection techniques are called upon as well as they are needed. Not before. I do not need a slew of indicators just to confuse me. I can do that very nicely without any help. But when I need clarification, there is something in our arsenal of techniques that we have covered that would be a fit for the problem.

Now we have a Stochastics signal present that is like being hit in the head with a baseball bat. I cannot ignore it. I know what it feels like to be hit by the market's bat, and I have been taught to pay attention to this signal. While the Composite Index diverged with prices near the bottom, both the RSI *and Stochastics oscillator did not diverge.* This is important for Stochastics. This is a trending market in this time horizon, and Stochastics has not "locked up" where it becomes a flat line at the bottom of our screen, but it is clearly spending the majority of its time below the 40 level. At the first chance this indicator is given to alleviate the oversold condition, it pops up to the top of the screen. Look at the pop into the high that became wave (2) up (or wave B up as we still don't know which will be correct). Again we see that the indicator has popped to the top of the screen and has formed a peak at the same displacement that developed wave (2). This pop out of an oversold market condition is what George Lane calls a "pop." The reverse? A "poop." It offers us an immediate signal and a price projection to go along with it. If you look at the RSI and Composite oscillators, there are no similar patterns present. This signal is unique to the Stochastics formula.

I know I covered this earlier, but here's how to make the price projection from the Stochastics signal. Measure the distance of travel in the Stochastics indicator preceding the current pop, and take the corresponding price move to make the price projection. (You can use the Stochastics bottom, but let's be conservative first.) This price decline can then be used from the high that formed the Stochastics pop by projecting 1.00, 1.618, 2.00, and 2.618 targets. In this chart from the top of wave 4 up is a projection to equality and two times the first measurement. The market will make a new low.

In addition to this signal, it is important to view the longer-horizon charts so that we can determine how the current market decline fits within a larger picture.

The following chart in Figure 10-26 was displayed in my Internet report for August 10, 1998, to address-longer-horizon analysis.

Suddenly all the Elliott Wave traders have been lost to the chart in the middle of Figure 10-26. Don't jump to conclusions. You need to understand that I label every subdividing five wave pattern as wave (1) up to start the move. The 120-minute DJIA chart also used waves (1) and (2). This situation is no different. Everyone quickly assumes that I am making a statement about the relative subdivisions in context to a Grand Supercycle top. Sorry. Not this Elliott Wave practitioner because as the bottom of the 1987 low in my view was a second wave. We will return to a big-picture outlook near the end of this chapter.

In Figure 10-26 the middle chart is the Toronto Stock Exchange. It is interesting relative to the American stock indices because it has a high correlation, develops very clean wave structure, and frequently tracks with a timing displacement compared to the American market as it did in this decline. Toronto was already declining when the American markets where developing their fifth waves into new highs. Toronto formed a second wave up as wave 5 developed in the S&P. So the Toronto Index is used to show how the market is forming a fourth wave decline that has realized the first Fibonacci target before the American Indices. Globally I might add the German Dax Index is the leader at this time.

Someone is going to ask me, "Why did you use the price spike to calculate the Fibonacci retracements in the Toronto Exchange?" Much time was devoted to

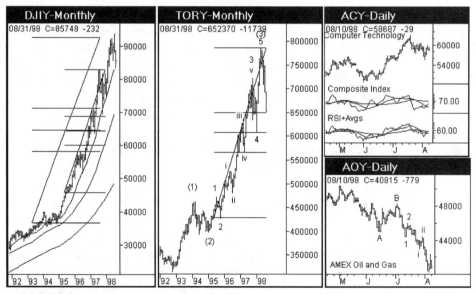

FIGURE 10-26

setting Fibonacci ratios based on prior market action. Look at the lows that form at waves iv and 4. The market tells us if we should use the spike or not. That's why I did not ignore the spike this time. The decline that has developed has now realized the 0.382 retracement. The market is suggesting that this was the right calculation.

On the far right is the daily AMEX Computer Index and AMEX Oil and Gas Index. As these two sectors make up more than 10 percent of the total S&P 500 Index, they have a strong influence on the direction of the S&P. Both indices display incomplete patterns.

On the left in Figure 10-26 is the DJIA. It shows the market has now declined to a very long term trend and to the top of the previous fourth wave. *The Fibonacci grids within this chart show how the Toronto Index was used to define the start of a large third wave.* We have balance as the midpoints overlap if we align the American Index with Toronto's. So we have a short-horizon opinion that a new market low will develop. But my guess is that we will form a Zigzag decline within a large fourth wave from the high. We will track only one more short-horizon chart in our real-time scenario to see if the Stochastics signal is correct or not. Then we can move forward and begin to look at the longer horizon.

Good place to end the short-horizon journal. Figure 10-27 shows today's action for August 11, 1998. The Stochastics pop correctly warned that market weakness would be seen today. New price lows have developed in the S&P and DJIA to confluence levels defined by Gann and Fibonacci. The Stochastics objective has been exceeded slightly from that projected in Figure 10-25 (lower target at 2x). The daily chart is being used to show that this latest decline is occurring into a cycle low. The Derivative Oscillator is clearly diverging. The Stochastics pop described in Figure 10-25 is now present in the daily DJIA chart in the reverse. The Momentum Extreme indicator we discussed earlier in the price projection section of this book is diverging. The DJIA should rebound tomorrow. I need to look at the indicator positions and wave structure into the advance. Will it just be a corrective pattern up? I do not know. I can only try to stay one day ahead of the market. I think tomorrow will be an up day. Our day-to-day scenario will be dropped now because we have the much longer horizon outlook to consider.

What will the market do next in the bigger picture? Will wave x up follow after this Zigzag decline that will lead to a larger correction? Will a large wave b rally form the second leg up within a triangle? Will the market develop five waves down from the high? I cannot tell today, but the indicators will tell us and will paint a picture for us every step along the way. For this reason I never know timing as I have to see the footprints made along the indicator trail. At this point you have a very good idea of how the day-to-day indicator signals can be used *to create a wave count.*

Always keep in mind that balance and proportion are of much greater importance than having all the internals perfectly cataloged. If the balance and scale is

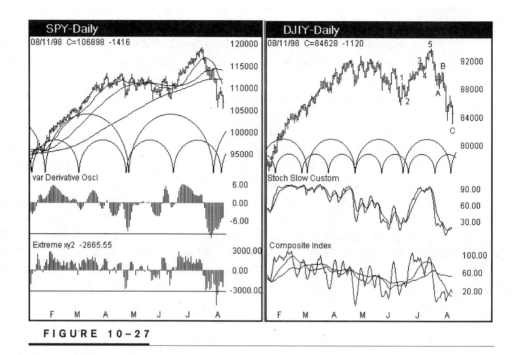

FIGURE 10-27

not right, fix it. This is the same as making adjustments to cycles as required. The longer the time horizon, the more time you should devote to the balance, proportion, and symmetry of your wave scenario. With practice the balance becomes more than just playing the right notes on the piano. We were fortunate to have a market reaction to a key objective that could be turned into a choreographed dance. It can happen. Not always. But it is worth the effort to study all you can because you can now understand what it is like to fall in step for even a brief period.

Once you experience this flow and harmony, it becomes an addiction. You will easily become motivated to work hard to find the next sonata that may grow beyond just the notes within a chart. The right notes in perfect harmony can become music to your ears and your accountant's. Might not the Elliott "Piano" have a bit more potential than you first thought? I cannot convert anyone, but the Elliott Wave Principle is clearly a viable technical method that has its own strengths and weaknesses. We have seen both illustrated over the last few days.

There are two patterns remaining that we have not discussed. However, the daily S&P 500 data will provide us ample opportunity to discuss both patterns. We encountered a small triangle in Figure 10-24. The pattern that developed in the DJIA is in fact the most common way this pattern develops. Figure 10-28 displays a contracting triangle in a short-horizon DMK/$ chart. Most people have tremendous problems with this pattern because it is common for wave b to exceed the origin of wave a. The problem might be that most illustrations in books that show line charts nearly always show a perfect pennant formation. A dotted line in the contracting triangle pattern in Figure 10-28 is the pattern most books use to illustrate this pattern. However, markets are permitted and will frequently produce a wave b second leg that breaks the origin of the orthodox high.

We actually had two triangle examples in our real-time market scenario, and I tried to squeeze past the first triangle when it developed. In Figure 10-18 there is a Zigzag rally. Wave c in this rally may have bothered some people as the five wave structure is made more difficult to see by a sprawling fourth wave contracting triangle. It was not a three wave structure if you wondered about it at the time. Also the market clearly fell to new price lows when the Zigzag was complete, confirming the pattern. In Figure 10-18 the three wave decline that is just prior to the high marked wave c up, is actually wave c′ of four in this small five wave advance. I would have had to compress the data to make it very obvious that the fourth wave was indeed a triangle, and that might have confused some people.

There is in the industry a lot of misunderstanding about triangles. I say this because there are so many examples in our industry to illustrate a common error. Suppose that five swings develop within a triangle pattern. That part is easy. Each swing is called wave a-b-c-d-e. That too is easy. Here's the catch. Every single leg you label as one of the swings within a triangle *must be a three wave structure*. Case closed. No exceptions. If any of the waves in your triangle has five waves, it is not a triangle. The most abused market in recent years was the weekly chart data for the U.S. T-Bonds. Most people used the outer dimensions of a contracting price structure to suggest that a contracting triangle was forming. If you go back to look

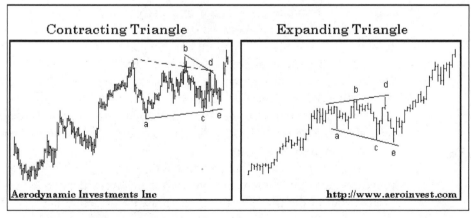

FIGURE 10-28

at these wave interpretations, you will find a five wave pattern in the first wave position. That should have been an early warning that this market was not developing a bullish contracting triangle. When the second wave became a five wave pattern, it ruled out the possibility that the market was forming a bearish contracting triangle. Bonds did not form a triangle.

When the first leg of what is thought to be a contracting triangle is a distinct five wave pattern, it can be used as wave A, let's say for a decline, and then a bearish triangle will develop to form wave B up. The resolution from wave B up would be a wave C decline. That's how people got caught on the wrong side: they used a five wave pattern for their first wave.

In a triangle the first leg down is generally sharp. That is why the current decline in the DJIA may develop into only a long-horizon triangle if a Zigzag decline from the high is the correct pattern that the market wants to preserve. Wave B up is then permitted to make a new high.

Wave C within a triangle is very sneaky. It usually takes the most time to develop, and every time you think it is complete, it comes back to form another leg in the complex structure. In a contracting triangle, wave C may not break the termination of wave a. If it does, you have to consider an Expanding Triangle. This is displayed in Figure 10-28 also. In a contracting triangle, it is well known that wave D may not break below wave C. Do not put your stops just below wave C for this very reason! The slippage exposure for stops below wave C is horrendous (above wave C in a bearish triangle). Use another price projection method to determine stop placement.

Wave D is not as tricky because it frequently forms a Fibonacci relationship relative to wave B. Wave E's, on the other hand, may form their own contracting pattern, which can be very confusing. They are hard to identify. Be aware that wave E's in financial markets are frequently a last leg down that will throw off your timing. Expect this because it happens often. A lot is said about wave E's forming on market news. While it can happen, it does not have to be the cause. One way to determine where the triangle pattern *must* be complete is to extend the converging trend lines of the lower highs and higher lows to mark a projected intersection. Where these two exterior trend lines converge marks the time allowed for this pattern to end. It is the maximum amount of time allowed, not a time projection for resolution of the pattern. The intersection of these two trend lines is the apex of a pennant chart pattern.

The triangle is a coiling pattern building energy within a market for the next move. At the completion of the pattern, the market will explode in what we call a "thrust" out of the triangle. The thrust must occur before the market exceeds the apex of the pattern. If the market crosses through the apex and it is still in a consolidation, the pattern is not developing the triangle you believed to be forming.

There may be a larger triangle, or perhaps the first leg of your triangle is not part of the original structure. A triangle that is just one leg off is coiling in the opposite direction, and it will produce a thrust out of the pattern in the opposite direction of your original expectations.

Once the market has developed a thrust out of this pattern, you can make a price projection. Measure the distance traveled by the market in wave B, and then calculate 0.618, 1.00, 1.618, and 2.618 swing relationships. Then project these ratios from the termination of wave E. The resolution of the triangle interpretation in Figure 10-29 is simply called a "fourth wave" because we have not considered the larger picture for this market. Deciding which degree best fits this fourth wave correction will be deferred until we address the longer-horizon analysis.

When we discussed Figure 10-10, we briefly mentioned that there was a great debate within the S&P Elliott Wave community over the price structure that developed from August 1997 to January 1998. The debate concerned whether a triangle had formed or not. In Figure 10-10 the data is compressed. Let's take a closer look at this wave structure now in Figure 10-29.

There are several ways to label this triangle in the middle of the daily S&P 500 futures chart. Move wave a' over to the adjacent low on the right, and you will have a five wave pattern into the high called wave b' up. That could end the prior advance. Therefore, this triangle can have a sprawled-out first wave a down or a sharp first leg. It will not change the debate. I can give you a triangle with much better proportions,

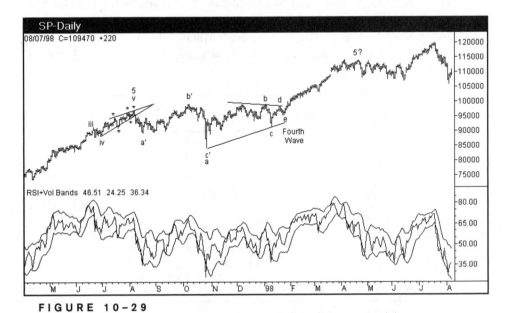

FIGURE 10-29

but it does not change the outcome. Each wave within this structure is a three wave pattern, and it does not matter how you interpret each wave. A valid three wave swing can be defined. I would also argue about the placement of wave b up in this chart. But whether or not this structure is a triangle will have no impact on the larger issue. *The debate over this pattern was ended once and for all when the decline that developed in April and May 1998 moved the RSI only to the 40 to 45 range for this indicator.* That is a decline within a bull market based on the range rules defined in Chapter 1. Case closed. If you viewed indicator signals as more important evidence than wave structure, the only conclusion that you could derive would be that the market needed to develop a fifth wave advance from the June lows.

It should be noted that those in favor of the triangle scenario were forced to use the choppy structure into the high marked wave "5?" as the end of the advance from the resolution of the triangle. When a fifth wave cannot exceed the third wave in a developing five wave structure, it is called a *failure*. It failed to make a new high in this case. Both interpretations correctly called for a decline. But the indicators made the more accurate call compared to using wave structure on its own. Elliott Wave structure by itself is deadly in my opinion. The RSI has an upper and lower volatility band displayed in Figure 10-29. We will discuss this analytic technique in the next chapter.

If a five wave advance developed, it raises a significant question: "Where is the first wave and from what price low does it begin?" To discuss the first wave, we need to look at a distant cousin of the triangle pattern: the diagonal triangle, or rising wedge.

In Figure 10-30 we have an actual bullish diagonal triangle pattern that formed in a financial market. These patterns will occur at the end of a larger trend

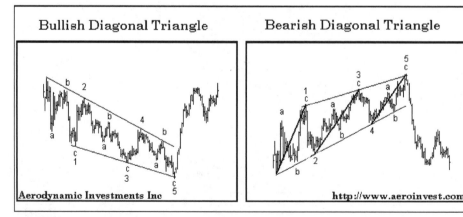

FIGURE 10-30

when the market is running out of steam so to speak. While a contracting and expanding triangle will develop in wave positions 4, B, and x *only,* the diagonal triangle will develop only in wave 5 or C. The internals are similar in both patterns since each swing or leg will develop a three wave structure. Waves 1, 3, and 5 in a textbook environment will develop Zigzag patterns. Do not get hung up looking for Zigzags in a real market environment. As long as the price structure internals are choppy, they will do. The wedge shape should be quite apparent when the exterior trend lines converge. What is more important is that you use a guide to help determine where these rising or falling wedges will end. Once the pattern is complete, the market rapidly returns to the origin of the wedge.

Tracking these patterns can be very tricky in a real-time environment because an error can easily be made in the third wave by prematurely thinking it is complete. Here's a useful guide: The same data displayed in the falling wedge that ended a market decline have been horizontally flipped so that I could illustrate a bearish diagonal triangle. You will find three lines in the bearish diagonal pattern to connect the start and end of each impulsive wave. Look at the slope of these lines. They are progressively becoming less steep, and the declining slope of each line gives the impression that they are falling forward. If your third wave has a slope that is steeper than your first, your third wave in the wedge is not complete. The same can be said for the fifth wave relative to the third. The three lines displaying a declining slope between each successive impulsive wave within this pattern will save a trader a lot of money. This pattern in real life can chop your trading account into shreds so that you end up trading the final resolution poorly. The slope is the key to surviving this pattern.

In Figure 10-31 we are viewing the same daily S&P 500 futures chart as displayed in Figure 10-29. However, Figure 10-31 is the better interpretation. This chart shows a five wave pattern that needs explanation. We'll come back to this in a moment. First look at the structure to the left in 1997 that defines wave v of 5. There are five asterisks to mark waves that form a rising diagonal triangle pattern. You can see that the resolution from this pattern is sharp, and the market declines back the wave iv in June 1997, which is the start of the wave v diagonal that later ends in August 1997. This is the pattern that always marks the end of a trend and leads to a correction.

There are 13 Elliott Wave patterns, and we have discussed or used every single one except number 5 in the list that follows. The fifth pattern is quietly mentioned when all the patterns of the Elliott Wave building blocks are cataloged. The 13 patterns are:

1. A simple five wave pattern
2. An extending five wave pattern
3. Truncated Fifth Wave or failure
4. Ending Diagonal Triangle (Wedge)

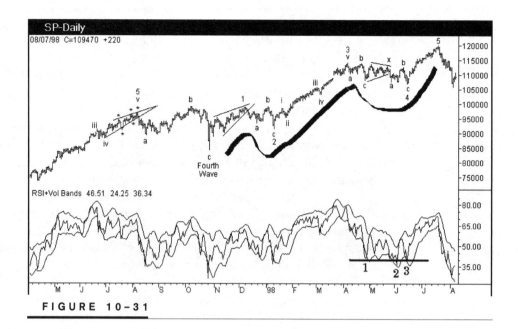

FIGURE 10-31

5. *Leading Diagonal Triangle* (Wedge)
6. Zigzag
7. Double Zigzag
8. Flat
9. Expanded Flat
10. Contracting Triangle
11. Expanding Triangle
12. Double Threes
13. Triple Threes

Pattern 3 in this list is the fifth wave failure when wave 5 is unable to exceed the termination of wave 3. The term *failure* is used more often than *truncated.* It is a common trading signal when the Cash S&P makes a new low when the futures do not in intraday data. The reverse is also common: The Cash makes a new high as S&P futures fail to form a new high. Futures in these situations are often forming fifth wave failures. We had to consider a failure for Figure 10-29.

Patterns 12 and 13 are just complex corrections that use connected corrective building blocks together in a group. We will look at these in a moment.

It is pattern number 5 in this list that is the key to the chart interpretation shown in Figure 10-31. A diagonal triangle forms three wave structures for each wave in a termination pattern. However, there is another wedge pattern. It is the

Diagonal Triangle type 2, or the leading wedge. The internals are 5-3-5-3-5, and the fourth wave breaks the top of wave 1. Is that not a rule violation? Yes, except this pattern must be a distinct wedge, and it is permitted in only one of two positions; wave 1 or wave A. Figure 10-31 demonstrates a diagonal triangle in the first wave position that ends into the market high of December 1997. It is a rare pattern within currencies and equity indices and should be used only in hindsight. However, you will find that this pattern develops more often in bonds because bonds generally are slow to establish a new trend.

In Figure 10-31 the RSI indicator has three oscillator lows marked 1 through 3. The low at point 3 is equal to point 1. Point 2 makes a new low, so the guidelines we discussed that an oscillator will test the prior range are demonstrated once again. However, the indicator level clearly warns that the bull market is leading into a fifth wave, which negates the triangle.

In the list that cataloged the 13 Elliott Wave patterns, the two complex patterns did not develop in our real-time market scenario. We were close—I thought we had one developing in Figure 10-23, but it turned into another Zigzag. So Figure 10-32 allows these last two patterns to be highlighted. A Double Three is just any three complete corrective patterns that follow one another. The minimum is three complete patterns, and the puzzle pieces will be constructed from Flats, Triangles, and Zigzag patterns. Figure 10-31 shows another real-life example as wave 4 is a complex Double Three.

A common error made within our industry can be discussed from the Double Three chart in Figure 10-32. If wave x up were higher than wave b, which is at the price high, would it still be wave X? No. How do you know that the market is not forming a Flat or Expanded Flat? Waves a-b-c would be labeled wave A, and the

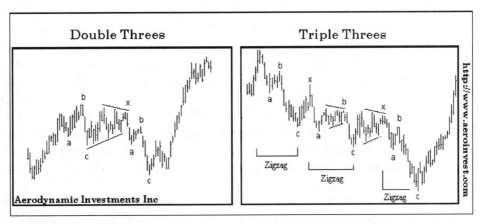

FIGURE 10-32

x wave would become wave B in a larger pattern. You would then have to see a five wave pattern develop in the market to complete the Flat or Expanded Flat pattern. Wave x's into new highs or lows are usually wrong wave counts. I'm not saying they will never occur, but I have not used an x into a new high or low for any time horizon or financial market within the last six years. That means it is far more rare than the elusive leading diagonal triangle.

Finally, the market may attempt to extend a correction one more time by forming a Triple Three pattern. Two x waves serve to connect three corrective patterns. Both x waves must themselves be valid corrective patterns. You now have all 13 Elliott Wave patterns at your command to use as pieces to solve any market puzzle. I would like to add a fourteenth puzzle piece to your arsenal: a blank. Blank? No pattern at all as you cannot make one out. Blank. When this wildcard is present, don't make a pattern up from which to trade. Wait. Be patient. Don't move until you see it. Same as playing chess.

Long-Term Analysis

If the S&P decline we tracked together in this chapter were a game of chess, I would refer to that market decline as a game of chess using a standard two-dimensional board. However, the analysis work is not two dimensional. It is synonymous with playing chess on a three-dimensional board. I would use the indicator signals from underlying components within the S&P 500 Index in conjunction with Global Equity Indices and the key financial markets of currencies, bonds, and gold. The balance between indicators and wave structure must balance in my three-dimensional game of chess. When they align and you see the pattern as a three-dimensional model, you have something to get excited about. I will not go into great detail about how to take the information we have just covered up to yet another level by showing you a three-dimensional model. It could easily be done, but that's why people pay me for my market opinion, so I'm not going to be stupid and give everything away. But I did promise that I would show you why I had a bullish outlook for equities by utilizing the Wave Principle when others had a different view.

First, you know I construct wave counts from indicator signals, not just from price data structure. That alone will lead to conclusions and market interpretations that are different from those of conventional Elliott Wave practitioners. But I also construct my larger market opinions from components within an Index rather than depending totally on indicator signals developing from the Index itself. Let me show you.

The S&P 500 Index is made up of 500 stocks, but most stocks within the Index have no weighted significance in terms of the actual movement of the Index itself. *In fact, there are numerous S&P Sectors within the Index that have no*

	A	B	C	D	E	F	G	H
1	**AERODYNAMIC INVESTMENTS INC**						**April 1998 US Equity Index Summary**	
2	http://www.aeroinvest.com							
3			**S&P 500 Index**				**Russell 2000**	**Nasdaq 100**
4	**Sector**		(Sector Subset) **% of S&P**		(stock)	% of S&P		
5	Financials	16.03%					23.30%	
6			Mjr. Reg Bank	5.08%				
7			Money Ctr Banks	2.99%				
8	Technology	15.68%					13.40%	
9			Computer (hrdw & Soft)	8.81%				68.94%
10					IBM	1.44%		
11					INTC	2.17%		
12					MSFT	2.27%		
13	Consumer Staples	14.38%					2.80%	
14			Beverages (non)	2.92%				
15					KO	2.02%		
16			Consumer Discr.				16.00%	
17			Foods	2.57%				
18			Household Prds	2.14%				
19					PG	1.27%		
20			Tobacco	1.43%				
21					MO	1.52%		
22	Health Care	10.39%					9.90%	
23			BioTechnology	0.17%				3.08%
24			Health Care (Div)	4.05%				
25					JNJ	1.11%		
26			Hth Care (Drugs)	4.41%				
27					PFE	1.06%		
28					MRK	1.59%		
29	Capital Goods	9.74%						
30			Aerospace/Def	1.21%				
31			Elect. Equip	4.21%				
32					GE	3.04%		
33			Manuf. Diversified	2.29%				
34	Consumer Cyclicals	9.27%						
35			Autos	1.77%			4.10%	
36	Producer Durables	n/a					8.60%	
37	Energy	9.00%					3.90%	
38			International Integrated	6.41%			0.50%	
39					XON	2.16%		
40					RD	1.62%		
41	Communications	5.95%						8.22%
42			Telephone	3.72%				
43	Industrials							19.11%
44	Basic Materials	5.33%						
45			Chemicals	1.67%				
46			Gold Mining	0.35%				
47			Mat. & Processing				9.87%	
48	Utilities	3.06%					6.41%	
49			Elec. Companies	2.38%				
50	Transportation	1.17%						0.65%
51	Other						1.22%	
52		100.00%		58.58%		21.27%	100.00%	100.00%

F I G U R E   1 0 – 3 3

weighted significance on the future movement of the Index. In Figure 10-33 you will see that 19 S&P Sectors contribute an underlying weighted value of 58.58 percent within the S&P 500 Index. In addition, 12 stocks make up 21.27 percent of the total S&P 500 Index in April 1998. The underlying components of the Index change. A market leader with significant weighting within the Index today may be less influential in a year's time. Therefore, to base all you analytic work on the Index itself is the same as swimming in an ocean and never looking for a shark or barracuda passing under the surface that could ruin your day.

When you consider that Energy and Computer Technology alone contribute an underlying weighting of 25 percent to the S&P 500 Index, you can see why Figure 10-26 had the AMEX Composite Indices for Computer Technology and Energy on my computer screen. If you know 25 percent of the underlying weight in your index, you have a higher probability of being right. So I analyze 20 S&P Sectors that have nearly a 60% weighting and align their wave patterns and indicator signals to construct a wave interpretation for the Index. I use the same approach then for the German Dax and Nikkei. I then have three opinions from underlying weightings of these individual indices. Finally, you can weight the Global indices themselves. Yes. It is a lot of work. But it is worth it to try and stay on the right side of the market.

Bond markets require a similar approach, but the yield curve is weighted and then the Global rates. Currencies become a puzzle between crossrates, bonds, and gold. The markets where I have been caught dead wrong are usually markets where I am either unable to look at underlying charts or I failed to do so. I will never trade the markets I refer to as "roots and hooves." We do not get along at all.

With your understanding of how the underlying analysis is approached for longer-horizon work, we can take a look at the big picture for Bonds and U.S. Stocks. Let's start with a few sample S&P Sectors that offer current data up to August 7, 1998. The four Sectors in Figures 10-34 to 10-37 are wave interpretations that my clients know have been unadjusted wave scenarios since 1993. It explains clearly why I have been so bullish. In the bigger picture I am still looking for the end of wave (3) up. Wave (4) is then expected to form a massive contracting triangle. Why a triangle? We are due. The market has not used that puzzle piece in the really big picture. It will at some time. Within 22 Sectors that I monitor, only 4 have needed a significant wave change in four years, excluding adjustments for the developing extension. We may well see a fifth wave blowoff to end wave (3) up in the future, but the entire rally is not a blowoff since 1987 to end a Grand SuperCycle fifth wave in my opinion.

It should be very clear now that my wave interpretations for the S&P 500 Index have been derived from aligning key wave (2) Sector declines that have the strongest weighting within the Index itself to "construct" a wave scenario for

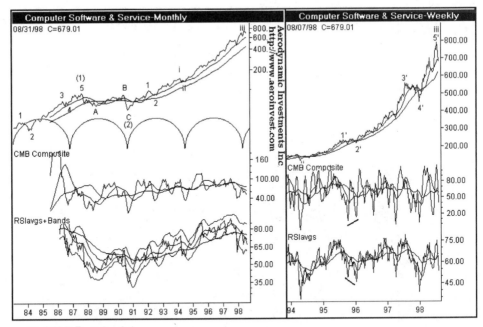

FIGURE 10-34

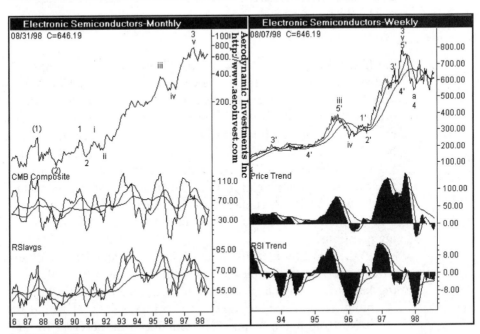

FIGURE 10-35

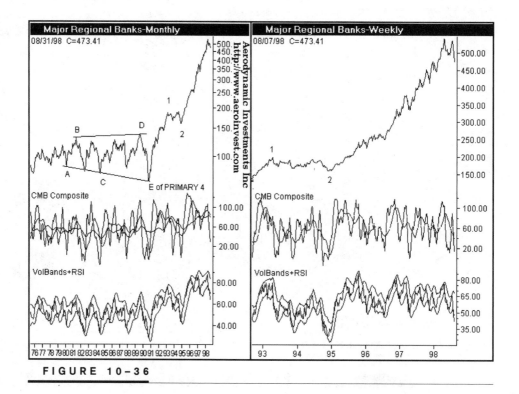

FIGURE 10–36

the Index. Keep in mind that the weighting changes within the Sectors change and must be monitored for future wave interpretations. Corrections like the present one have and will change leadership in the underlying Index. This is not an orthodox way to apply the Elliott Wave Principle. But, as I mentioned earlier, this is war. Grab anything you know works to win a battle! This approach has been working in a Global environment as well. The last two Sector charts in Figures 10-36 and 10-37 have the internal wave counts deliberately removed so you can use the thumb nail method. The market will answer you if you are right. By the way, Major Regional Banks is a composite sector that is an interest rate sensitive Index. When you look at the Bond chart, this will raise a few interesting questions.

When do I look at the Stocks listed in Figure 10-33? When I need to see what is brewing under the surface within each Sector, I will study the underlying key stocks for that Sector. Gold is a Sector where a large Expanded Flat is unfolding, and wave C down is developing now. It would be very hard to see wave B up if the major weighted stocks in the Gold Mining Sector were not viewed.

Now the big picture. But keep in mind that I need to be on the right side of the market only tomorrow. The decline we tracked is a fourth wave, and I am not even concerned with what degree the fourth wave will become until we start the fifth wave up. Then the focus will be on calculating objectives for wave (3). You have the idea now, I'm sure. I'll leave the final charts in your hands for review without further comment. It is time for me to move on to the next chapter.

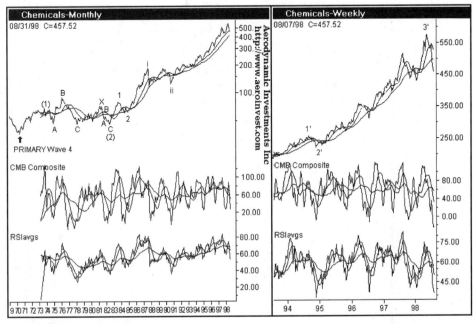

FIGURE 10-37

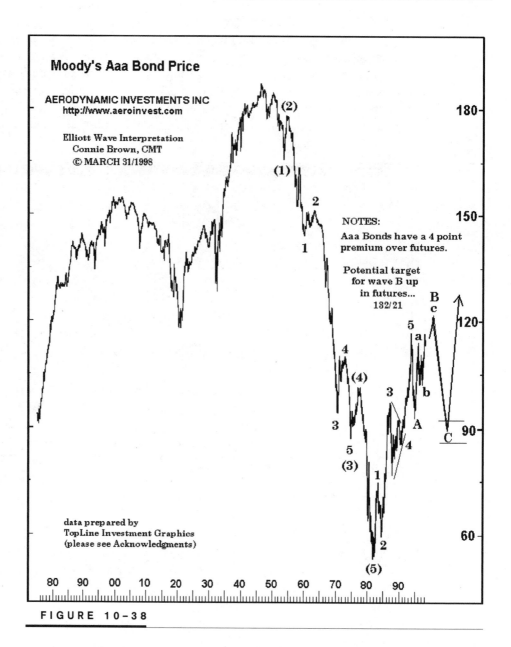

FIGURE 10-38

As this book was going to press, Bonds realized the 132/21 objective. This target marked where waves a and c formed equality within wave B. Now the 1.618 relationship for wave c relative to wave a of B should be considered.

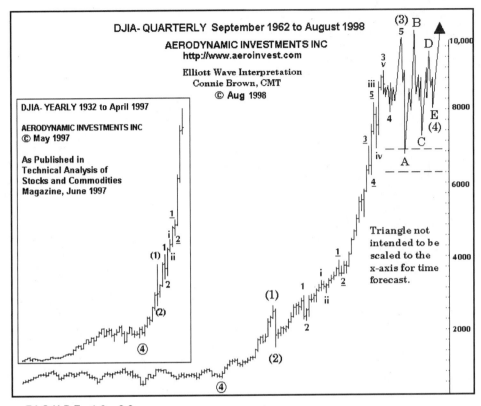

FIGURE 10-39

Wave 5 of (3) is not drawn to scale. Intermediate wave (3) could realize 14485, which is a 1.618 Fibonacci relationship projected from the 6971 low. Timing? Always the emotions affect the future, Yoda would say. There is a Gann time cluster forming in May, 2000, that might be a consideration. But it is more important to allow your indicators to dictate the timing. Be patient. Remember patterns take longer to develop in the markets than they do in our minds.

PART THREE

New Methods for Improving Indicator Timing and Filtering Premature Signals

Volatility Bands on Oscillators

By the end of Part 3, you will feel certain that no conventional indicator is safe in my hands. I will invert it, smooth it, compound it, disassemble it, superimpose it, and even imbed it—all in an effort to understand it.

Nearly everyone views common indicators such as the MACD, Stochastics, and RSI as sacred entities. Most believe an underlying formula must never be altered. Not even the conventional display of an indicator must be changed. But what if Stochastics shouts out a signal to you more clearly if one line is plotted as a histogram? Would you not change it? Chances are high that you do not know because you may not have considered looking at a conventional indicator plotted in an unconventional manner. Therefore, in Part 3 my mission is to challenge your perceptions about indicators. The time has come to push the boundaries of convention, to show you that we can mix and match the elements we like and then, more importantly, discard or minimize the elements we do not like. The next five chapters will, I hope, give you greater flexibility and broaden your options in your work with indicators.

In this chapter we present a method with which to address a specific market problem. The problem is, "Just how overbought or oversold can a market become?" Specific questions of this nature are sometimes answered by indicator formulas expressly designed to answer that one particular question. The method or indicator is used only when the question arises in the market. It is monitored for only one specific signal at one critical market juncture. The rest of the time you might ignore the indicator or method entirely. The method you choose or develop may not always provide an answer to the same question every time the market comes face to face with that problem, so it is advisable to use more than one method that displays information in different manners. For example, the momentum extreme histogram displayed in the reverse-engineering chapter is one method that compliments the method we are about to look at now.

Using volatility bands with indicators rather than on prices can answer the question, "Just how overbought or oversold can a market become?" It will not answer the question every time, but when this method steps forward and makes a statement, it should be respected.

The formula for volatility bands that I use was given to me by Manning Stoller. Stoller uses this formula on price data while I have found the same formula with a modification can be used with oscillators. Figure 11-1 is a weekly chart for German Government Bund futures. A 14-period RSI is plotted with volatility bands. The reason I like this formula is *that it gives very few signals that warrant attention.* But it produces one particular signal that nearly always demands respect and states, "Pay attention and look at other methods now because a trend reversal could be near, and you may be missing it." I need blatant signals. Especially at emotional market extremes—not ones that can be easily missed after an exhausting week of trading when you are doing analysis at all hours of the night. This one signal is a good wake-up call.

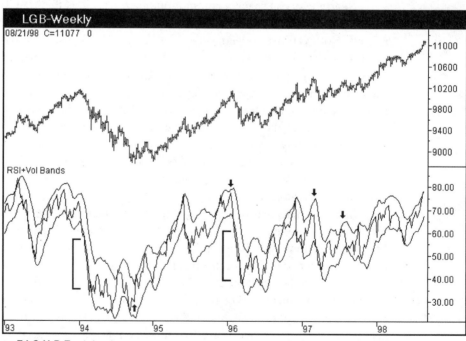

FIGURE 11-1

The signal itself is very simple. Look at the upper and lower extreme ranges for the RSI. When the RSI is *near an extreme high or low* and is touching the volatility band, the indicator will follow the strong move with a pullback from the band. The market signal occurs when the RSI attempts to resume the former trend and fails to challenge or reach the outer band a second time. That is it. Period. Nothing more to add. The RSI does not necessarily have to display divergence or create a reversal signal—just fails to touch the outer band on a second attempt. There are four signals in Figure 11-1 that have been highlighted by black arrows. Other interpretive relationships you might extract elsewhere between the RSI and outer bands in this chart are not used because other methods we have covered are less risky and offer better timing. Just monitor the extremes for this signal and keep it simple.

Before we move on to the formula itself, we need to set the stage for correctly setting these bands up relative to the oscillator. Observe the upper band relative to the RSI. The RSI violates the upper boundary only four times in a five-and-a-half-year period. That is a correct setup placement for this band. Now look at the lower band. There are two square brackets to mark an area where the RSI travels outside the boundary of the lower volatility band for a period of time. You do not want this to occur. The RSI may travel in extreme moves along the boundary of the band, *but not outside of it*—at least not until you are familiar with the character of this signal.

I tend to use a default period because my eye can make any necessary adjustment needed to shift the placement of the band. However, until your eye is trained to automatically make any adjustment required, you will not want an indicator on your computer screen to exceed these bands except on rare occasion.

As markets decline much more rapidly than they rise, it is important for volatility band formulas to accommodate independent coefficients that allow independent setup of the upper and lower bands. It is for this reason that I do not care for band formulas that operate on the premise of using equally proportioned moving average envelopes or moving standard deviation bands from a simple moving average.

The formula that creates the band displacement in Figure 11-2 is derived from an average of the true range of prices to accommodate data gaps. Each band then applies a separate coefficient so that the user has independent control of the upper and lower perimeters. The formula in Figure 11-2 has been modified from Stoller's original formula. Oscillators do not experience gaps so it is unnecessary to imbed the true range function within this formula when an indicator is being plotted. However, as the Average True Range is always needed for price, it is easier to create a formula that will easily accommodate a similar format for both prices and indicators. If you want to use this formula for prices, just replace the three imbedded 14-period RSIs that define the inputs for the "TrueRangeCustom"

```
Indicator: RSI+Vol Bands
Input: Coefdwn[2.1],Coefup[2.3];
Plot1 ((Average((RSI(Close,14)),6))+(Coefup*(Average(TrueRangeCustom((RSI(Close,14)),(
RSI(Close,14)),(RSI(Close,14))),15)))),"Plot1");
Plot2((Average((RSI(Close,14)),6))-(Coefdwn*(Average(TrueRangeCustom((RSI(Close,14)),
(RSI(Close,14)),(RSI(Close,14))),15)))),"Plot2");
Plot3((RSI(Close,14)),"Plot3");
IF CheckAlert Then Begin
  IF Plot1 Crosses Above Plot2 or Plot1 Crosses Below Plot2
  or Plot1 Crosses Above Plot3 or Plot1 Crosses Below Plot3
  or Plot2 Crosses Above Plot3 or Plot2 Crosses Below Plot3
  Then Alert = TRUE;
End;
```

FIGURE 11-2

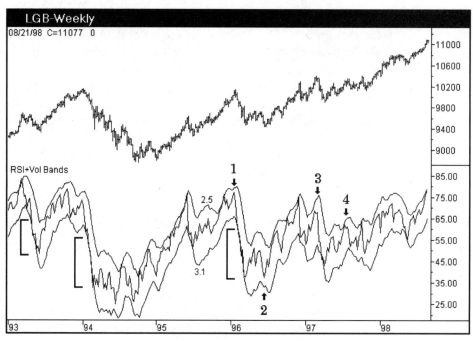

FIGURE 11-3

calculation with data for price "High, Low, and Close." That is a change that would be required to apply this formula to the price data itself. The modified formula in Figure 11-2 continues to use Stoller's original 6-period average with a 15-period Average True Range. The trickiest part of the entire conversion is converting a fairly simple formula into a *TradeStation* formula that is linear. The indicator in Figure

11-2 can be downloaded as an ELA study for TradeStation from our Web site at the address http://www.aeroinvest.com.

The coefficients that I start with are 2.1 for the lower band and 2.3 for the upper band. Stoller uses a double set of bands, but as I am looking for only one specific signal in relationship to the RSI, I find that one set of bands is sufficient.

The same weekly chart for the German Bund futures is displayed in Figure 11-3. The lower band is now using a coefficient of 3.1 instead of 2.3. The 3.1 was selected by appearance alone knowing that the RSI should rarely exceed the band. The upper band has been "tweaked" by using a coefficient of 2.5 instead of 2.1.

The lower band now shows the RSI traveling down the same boundary as the band in the areas marked by square brackets. At signals 1, 2, 3, and 4, the signal forms with an M or W pattern in the RSI, showing the second peak or trough failing to reach the outer band. The width of the oscillator pivots within the M or W pattern will vary considerably. The personality of the W or M will remain fairly consistent for an individual market, however. The number of periods or spread between peaks or lows is relative to the character of the indicator used. Nine periods in the RSI has already been defined as a strong signal in earlier chapters for financial markets.

Signal number 3 shows the second peak well under the rise of the band. The first peak, however, did not touch the band. This is an example of considering the relative displacement to the outer band.

Figure 11-4 contains the most memorable indicator signal that I have personally experienced in my career. The signal first develops in the monthly S&P 500 Index and is then repeated in the monthly London FTSE Index and German Dax. These signals are the cleanest, strongest, most aggressive confirmations you will ever experience using these bands. The RSI is forming a bottom between a range of 40 and 50. The zone between 40–45 marks the end of a correction within the context of a larger bull market. This is the range rule concept that was demonstrated in Chapter 1. Unfortunately, the signals in Figure 11-4 were in direct conflict with my employer's very long horizon diagonal triangle interpretation, which implied the end of the bull market. I would not wish such a strong signal confirmation on anyone at a more difficult juncture in a market.

There is a sell signal marked in the London FTSE data that has a question mark. This one signal has been highlighted to reinforce the importance of not staying short when the indicator declines and the price fails to follow. The indicator falls nearly to the lower band, and the price just fights the indicator all the way down by forming a choppy corrective pattern. But it is more important to recognize that the RSI declined to the 65 level, which is the upper zone that defines resistance for a bear market. A market that can allow an indicator to hold this level

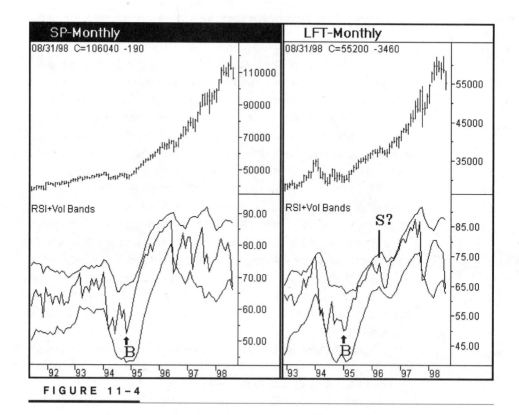

FIGURE 11-4

generally explodes into a third wave in prices and allows the indicator to break into a new higher range for that time horizon. When you consider that all this was coming together in a monthly chart, it was a massive buy signal.

Figure 11-5 is used to show that Bollinger Bands applied to prices are very different in character from the band formula applied to the RSI. This would be true even if the band formula on the RSI were displayed with prices. In the monthly FTSE chart the standard deviation bands on prices offer an analytic tool, but timing is a problem. The market is able to track the upper boundary for several years. The Bollinger Band narrowing in conjunction with a choppy price decline, that corresponds to signal 3 in the RSI relative to the upper volatility band, is of value. But if timing is important, Bollinger Bands alone will offer limited help.

On the other hand, let me strongly caution you about the RSI signal relative to volatility bands displayed in these figures. It is essential that they be used with a price projection system. To simply buy or sell based on this indicator pattern alone would be financial suicide. You will be hoping that the run-away freight train will stop near your market entry. Please keep in mind that *these signals are based on an indicator that sees only a closing price!* The spikes above or below a close in a monthly chart could permanently blow out any trader. Then the market will move in the direction you had been anticipating, but you will not be around to trade it as you will have become a mere statistic added to prior road kill tallies. Clear? Please do not view the clarity of these patterns as an easy signal to trade. This is only an analytic method and not a trading signal.

Figure 11-6 is a chart showing the 10-Yr Treasury Note market in a monthly time horizon. The band formula can be applied to other indicators, but how much value it really adds is questionable. Signals 1 and 2 display the pattern that is watched for, but it is the divergence between the RSI and Composite Index that offers the stronger signal. More is not necessarily better—sometimes just redundant and unnecessary noise.

We have discussed how to apply moving averages to the RSI and Stochastics. Adding volatility bands is the more common chart layout that I will use with these bands. I have had three quote vendors explain to me why traders will never require the ability to plot more than four lines for any given indicator study. Their belief becomes a limitation that makes our life more difficult. However, we can navigate around the obstacle. In *TradeStation* it will be necessary to create two windows

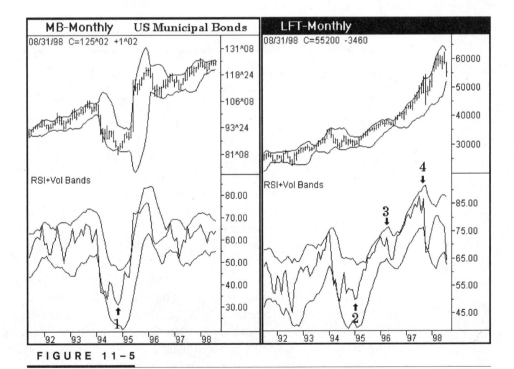

FIGURE 11-5

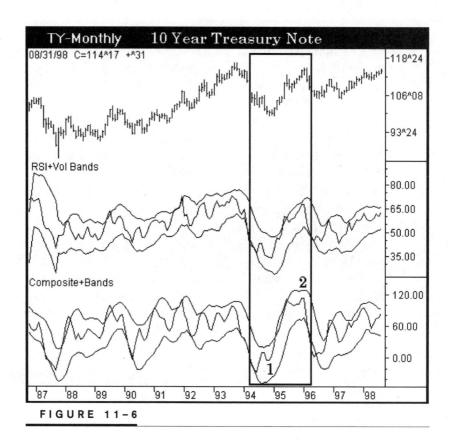

FIGURE 11-6

with the RSI and Volatility bands in one, the RSI and moving averages in the other. The key is to then pick up one study and overlay it on top of the other. The problem will be that the RSI indicators will then be out of registration. The solution is to establish a fixed scaling for both independent RSI studies. The scale you select will depend on the range of travel of your indicators. The bands may not exceed the plot scale or the indicator will again step out of registration. Figure 11-7 illustrates how the indicator scaling can be set in *TradeStation*. Other quote vendors will also have similar limitations. The visual image you are striving to obtain is offered in Figure 11-8.

The weekly Yen/$ spot market is shown in Figure 11-8. First examine the band placement relative to the indicator. The upper band is ideal; the lower band coefficient needs to be increased so that the RSI does not exceed the outer perimeter. Is signal 1 a volatility band signal? No. It is an M pattern, but it has no relationship to the upper volatility band. Signals 2 and 3 are clear. Signal 2 shows why other methods should be used in conjunction with this signal. This same chart has

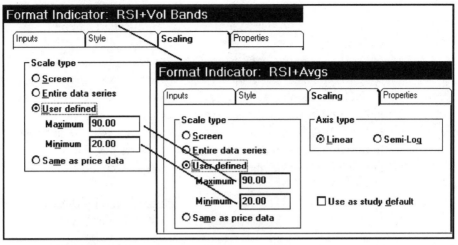

FIGURE 11-7

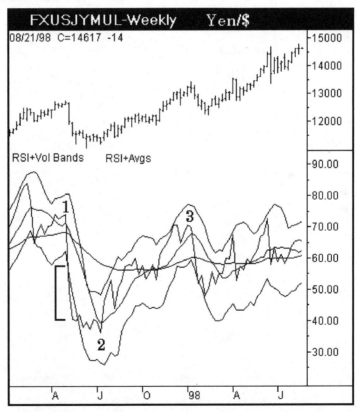

FIGURE 11-8

been discussed earlier to focus on other methods viewed more useful. Other signals you may see relative to the bands in this chart can be ignored. We'll move on to Figure 11-9.

The monthly DMK/$ spot market is offered to reinforce the pattern being sought. Signals 1 and 2 show the ideal scenarios to answer the question of when a market has become too oversold or overbought. They are the only signals of this nature in this chart. Signal 3 is the Composite Index diverging with the RSI. The fact that RSI fails to reach the upper band does help to emphasize the divergence, but it is just a redundancy and adds very little new information. The most important factor to remember when using bands on indicators can be illustrated in Figure 11-10.

In Figure 11-10 are the 120-minute September S&P and 240-minute Bond futures charts for Sunday, August 16, 1998. In the September S&P, signals 2 and

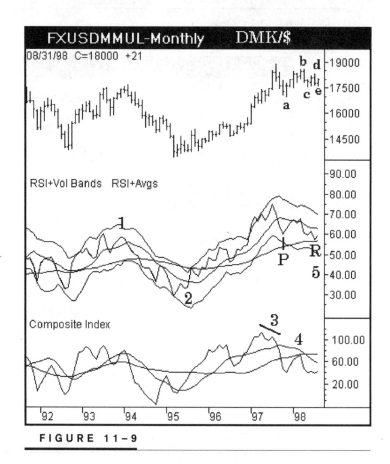

FIGURE 11–9

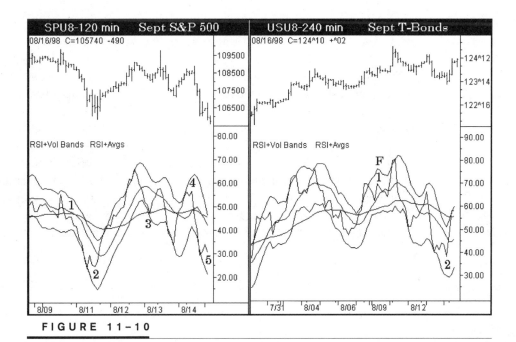

FIGURE 11-10

4 are distinct and clear. Signal 5 is again warning that a market rebound is near, but so too is the Elliott Wave structure. A minor decline is needed to complete the prior day's pattern. It was then believed that a significant rally could develop from signal 5 in this chart. The target was 1143 to 1146.50. The actual low made during the Globex session was 1148, and then a sharp rally unfolded toward an 1102 target. That is a major signal, and such reactions are common when the bands are used at an appropriate market juncture.

Having a precise target is essential because the alternative would be very damaging. The alternative would be a sharp freefall wave iii of 3. This is a common alternative scenario at this extreme position. Had the signal failed, the indicator would have broken down and fallen to 10 or lower, then remained frozen as the market continued to plummet. Early in this book I discussed the formula weakness inherent in the RSI. The question was asked, "How long would it take for an atom to reach a fixed object if it moved half the distance between its current position and the fixed object?" The answer: infinity or until the outer dimension of the atom became a factor. That's as good as saying never. That is the RSI position you are witnessing at point 5 in the S&P chart. You need to be caught only once to understand that this is not a trading signal to use by itself without other factors that reinforce it.

The 240-minute September Bond chart in Figure 11-10 shows correct signals relative to the bands at points 1 and 2. Are the signals marked in this bond chart correct? No. Bonds have been developing a five-wave rally that still requires the fifth wave up *in a normal market environment.* The fact that bonds require a fifth wave up after signal 1 is not the reason you would not sell into this signal. The reason you would not use either of these signals is that bonds are in a normal market environment. I just don't want to see you get overzealous on this one signal and use it at times when an extreme situation is not present in the market. We know the application in the September S&P is appropriate. However, it is not an appropriate time to look at this analytic method in the bond chart as the market was not overbought or oversold within a larger market move. I hope this comparison clarifies the original objective set for this chapter; this is a signal to be used in an isolated market situation near an extreme. Just ignore it the rest of the time.

CHAPTER 12

The Composite Index

Most custom formulas that you develop will be designed to provide additional guidance for a specific market character or problem. You will not use the indicator all the time, and that was never your original goal.

Some of the formulas you will develop will prove to be of more value, but the markets that they apply to, or the time horizon they work well in, will be limited. The Derivative Oscillator will fit in this later category. The Derivative Oscillator will be used later to examine the development cycle of a custom formula.

The third type of custom formula, and one that will take much more time, effort, and expense to develop, will prove to be the rare gem that becomes a foundation for all other techniques that you use. The Composite Index is a custom formula that can be used in all markets, under all market conditions, in any time horizon.

Because I use the RSI for a price projection method, I required a formula that would give a clear warning when the RSI would be caught on the wrong side of the market. Over 20 different formulas preceded the final version that became the Composite Index. This name was selected because it is indeed a Composite, but the internals in this equation resemble no other oscillator, which was one of the primary objectives. You have seen examples throughout this book of how it is used with the RSI and Stochastics. The formula forms bullish or bearish divergence with the RSI to identify when the RSI is failing to detect a market turn or is producing a low-probability signal. It is an inseparable companion to the RSI.

The chart on the cover of this book is displayed in Figure 12-1. The three monthly charts from left to right are the DMK/$ spot market, the U.S. T-Bond

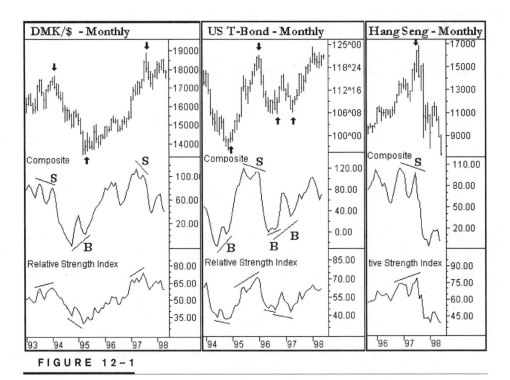

FIGURE 12-1

futures, and the Hong Kong Hang Seng Index. We chose this chart because we wanted to show a currency, bond, and equity index with distinct signals. It was easy to select the markets for the cover as this indicator develops divergence signals at many important pivots, regardless of the time horizon. The formula will work in thinly traded markets or any major global market. The major pivots for the markets in Figure 12-1 are marked with black arrows. Probability is extremely high when divergence occurs in weekly or monthly financial charts. The signals are very clear with the exception of the last signal starting to take shape in the monthly Hang Seng Index, which needs further clarification.

We discussed using longer time horizons to filter signals in shorter time horizon charts. As an example, a buy signal in a daily chart would warn a trader viewing a conflicting sell signal in a 120-minute chart to reevaluate. One would either trade a smaller size or step aside until both the daily chart and 120-minute chart displayed signals heading in the same direction. Another very important point we made much earlier concerned the domino effect of signals you will see through an entire time sequence. As an example, a signal, as we have in the monthly Hang Seng chart, is attempting to form bullish divergence with the RSI. After a major trend, the domino effect of transcending signals from long to short time horizons becomes especially important. Be patient. First the buy signal will be seen in the monthly chart, then the weekly, followed by the daily and finally an intraday trading chart. When the monthly, weekly, and daily charts all align in a relatively short period of time, the diverging peaks will rarely exceed the two required to form the divergence signal.

The character of this formula is that it forms the W pattern for bullish divergence that marks a bottom (or M for tops). The oscillator lows or peaks should always have a trend line extended from these key pivot points. When the underlying shorter time horizons are strongly aligned *against the monthly signal,* the longer-horizon chart, in this case the Hang Seng monthly chart, will likely form additional V's that mark divergence as the shorter time horizons form new lows. The V's must track up the trend line radiating from the first signal in the monthly chart. The reverse would be true of tops. If the monthly chart should break through the trend line defined, it would be a warning to reevaluate. This would be a complex pattern, and I suspect that the Hang Seng signal in place as this is written will develop into the more complex oscillator pattern being described.

How do I know to expect a complex bottom in the monthly chart for the Hang Seng? A few technical signals have been mentioned earlier. We know the Hang Seng was sitting on a support cliff with a void of Fibonacci support levels directly under the market. This would mean a fast break as the market would accelerate through the support void. You might want to review the end of the Fibonacci chapter to see examples of support voids. In the shorter time horizon, Negative Reversals are still developing so a bottom is not in place. If a bottom is not in place, the Elliott Wave pattern will extend its fifth wave down. (The entire decline could be a wave *C* decline.) That will push the market over our support cliff. That in turn will develop the complex pattern in the monthly Hang Seng chart that is not present at the moment. This signal I'll leave for time to tell. But next spring we will know how the story ended. Check the web address http://www.aeroinvest.com for a more recent chart.

In the DMK/$ and U.S. T-Bond charts in Figure 12-1, simple divergence is seen at all the major pivots. With monthly time horizons, it is generally extremely hard for oscillators to define clear signals without excessive lag. You will not see another common oscillator that handles these major trend changes as easily. Just a note about the double buy signals in U.S. T-Bonds when a second divergence signal between the RSI and the Composite Index develops. Do not interpret this indicator to be forming the 1997 buy signal at the lower range defined for bull markets. Range rules generally do not apply to this formula because it has not been normalized. The range rules were always discussed with normalized oscillators, meaning that their maximum range of travel has been fixed. I needed an oscillator that could stretch upward or downward as far as it needed. Why? You have seen the answer to this question in prior chapters:

1. We marked the oscillator extremes as important horizontal trend lines.

2. We also knew when new range extremes were established that the market would come back to test the prior extreme range.

3. You might recall the horizontal channel of Sell signals in the Elliott Wave chapter that warned that we were about to see a market rescale its proportions. Therefore, we would adjust the starting price levels for Fibonacci price projections.

4. Most importantly, it is the fact that the Composite Index is not normalized that it is able to form divergence signals in sideways markets and powerful markets equally well.

These points summarize only a few of the ways we have used this indicator without my looking back over the chapters to list all the methods with which it has shown to be of value. The formula is clearly a major contender in our current menu of technical formulas. We will address the formula itself shortly.

So far all the interpretations derived from this formula have been coupled with conventional Western Analytic indicators. The original reason the formula was developed was to identify when the RSI was about to be caught unaware of an approaching trend change. However, a point was offered much earlier that it is wise to study widely used methods of traders who have an influence on a market. In the case of very short horizon S&P intraday trading, one should develop a working knowledge of the Elliott Wave Principle. The locals in the S&P pit are well versed in wave patterns. In Asian markets, clearly Japanese Candlesticks are widely followed.

In Figure 12-2 we have a daily chart of the Nikkei Index. The Composite Index is plotted below it with two moving averages. There are numerous Candlestick patterns in this chart. My goal is not to identify all the Candlestick interpretations that could be made but to focus on signals that are associated with key pivots in the Composite Index. The Composite Index and Candlestick charting techniques compliment one another well.

Point 1 is a *Bearish Engulfing* pattern that forms when sellers engulf the weak buying action of the former period. This topping pattern develops at the same time the Composite Index is forming a peak under the resistance level defined by moving averages.

Move to point 2, which marks five Candlesticks known as a bullish *Rising Three Methods* continuation pattern. The tall white Candlestick is preceded by three small black real bodies. The fifth Candlestick closes the pattern with a strong white candle that ideally should close at a new high for the range. In this chart it does not, and it may have challenged the suggested pattern. It is a confusing pattern regardless when it follows clear indecision by both bulls and bears in the preceding three Candlesticks where a bullish pivot may have occurred. The

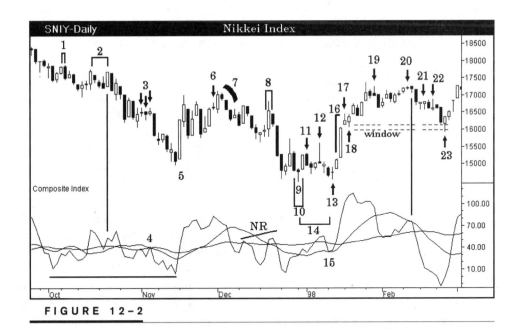

FIGURE 12-2

Composite Index would suggest that the trader wait for confirmation as there is divergence with price and *the moving averages on the Composite Index are showing a negative spread.* Confirmation does not appear, and the next day the downtrend resumes clearing up the question raised at point 2.

Point 3 consists of three Candlesticks that each make their own contribution—from left to right: a *Doji, a Hanging Man,* followed by a *Spinning Top.* While I am only a novice student of this methodology, I also wonder if the Spinning Top and Hanging Man would have been viewed as a Bearish Engulfing pattern. Perhaps the real bodies of these two Candlesticks are too small. Regardless, engulfing pattern or not, the three individual patterns spell trouble. The interpretation of a Doji can be read in any language. A market that opens and closes at the same level is a red flag for a possible trend change. The red flag is immediately followed by a Hanging Man candlestick, which, as the name implies, is not a healthy outlook for the market near term. This is an important topping signal. The third candlestick, a Spinning Top, is a small real body that shows neither the bulls nor bears are in control. However, considering the two bearish warnings preceding the spinning top, it is not surprising the bears gain the upper hand the next day.

Signal 4 in the Composite Index is extremely important. The oscillator peak at point 4 is directly under a crossover where the shorter moving average falls below the longer. That is a strong sell signal by itself. However, look very closely to the immediate left of point 4. No. Too far. Not the peak that forms the double top at point 2 but the more subtle one right beside point 4 that is just to its immediate left under both averages. The oscillator at point 4 is higher than the one beside it. The closing price at point 4 is lower than the close of the peak to its immediate left. Yes. A Negative Reversal of immense significance. The Reversal patterns that were defined in the RSI chapter will also be seen in the Composite Index. The acceptable amplitude of the signal will be larger because the formula is not normalized. We have not spent a lot of time on this. But in this Negative Reversal we have a shallow amplitude, narrow spread between peaks, *and* point 4 is directly under a crossover. This is very strong confirmation. The confirmation for the second oscillator peak occurs at the same time as the Hanging Man candlestick. So a one-day lead might have been gained for traders working to establish large positions.

The long white candlestick with a shaven bottom at point 5 does not follow a signal from the Composite Index. However, the Composite Index was at a Fibonacci ratio relative to the first part of the decline in the oscillator. (The oscillator high is not displayed and is to the left of this chart's view.)

Point 6 is a small Doji that would need further confirmation. While the trend continues upward the next day, the three down days under point 7 form a bearish *Three Black Crows* pattern. This pattern is an example of why we should all be students of each other's techniques. This particular bearish pattern would have required great caution. Be suspicious of this pattern because the Composite Index warns that underlying market strength could still be present to form a more complex top. The majority of sellers would have established their positions in the second and third candlesticks within pattern 7. The cause for concern is that the Composite Index is neither diverging nor displaying averages with a negative spread.

When the last-gasp market pop does occur into the *Harami* pattern at point 8, the market actually places all the sellers from the second and third day in the Three Crows pattern in jeopardy. The shorts are squeezed out of their positions as seen by the first candlestick forming the harami. The short squeeze was a setup caused by the majority of participants' trading this market recognizing a specific pattern. The true sell signal occurs at point 8, and it develops in conjunction with a Negative Reversal signal in the Composite Index. The Negative Reversal also offers a price projection that the Candlesticks cannot define. The strong selling that follows should not be a surprise as the second peak within the Negative Reversal is again at a crossover of the averages on the Composite Index. Such a juxtaposition in this oscillator's averages can be viewed similarly to a *dead cross*. The opposite occurs when the signal tests the rising short average that is crossing the longer period—similar in interpretation to a *golden cross*.

Point 9 is a *Hammer* that begins a complex progression of conflicts as the bulls and bears fight to gain control. Point 10 is similar to a towers pattern except that the congestion between the towers should have covered more than a single day.

Regardless, it certainly would have been watched with great interest. Point 11 is a two-candlestick pattern called a *Dark Cloud* and correctly warns that the market is still not ready to change trend. Point 12 marks a *Shooting Star* generally viewed as bearish in an uptrend. From the lows, this is not much of an uptrend. But after eight days of indecision over who has control, this is evidence that could tip the scales over to a bearish view. In the short horizon it would have been correct.

A *Harami Cross* develops at point 13 between the Doji and preceding black-bodied candlestick. These two candlesticks would have been widely recognized as a Harami Cross denoting a major bottom. It is also possible that this strong individual bullish pattern combined with the Hammer at point 9 would be viewed as a *Tweezers Bottom* marked at point 14. This very bullish evidence is coupled with the Composite Index signal at point 15. Though not marked, it is an oscillator pivot that also occurs on a trend line for the oscillator as well as the moving average. If you look at the Composite Index relative to the moving averages, this is the first time the oscillator is testing the averages above their lines since the test prior to point 2. Therefore, this is the first occurrence in three months.

With such tremendous bullish evidence, it is no surprise that *Three Advancing Soldiers* follow at marker 16. The group of strong candlesticks has consecutively higher closes, and the third, at point 17, gaps upward on open, opening a *window* of support. The market fails to close the window the next day at point 18. The continuation pattern established by the window is respected by the market, and it proceeds to establish further gains. Point 19 is a Shooting Star leading to a minor pullback. The candlesticks leading into point 20 clearly show a market overextended. The rounding top coincides with an extremely bearish signal in the Composite Index. Point 21 where two hammers develop could be confusing, but not when compared to the oscillator. Point 22 warns to look for renewed selling, and the market goes to the window at point 23. A rebound then follows that is not unexpected. The window was successfully tested, and the Composite Index has formed an extreme oscillator low where the pivot forms a Positive Reversal. These two chart analysis techniques clearly compliment one another extremely well at important market pivots.

Another important topic for discussion is the use of Volume to confirm oscillator signals. Volume can be viewed as actual or tick for intraday charts. I will admit I did not understand the correct interpretation of Volume until I attended George Lane's seminar. The terms *high* and *low* mean something quite different when applied to oscillators. The mystery that was clarified for me was that Volume is only a relative comparison between the points you are studying. Therefore, high Volume does not actually have to be a histogram spike that extends into the upper end of the scale. The bottom line that trading signals in oscillators should be executed only on lower volume. Let's take a closer look.

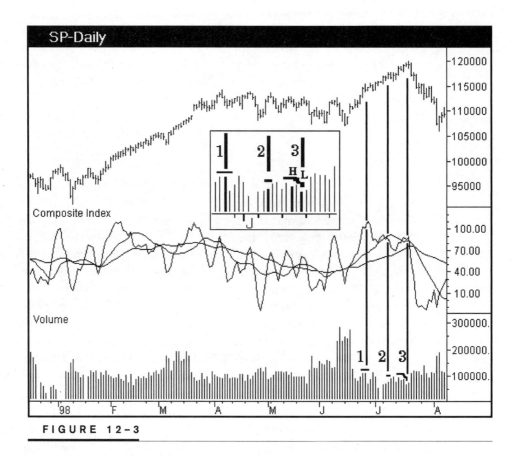

FIGURE 12-3

In Figure 12-3 we have the daily S&P 500 chart. Into the high there are three key oscillator peaks. The chart marks three corresponding lines to show the Volume bars that correspond to the oscillator peaks and price position. As they are really hard to see in this scale, an enlargement of this section has been imbedded into the same chart. Each of the three Volume bars at points 1, 2, and 3 display *declining volume.* The key is to look for relative comparisons. Bar 1 would be viewed High Volume and bar 2 as lower Volume into a price high. It has nothing to do with the fact that extremely high volume days developed June 3 to 16. However, while we are looking at volume into the June price lows, the volume where the market actually bottomed is lower volume compared to the extreme volume high made four days earlier. This shows that the guideline is to *trade oscillator signals only when they are accompanied by lower volume.* Finally, point 3 in the Volume study is actually a narrow double peak in the oscillator. The small M pattern in the Composite Index near line 3 is the signal being highlighted. If you look very closely, the two bars in the insert that correspond to the M pattern in the oscillator show that the High-Low relationship exists.

I do not actually use Volume because my primary market is the S&P, and the Globex data must be used in my charts for wave structure analysis and supporting indicator development. The Globex data would require changing the scale to display Volume so that only Globex data are compared at night. The scale would just have a maximum set much lower to expand the range of the evening session. As a result, I do not use this information.

It is strongly recommended if you trade the S&P market that you do not use just the day session. Many black box system traders use just the day session. In my opinion the market conditions have changed so that we truly have a 24-hour market now in the S&P. I developed this opinion from observing price projections that have been derived just from the day session versus using pivots from both day and Globex data. It would be similar to analyzing currency futures only during the IMM trading sessions. You do that too?! You might want to purchase spot data as well, if for no other reason than spot prices can lead futures so you can have a clearer warning before the pit. Then there is the problem that indicator signals for currency futures can easily miss critical formations because you cannot see all the trading hours. You might want to reconsider this one.

I have no use for Open Interest as it is an analysis indicator only and offers no timing value. I have enough to monitor without adding a signal of this type. However, as I've said before, this is war, and I'll turn to anything if I get lost to regain my bearings if I need to. I understand how to interpret Open Interest, and I might take a peak maybe twice a year, usually at times leading into contract rollovers, a period of time I dread as all the numbers etched in my brain have to be erased and recalculated right from scratch. Contract rollover days to a new front month is time I usually schedule to work with my four-legged friends in the barn. This usually saves me a lot of money and gives me a forced day of R&R. Then once the dust settles on the first day for the new front month, I recalculate all the tables of targets incorporating the new data that have respectable intraday volume.

By now you are probably trying to find the formula for the Composite Index. This indicator has too much to offer to be sealed forever more in a vault. Well, at least in one person's computer. But, on the other hand, I owe it to my investors participating in my pool to not release it immediately to the general public. What to do, what to do? What a dilemma. In the hands of professional traders, the formula is not a problem as everyone is establishing different kinds of positions. Some are outright traders, some are delta neutral, some use different time horizons, etc. However, investors in my funds do not want the formula released at this time. So you see, I do not have all the answers at the moment. Forgive my inconveniencing you, but look toward the Aerodynamic Investments Web site at http://www.aeroinvest.com for the outcome of this sticky dilemma. There will be a decision made. The time from manuscript completion, to publisher, to book launch date is a seven- to eight-month window. I hope to know much more by then.

The final chart in Figure 12-4 is a weekly view of U.S. T-Bond futures. We will make an observation in this chart that will be developed more fully in the next two chapters. We will go through the progression of how to isolate indicator signals that you like or dislike, how to develop new ideas for indicators, and then finally how to develop your own formulas from these ideas. The considerations and evolutionary steps that occur will be discussed as an indicator evolves from idea to statistically viable formula ready for battle. I think the next chapter will be of particular interest as it will discuss why personal bias will impact perceived strength and weaknesses of comparative indicators.

The observation being made in Figure 12-4 is in the moving averages applied to the three oscillators from top to bottom: Stochastics, the RSI, and the

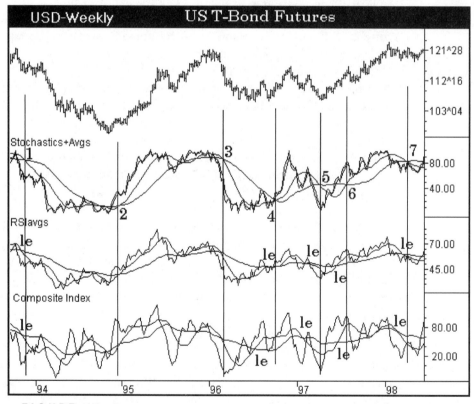

FIGURE 12-4

Composite Index. The periods for all three oscillators have been set up so that key oscillator pivots align. Now look closely at the moving averages on these oscillators. They are crossing at different time intervals. A line is drawn from the moving average crossovers that occur in Stochastics to bisect the other studies. This line is then used to compare the relative timing of the moving averages that cross over in each study. The periods for these averages are all the same. Where you see an "le" marked in the RSI or Composite Index studies, a lead signal has occurred with the study above it. We will use this observation to see if the spread of these averages, or something similar, could be used to develop a custom lead formula to improve the timing of our original Stochastics study.

CHAPTER 13

Evaluating the Comparative Strengths and Weaknesses of Common Indicators

To really understand the personality of any indicator, you need to allow yourself time to have a little fun with it. The more creative you can be, the more useful will be the observations you derive from this process.

Break an indicator apart. Look at it from different angles so that you can see its unique personality or character. We have an objective: to extract or visually enhance the signals we like in Stochastics and to minimize the attributes we could do without. We might even be able to create two studies so that attributes that used to be imbedded in one study formula can be manipulated independently.

Have you ever superimposed one indicator formula on another? (I do not mean using averages with an indicator as we have done in prior chapters.) As an example, the Parabolic study (or Stop and Reversal) has an imbedded acceleration factor. It therefore has greater potential to warn when a momentum oscillator is losing steam than when it is used on price data for which it was designed. In addition, when the Parabolic signal reverses its orientation, it can be used for price projection. You might like what you see when the parabolic formula is charted on the RSI. I will leave that idea for you to explore.

Just when you think you have a firm understanding of the quirks and personality of your formula, go the extra mile or kilometer and chart the indicator in *a totally new way*. The conventional presentation for charting a common indicator may not be the best signal communicator for you. Have you ever considered how your own visual biases will affect your judgment within a two-dimensional chart environment?

A topic that I have not seen discussed relative to technical analysis is how visual distortions can occur from the juxtaposition of indicators. Anatomical considerations do have an influence on our ability to interpret a technical chart. This is an immensely important topic in my opinion, and it is given little consideration by an industry that requires it. I know it will be difficult to understand my bold comment without any background to establish my credibility. So let me digress for just a brief moment.

If a cat has nine lives, you might say I am in my fifth life now. In one of these past lives I served as technical advisor to the National Geographic Society and the Jet Propulsion Laboratories on behalf of the Eastman Kodak Company. That particular job function was only one position during my eleven-year tenure. My last assignment was serving as Brand Manager of Kodak's Professional Color Films. That is not the consumer division. I had the opportunity to work with the best people in the industry who spend their lives studying the technical and psychological aspects of a two- and three-dimensional image in every conceivable way. My comment that technical analysis is overlooking something important is not an uneducated observation.

Kodak had technical evidence to show that the majority of people have less than 57 percent color accuracy. Many men fall in a range below 30 percent. I was cautioned to not evaluate technical charts if they were plotted in blue shades, and I was tested to have 94 percent color accuracy. The reason for the caution is that just one small limitation will translate into other perception errors. I will demonstrate a problem of this nature in a chart for you. You may think, "But how? This is a book that has black-and-white charts!" That is the point. It does not matter. I left Kodak when the Hunt Brothers' Silver crisis and Foreign exchange exposure ignited my interests about markets. I loaded up my wagon and headed East to begin my "fifth" life on Wall Street. This chapter has been intentionally placed just ahead of the chapter that discusses the development of a custom indicator *because understanding your own perception biases will be as important to you as evaluating the indicator formula itself.*

In New York City there is a sidewalk game called "find-the-pea-under-the-shell." The sidewalk "artist" has three shells. He lifts one shell to reveal the pea hidden beneath it. He then instructs you to keep your eye on the shell that hides the pea as he picks up the other two shells to show you that no other peas are hidden. He quickly shuffles all three shells. If you can correctly point to the shell that has the pea under it, you win the money on the table. This is my version of find-the-pea-under-the shell. In Figure 13-1 we see three windows displaying the Daily Yen/$ chart. The data are compressed so that you can see as much of the indicators as possible in these narrow windows. All three windows contain studies called "Stochastics" below the data. You know what Stochastics looks like. Which window has the actual Stochastics study?

What did you pick? The first chart? No. Try again. However, it is the right character for it to be a Stochastics study.

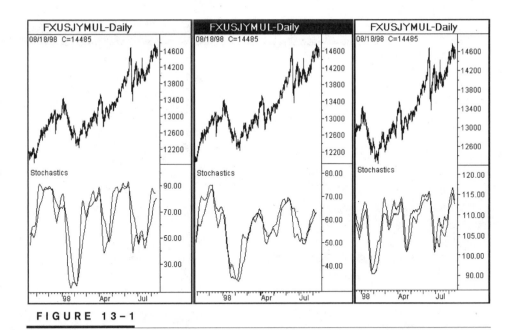

FIGURE 13-1

Ah, you picked the second chart. I like that one too. But it is not Stochastics. Try again.

Then it has to be the third chart, and I did something to the formula. Right? No. Wrong again. In the game of find-the-pea-under-the shell, you have zero chance of winning because the con artist has removed the pea from the first shell. You assumed I offered a correct answer in Figure 13-1 from the way I described the shell game to you. But, like the person who falls prey to this game on the streets of Manhattan, you could not win my game as you could not answer the original question: "Which window has the actual Stochastics study?" None of them.

So what do I really have in these first three charts in Figure 13-1? The chart on the left actually has the Stochastics study removed. These are the averages on the Stochastics study. I'll show you the real Stochastics in a moment. If you want to press this issue, I'll go along. If you know the Stochastics formula well enough to know that the second line in a slow Stochastics study, Slow D, is just a moving average of the signal line, then you could ask, "Is this first window not still Stochastics?" No. The first line plotted would be Slower than Slow Stochastics and technically half of a Stochastics study, but the second line would be a third-generation signal. It is the third line that evolves into something other than Stochastics. We can use this idea later when we want to remove noise that is present in the Stochastics study *without changing the correct setup period for the underlying study itself.*

FIGURE 13-2

Figure 13-2 is the actual Stochastics study using correct setup periods that you can use for comparison. By viewing the separated average in Figure 13-1, with the original study in Figure 13-2, you will find that the indicator low in early 1998 actually forms *bullish divergence* with the Stochastics indicator itself. With the Stochastics study plotted in the same window as the averages, you may not have ever known that divergences frequently develop at key pivots. You will find this to be true when comparing all the major pivots in these two charts except for the pivot high into the April 3, 1998, dollar highs. We need this chart to establish a milestone record before we begin to make evolutionary changes to this study.

In the second window of Figure 13-1 there are two RSI indicators plotted together using different periods. It is important to compare what signal characteristics you like in the Stochastics study and what attributes you would have preferred in the double RSI study. As an example, the 1997 top in the double RSI study is a single peak. The Stochastics study is a triple peak. There is no right or wrong. This is personal preference. Notice after the decline to 127.37 on April 10, 1998, that the double RSI study develops bullish divergence with the Stochastics formula in Figure 13-2. Differences such as these are extremely important observations to make.

What was the study in window 3 of Figure 13-1? Let me first ask you a question before I answer. Did you pick up on the fact that the scale of window 3 has a range outside the dimensions that is possible for a Stochastics study? Most people would not have seen that the oscillator peaks exceed 115. The scale for the real indicators was changed to point out that most people never look at scale anyway. I do not look at scale numbers either as I study relative scale within the chart.

One fateful day a trader visiting from overseas was given my office during the Asian trading session. The visitor went into my underlying CQG variables and changed my RSI period from 14. As you know, I use a precise signal for price projection and must use a fixed period. Anyway, to make a long story short, I was not told of the change, or of the visitor who did not put the indicator value back were he had found it. As my office door was always locked, I had no cause to suspect changes would occur. Later I had to unwind a trade when I could not duplicate a target, thinking I had made a calculation error. When I find one error, there are usually others, and it means that I am exhausted. So I double check everything and arrange to take time off. In this case, I spent two hours trying to find why the numbers had shifted in the RSI. Several hours later the RSI range rules that were slightly off track warned me to check the setup period. The number had been changed only from 14 to 18. That was enough to ruin my day.

We precondition ourselves by following similar patterns day after day. Trying to break up our indicators into different variations will help to break the preconditioning that we create for ourselves.

The third window in Figure 13-1 is what *TradeStation* calls a "Price Oscillator." All that means is that it *began* as a spread between two averages derived from the price data. I created two sets. However, I then set the short average as the long period and the long period as the short (that is, short = 27, long = 21). In doing this, the actual spreads were horizontally flipped. Why do this? Why not. Be creative. This is an exercise. It is just a tool to help study character and generate ideas for thought. Do not trade from the third window, especially since all the trading signals are upside down! You know that any oscillator, not just Stochastics, produces a swing called a *knee* or *shoulder,* when the short period line tests the longer without crossing it. Look more closely at the third window. The entire oscillator is upside when you think about the signal relationships relative to the price movement.

Now we are going to start the indicator comparison. Once individual attributes are identified in Stochastics, we will then separate them. We would like to know if different Stochastics attributes can be controlled or monitored separately. We are going through this exercise so that you might consider that conventional indicators are just optional starting points within a larger technical tool box. The well-known formulas are not sacred entities. We can mix and match components to our heart's content at this stage. This is the step where we can ask ourselves, "What happens when I try to do this?" Sometimes "this" does not look so good as we saw in the third window of Figure 13-1. But I will show you that discarded ideas like "this" could be the solution for "that." Don't toss anything out. However, permit me to turn to a quote from Albert Einstein that goes something like this:

> As one grows older, one sees the impossibility of imposing one's will on the chaos with brute force. But if you are patient, there will come that moment in time, when while eating an apple, the solution will present itself politely and say, "Here I am."

Therefore, the challenge is not to impose our will on the indicators with brute force but to patiently observe them and listen to what the signals have to tell us. At some point we will find the solution that says, "Here I am." Then once an idea has stepped forward with merit, we can begin the laborious work to define probability and establish merit for our new indicator or signal. This will be the focus of the next chapter. In this chapter our mission is to just find a polite solution that shows promise.

In Figure 13-3 we continue to chart the Daily Yen/$. The first indicator under the data is now correctly labeled. It is Stochastics with moving averages, except that the Stochastics study is plotted "white" to block it from view. The study below the Stochastics displays two moving averages derived from the RSI. The averages are a third generation as they are derived from the spread of the RSI study that was plotted in Figure 13-1 in the second window. Averages define a trend so we will call this an *RSI Trend*. The spread itself is blocked from view by plotting it as "white," similarly to the way the Stochastics was hidden.

We need to make some comparisons. At signals 1, 3, 5, and 7, the RSI Trend study leads the signals generated by the averages from Stochastics. Interesting. More interesting is the fact that all these signals are buy signals. Many indicator formulas have a bias between their buy and sell signals. Signals at positions 2, 4, and 6 have similar timing, but the appearance is very different. While signals 2 and 6 are fairly clear in the RSI Trend, the Stochastic averages are superior in signal 4. You are allowed to disagree at any time. What works for me may not work for you. But this is how you might go through the process of discovering what you like.

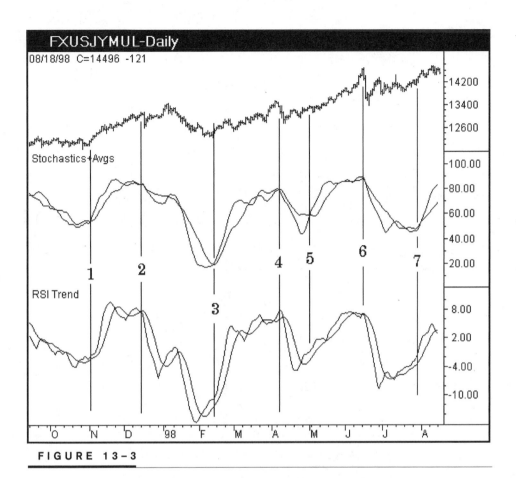

FIGURE 13-3

In Figure 13-4 we add additional information by plotting the slower Stochastics signal line. The fast Stochastics would just add noise to this exercise so it is not included in this step. Signal 1 adds no additional information to what we had in Figure 13-3. Signal 2 is much improved by adding the %D Stochastics line. Stochastics tests the averages after divergence with price and succeeds to move only up to the averages, but not through them.

It might be said that the averages on Stochastics give the illusion of rolling over and down more steeply in Figure 13-4 than in Figure 13-3. This will be hard for you to see perhaps. Photographic DlogE charts require an eye to see a 2 percent slope shift. The impact squiggles have when they are next to one another could of itself become a book. By having Stochastics visually extend the sloping line for your eye with the pop into the November oscillator high, the perception will be suggested that the slope is steeper in Figure 13-4 than in Figure 13-3. If

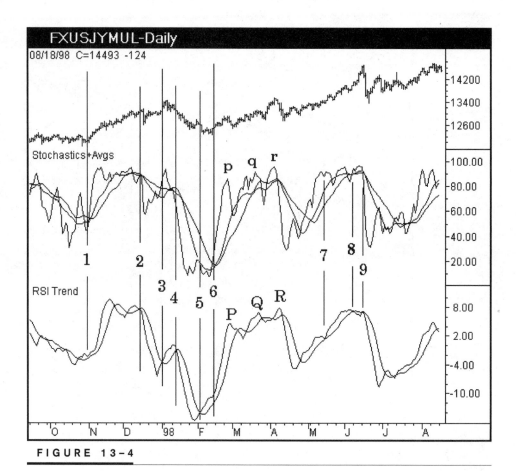

FIGURE 13-4

you do not see this at all, skip it for now; if you do, try to understand why this is occurring. Signal 3 in Figure 13-4 was omitted in the last chart and might as well have been missed in this one. It does not add much value overall in the way it is displayed. The timing between oscillators at signal 4 is slightly different. Signal 5 shows that the RSI is early, which warns that the accompanying Stochastics signal is premature. I like this signal a lot because it just saved money. Signal 6 is the true signal generated by Stochastics and confirmed by the RSI Trend. Then it becomes very interesting. Peaks at positions p, q, and r in Stochastics are similar to peaks P, Q, and R in the RSI Trend study. But, looking at the differences between peak q and Q, it could be suggested that there is a cleaner signal at Q.

Now move over to signal 7. I like the fact that the range in the RSI Trend is not as overbought as indicated by Stochastics. However, it is extremely important to know how to read the Stochastics signal at point 7. *The first time the Stochastics signal moves to the top of the chart at point 7 and then pulls back from this over-bought extreme to a level near 75 to 80, it is a buy signal.* The RSI Trend indicator confirms this interpretation. Because the signal just touches the rising average, it might be easier to interpret than its Stochastics countersignal. Two indicators, exact same interpretation, but they convey information in very different ways. We discussed in the price projection section how this Stochastics formation could then be used to project the next targets.

Signal 8 is early for both indicators, and the signals are easy to interpret with this conclusion. Signal 9 is again biased preference. I like sell signals that cross down and then challenge averages from below rather than triple peak patterns as displayed by Stochastics. That way the averages that the RSI signal is challenging become a way of determining where I could be wrong. Lane would use volume to confirm signal 9. Signal 9 should have lower volume than signal 8. Had there been lower volume present in signal r compared to q, that would also have given permission from Stochastics to sell. It shows you that similar interpretations can be derived from very different indicator patterns. What will work and shout a buy or sell signal for one person will not be the case for another. The differences that I am describing at signal 9 are based on my knowing the character of an indicator intimately. Buy Stochastics at 75 and sell with a reverse signal at 25 will be alarming to someone just learning to see very simple divergence.

I like the fact that signal 3 in the Stochastics study in Figure 13-3 was preceded by an earlier crossover in the RSI Trend indicator. The difficulty is that signal 7 in Figure 13-3 is much too early and might have caused an early market position, netting a loss. Let's try to see if we can balance these signals so that both can be more easily identified.

In Figure 13-5 the points 3 and 7 have been repeated from Figure 13-3. I have added the spread itself between two RSIs, and I have plotted the result as a histogram. When the Stochastics %D line was added to Figure 13-4, the additional information was then considered to see if it added value or just noise at key points along the chart. We need to do likewise for this new addition to the current chart. The averages we have been viewing in Figures 13-3 and 13-4 have not been changed, but the spread between two RSIs will be considered as a factor. We can look at two variations and call them RSI Trend2 and RSI Trend3. The first thing you will notice is what happens when we add a histogram. The study assumes a very different appearance. The use of three indicators shows a progression of signals at pivot points 1, 2, and 3. Point 1 leads point 2, point 2 leads point 3. The price low corresponds to signal 3 in Figure 13-3. The confusion in signal 7 from our evaluation of Figure 13-3 also appears to be easier to read. These two signals suggest that we should make a more detailed comparison to see what contributions are made at all the key signal points in this chart.

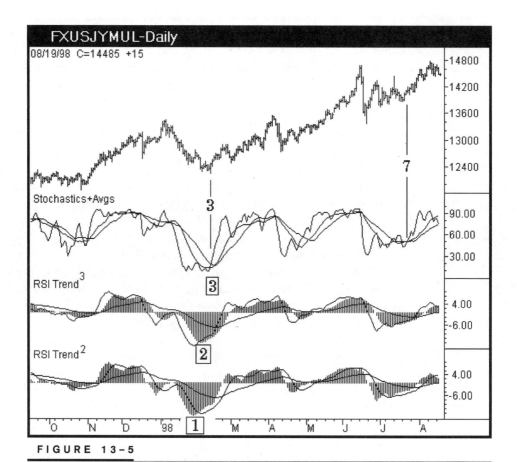

FIGURE 13-5

In Figure 13-6 we again have three studies, but we are not going to discuss them right away. You have just been caught in a depth perception trap. I warned you that I would do it at some point. You have been caught up in a depth of field problem. Indicators will reproduce this type of problem often, and you may not realize it consciously. I did not need color. But just think what I could do to you in color! RSI Trend2 and RSI Trend3 *are the exact same indicators* in Figure 13-5. I am hard to fool when I have been told to look out for it. So Figure 13-6 was added before I lifted your blindfold just in case someone, like me, would have noticed the discussion changes direction after the "ringer" chart. So we jumped one chart ahead to help with the disguise. In fact, we are not done with Figure 13-5. Not by a long shot!

Figure 13-5 displays RSI Trend2 and RSI Trend3. If you look more closely to these indicators at signal 3, you will find that RSI Trend2's histogram is the lower boundary of the single line in RSI Trend3. In RSI Trend3 the histogram is the lower boundary of the line in RSI Trend2. The two moving averages we simply called the "RSI Trend" in Figures 13-3 and 13-4 have been plotted as histograms. Therefore, the signals are mathematically identical as the crossover points cannot be changed. If you have a problem seeing this, it will become clearer in a few pages. The third line that was added is just another average with a longer period. Your mind played a trick on you, and you likely agreed with me when I suggested that RSI Trend2 was a lead signal for RSI Trend3 at the low. Both studies are identical, but the presentation of the information became very different in how it was interpreted. Therefore, I will use RSI Trend2 and discard RSI Trend3 in the next step. It is for this reason that we must depart from this comparative study to fully address depth perception problems in technical charts. Then we will return to Figure 13-6, the next step in our original discussion, and be able to make an educated judgment about our signal preferences.

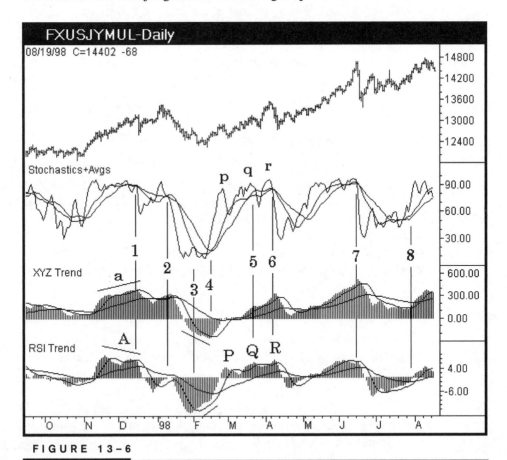

FIGURE 13-6

Why is depth perception so difficult, and why does it become a factor when we look at a two-dimensional chart? The world is three dimensional, but how does this fact change our ability to interpret a chart? Anatomically we can see only a visual representation of our environment in two dimensions. Somehow, we need to recover the third dimension, which is depth. As we cannot see depth, the problem we have with a chart is that our mind assumes *it must always recover the third dimension.* Depth is called the *median plane.* Our minds will unconsciously look for subtle cues to create a solution for the missing plane that has been omitted in our charts. To understand depth perception problems, as they relate to chart analysis, it is necessary to understand how we are able to see depth at all.

Generally, there is a great deal of information about depth available to us. The subtleties our mind searches for are *depth cues.* Some of these depth cues are linear perspective, texture gradient, elevation, interposition, clarity and aerial perspective, and visual angle. When you look at a chart, you will be very surprised to know that all six of these informational cues may have an impact on how you see it. Learning to analyze a chart is really a matter of learning to see. *To see correctly.* That means a good deal more than merely looking with the eye. We will look at all six depth perception types, and then I will refer to specific chart formations to demonstrate how these principles will have an immediate impact on traders.

LINEAR PERSPECTIVE

Linear perspective is perhaps the one with which you are most familiar. It is common knowledge that lines or edges that are truly parallel, such as railway tracks, *converge upward* as they recede from an observer. The greater the distance, the closer the lines will appear until they merge as one into the distance. The mathematical system for creating the illusion of space and distance on a flat surface originated in Florence, Italy, in the early 1400s. It was an architect, Leon Battista Alberti, who first wrote down the rules of linear perspective.

Technical analysts need to understand the mathematical components of linear perspective because these depth cues have a major influence on how we will see signals in a chart. The example of receding railway tracks is the simplest mathematical system called *one-point perspective.* When we look at charts, we will be applying *two- or three-point perspective* based on the chart patterns we are viewing. So let's review one-point perspective to ensure that everyone understands the fundamentals.

The basics of one-point perspective are illustrated in Figure 13-7. Whatever you are looking at, a three-dimensional chocolate chip cookie or a two-dimensional chart, there will be a *Horizon Line.* If you look out at an ocean's horizon from the cockpit of a plane, or look out from a seashore while sitting on the beach, the hori-

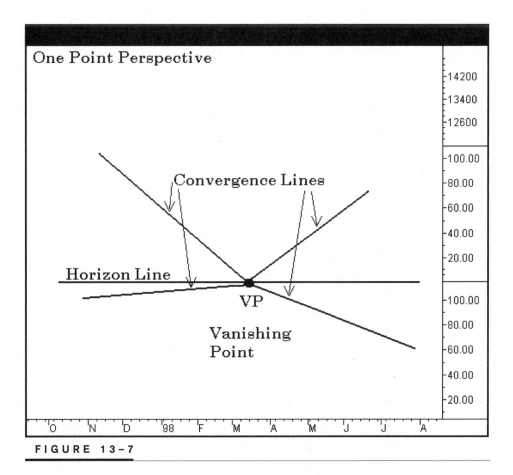

FIGURE 13-7

zon line will always be at your eye level. This invisible plane cuts through everything, including your chart! Your horizon line will always be at eye level regardless
of where you are looking. If you look down on the trading desk, the horizon line
does not change as your eye level remains the height of your eyes.

The *Vanishing Point* is the point to which all lines that are parallel to the
viewer recede. In one-point perspective only lines that are moving away from or
to a viewer seem to recede on the horizon at the vanishing point. Verticals and hor-
izontals stay the same. In a chart the vertical and horizontal lines of the chart grid
establish the reference points for our mind to then try to use the indicator swings
as points to define a vanishing point. *All the points that can be connected to suggest a line leading to the vanishing point are called Convergence Lines.*

In Figure 13-8 I have extracted the Stochastics signal from Figure 13-4.
Above it is the moving average signal that was displayed in Figure 13-3. I stated

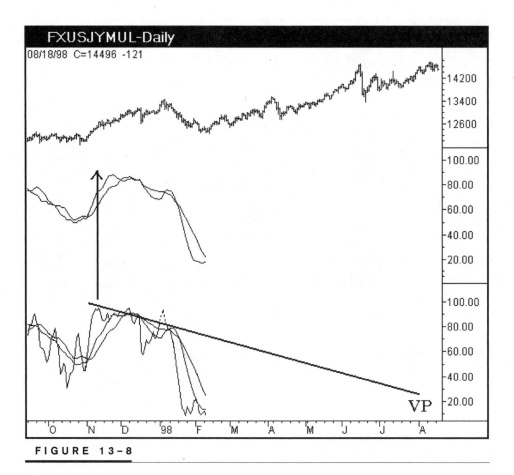

FIGURE 13-8

that the slope of the average with the Stochastics indicator appeared to be more steep than the chart displaying the averages alone. The reason for this is that our eye will use this first Stochastics oscillator peak as additional information. The new Stochastics peak adds a point that is closer to the edge of the chart's frame, making it easier for us to *unconsciously* determine where the Vanishing Point is located within this chart. As a result, our eye uses this visual cue to create a converging line to mark a vanishing point. It does not matter that Stochastics forms a peak at a later time that exceeds this convergence line. The peak is filtered out as noise and indicated as being filtered by a broken line for the Stochastics travel. Orthogonal lines are visual rays that connect points from an outer edge of a chart toward the vanishing point. The Stochastics peak in Figure 13-8 becomes more important than the inner peak that is a broken line because the first is closer to the outer frame. The first peak in Stochastics serves as the origin for an orthogonal line. The fact that the Vanishing Point leads to the far right, not to the center as was drawn in Figure 13-7, shows that the mathematical system defining one-point perspective is insufficient for this chart.

We know our brains are extremely complex computers. When we present an abstract chart to our central computer, it tries to reference known variables. The placement of an object defines two-point linear perspective. All we need is *one corner* and our mind will try to complete the shape. It is the angles of the object that define where the vanishing points are located. In Figure 13-8 our mind will assume it has located one of the angles for our abstract puzzle to define depth. The vanishing point leads to the right in the chart. Sometimes one vanishing point in two-point perspective *will not be on the page.* Our mind will approximate where the point falls beyond our chart dimensions. Distortions are minimized when our mind establishes where the horizon line is located. Some charts will have a horizon line

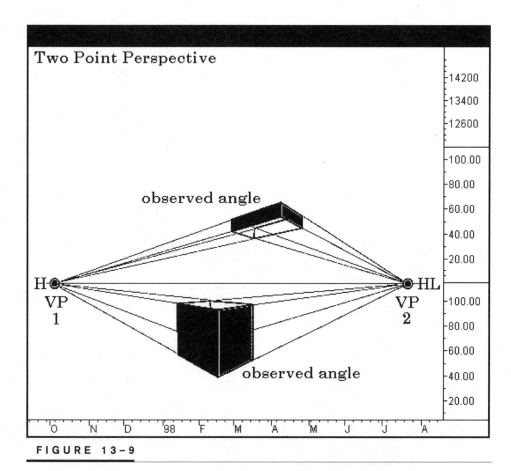

FIGURE 13-9

defined. That actually adds to our problem as the visual cue becomes stronger. An example would be the zero line for a histogram. When the object we are looking at does not have a perpendicular or parallel point, our mind's-eye will find a "corner" within the abstract from which to extrapolate a converging line to a vanishing point. That is what is forming in Figure 13-8. Each of the corners that mark the start of a convergence line in Figure 13-9 becomes the dominant point. Therefore, chart 13-8 has a dominant point predefined at the first Stochastics peak that is not a trading signal but becomes an influential point to all other information we are analyzing within this chart.

Because we are dealing with an abstract image, a third point can come into play that is normally used only with extreme heights or lows. Not only will there be the two vanishing points along a horizon line but there will be an upward or downward recession to a third vanishing point. *The third vanishing point will*

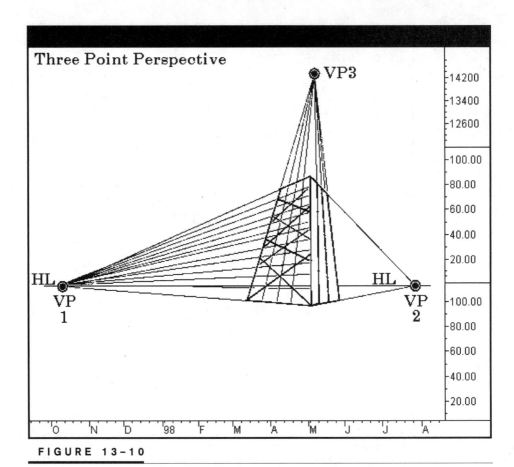

FIGURE 13-10

FIGURE 13-11

always be 90 degrees to the horizon line. Many complex technical chart squiggles will provide points that lead to a projected third vanishing point.

Figure 13-5 was the chart that I used to catch you visually in a depth perspective trap. The trap itself was an example of three-point perspective. The master of three-point perspective traps is M. C. Escher. Let's look at his work *Sunmoon* in Figure 13-11 and then return to look at the chart in Figure 13-5 to point out the similarities of the distortion that misled us.

In Escher's work, there is frequently a play on depth of field. Our mind alternates the dominant image in an effort to determine the correct vanishing points. Generally we see the darker image first and then allow that pattern to recede, allowing us to view the lighter pattern.

The chart in Figure 13-12 is the same chart as Figure 13-5 that was used to visually trick you. RSI Trend2 and RSI Trend3 appear to give different signals at points *A* and *B*. However, the indicator on the bottom of the chart shows you more

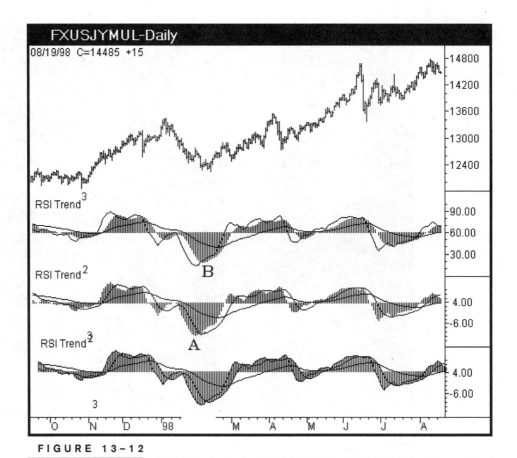

FIGURE 13-12

clearly that RSI Trends 2 and 3 are in fact the exact same signals. The only difference is that different areas have been selected to plot a filled histogram pattern. Be aware of the visual impact when you add a histogram. The vertical lines of a histogram are 90 degrees to horizontal, and everything else that follows in your chart will be processed as an image that has height and a third vanishing point. The histogram in RSI Trend2 at point *A* becomes even more significant because *it is closest to the outer frame of the chart* and is also an orthogonal line of convergence. Therefore, the pattern that must be used is Trend2, and we will discard Trend3 when we continue this indicator evaluation.

TEXTURE GRADIENT

Another depth cue that we use to define our missing median plane is called the *texture gradient.* This cue becomes important when there are no straight lines present in an image. This is the case in Figure 13-12. When linear lines are absent, our mind will process any element—such as a dot (parabolic), indicator peak, or pivot—to try to determine the rate at which the elements change size. Our mind's-eye sees objects that become smaller and more closely packed together as depth that has an increasing rate of change. This rate normally depends on the slope of the ground. When there is no ground within a chart, our eye may see the juxtaposition of certain indicator patterns as depth cues. You will not be caught by this problem, but it is likely one that motivated you to move your vertical line cursor over to a peak or low for further clarification.

ELEVATION

Objects that fall between us and our horizon will normally appear higher up the farther they are from us. The railway tracks receding into the vanishing point will always move upward to the vanishing point. This upward movement becomes a visual cue from which our eye will travel within a chart. Elevation cues are a given fact and help to set up a visual problem when combined with interposition cues.

INTERPOSITION

Normally texture appears to be more dense in a distant object than in an identical but closer object. However, some depth cues will be stronger than others. This is the case when one object obscures part of another. We frequently obscure another indicator such as an average when multiple studies are used as an overlay in a chart. The partly obscured object will be viewed as farther away. However, your mind may again trick you, as illustrated in Figure 13–13. The farther object appears to be closer because the cutout gives us a pseudo-interposition. It looks as though the smaller card is in front of the larger when in fact, the smaller is positioned behind the larger card with a cutout. Before moving away from Figure 13-13, can you tell if the card that is actually in back is the same size in both illustrations? I suspect you will have to use your PRC—that is, your precision ratio compass or proportional divider—to prove that these two smaller cards are identical in size. The image on the left I created from the image on the right, so all four cards are in fact the same. However, adding the width of one pixel line to the inside boundary of the smaller card on the left will make it appear larger than its counterpart on the right. That is because shadows are also depth perception cues. When you draw a trend line on a chart, you can shift the proportional dimensions within it. They will be relative if the line is long enough across your chart. But short lines can contribute to visual errors or distortions.

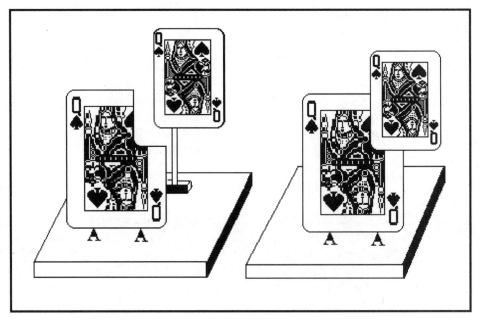

FIGURE 13-13

CLARITY AND AERIAL PERSPECTIVE

It is harder to see the details on objects that are farther away from us than on identical objects that are up close. This alone does not become a factor in a two-dimensional chart, but its near cousin Aerial Perspective does have a play in chart analysis. This refers to the fact that far objects appear bluish to us because the wavelength frequencies from ultraviolet to blue are scattered in our atmosphere in a higher proportion than reds that fall within the infrared segment of light's wavelength frequency spectrum.

Because we are used to associating blues as distant, these cues can be used to our advantage or disadvantage in a chart. *TradeStation* offers 16 colors that traders can use for their drawing tools and markings that we may add to any chart. Use them wisely. Fibonacci lines do not have to compete for attention with your price data. Select a soft gray for a Fibonacci line and watch it immediately fall a perceived distance behind price. Be very aware of the impact of the color you use for your signal line. It should not be the recessive one when viewing the technical study. The vendors that offer only colors of equal intensity (brightness) and saturation (color intensity) need to wake up and move out of the dark ages for charting capabilities. It is essential that the technical information on your chart be compatible with your depth perception capabilities. Get after your vendor to make changes if the only colors you can use force you to view needless noise. (As an example, CQG for Windows.)

VISUAL ANGLE

This is the sixth depth perception cue that will have an impact on our ability to analyze a chart. This cue requires anatomical considerations and elementary physics to relate lens equations into something useful that we can apply. *Visual Angle* is a depth cue affected by pupil size and lens power. Everyone sees differently, and that is why it is as important to know our personal biases as it is to know the indicator patterns and underlying formulas themselves.

Visual Angle refers to the size of the image on the retina. When we look at similar objects, the one farther away has a smaller image on the back of our eye. Whether your computer screen is touching your nose or sitting at the end of a table, the size of the object in terms of visual angle *is independent of distance.*

Figure 13-14 shows us mathematically why one degree of visual angle plus perceived distance can determine height. So how is it we can judge the size of an object when the visual angle of an object on the back of our eye is

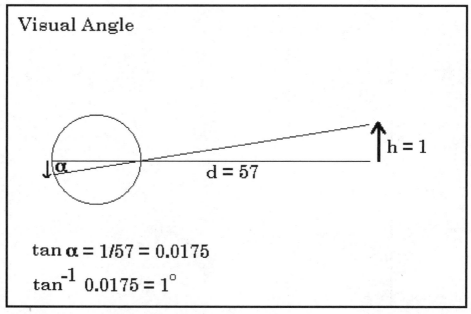

Visual Angle

$h = 1$

$d = 57$

$\tan \alpha = 1/57 = 0.0175$

$\tan^{-1} 0.0175 = 1°$

FIGURE 13-14

changing all the time? The fact that an object can look the same size regardless of changing retinal image size is referred to as *size constancy*. How this relates to analyzing a chart is that frequently the only cue our brain has to work with is visual angle. As it knows it must define the missing plane of depth derived from distance cues, our interpretive abilities may begin to get creative, and that is when distortions occur.

One of the depth cues of greatest interest to us as traders is *Retinal Disparity*. The term refers to the fact that, because our eyes are separated horizontally, each eye processes different views of any object. What does disparity do for us? It is the slight disparity between the two pictures on the back of our eye that gives us depth. Our two-dimensional image of a chart is the same as the image that forms in our eyes when we look out the window. The brain views two-dimensional views from slightly different visual angles and integrates them into one three-dimensional image. *Over 10 percent of humans are stereoblind.* There are great differences in our stereovision ability. If you are stereoblind, you will depend on other depth cues that are monocular. The aerial perspective we discussed, which makes distant objects appear less clear and bluish, will be monocular. Therefore, we have all developed different depth cue dependencies that match our anatomical abilities.

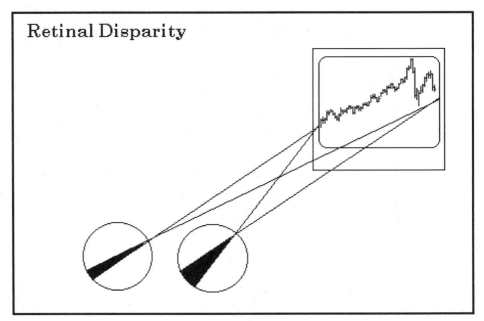

FIGURE 13-15

One of my eyes is stronger than the other, so I always offset my primary trading screen to the right. Figure 13-15 will show you why making this change produces a smaller visual angle in my left eye covering less surface area than what is being projected onto the back of my right eye. The purpose is to capitalize on a stronger visual processor and thereby reduce error. It is easy to determine which eye of yours is stronger or weaker. Cover one eye and read text. One eye will handle the task easily, the other will hurt. More likely the eye you first wanted to cover is your weaker eye.

Knowing how we process visual information allows us to return to our original discussion about the strengths and weaknesses of indicators. I cannot put together a table of numerous indicator studies and categorize their signals for you as one being better than another. *Only you can really determine what will work for you or not based on your own biases.* So may I strongly suggest that you spend some time and give some thought to which chart patterns and signals work best for you. With that in mind, we can return to the chart that was evolving from a Stochastics study. My personal preference is to view a clean histogram, so that the signals within Stochastics are evolving into a different presentation graphic. The signals will be nearly identical, but the different presentation of the information offers clarity for me in situations in which Stochastics alone would be hard for me to interpret.

Figure 13-16 is in fact the exact same chart as Figure 13-6. Stochastics with averages remains plotted under the price data, and the bottom is the stronger visual of the two histograms we viewed in Figure 13-5. The middle histogram with averages is called the *XYZ Trend* to disguise its origin for just a short period of time.

We are evaluating the combined signals in the XYZ Trend and the study called the RSI Trend as they compare to Stochastics. At points *a* and *A,* divergence is present. Pattern *A* clearly confirms signal 1 in Stochastics. However, the fact that pattern *a* displays strengths may warn that the market will have sufficient momentum to attempt another advance that would create a more complex top in the other indicators. At signal 2 this is indeed what occurs. The XYZ Trend is now diverging as well with prices. It is an extremely important observation to make that the RSI Trend is failing just as it tests the zero line. We must later test other market moves that occur in a histogram where the pivot becomes the zero line.

At signal 3 the reverse is developing from what we saw at signal 1. This mirror image between buy and sell signals is important. At signal 3 the RSI Trend is rolling up, but the XYZ Trend is suggesting that the market may have sufficient momentum to still attempt another bottom. At signal 4 both histograms are

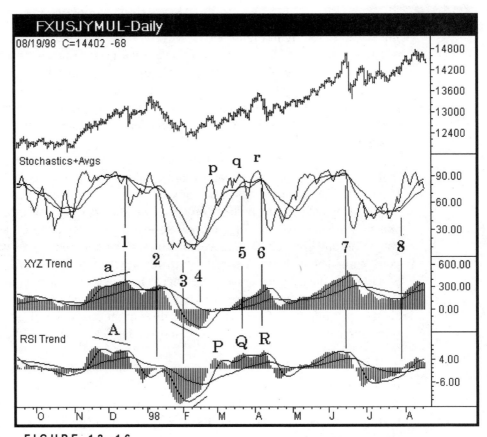

FIGURE 13-16

rolling upward. Points *p, q,* and *r* and *P, Q,* and *R* have been discussed in a prior chart. Signal 7 is much improved by the RSI Trend. However, notice that the moving averages at signal 2 in this indicator had a negative spread where the shorter-period average has crossed below the longer-period average. In signal 7 the averages are positive. This is an observation that would require back-testing to define statistically whether it is important or not. (It is.) In the XYZ Trend, the oscillator is not diverging prior to the intervention. However, the indicator is at a historic high peak within this chart. Extremes would have to be back-tested in this indicator to see if there is information at this peak that we are missing when it is seen as only an isolated case in the chart. Signal 8 offers perfect timing between the RSI Trend signal and the Stochastics indicator as we have seen at other points in this chart.

If using a histogram is useful when plotting the averages from the spread of two RSI indicators, what would we gain by applying this idea to Stochastics itself? Figure 13-17 shows Stochastics as a histogram. It is extremely noisy with all the long bars plotting an area under the averages.

We can fix this visual problem, as shown in Figure 13-18. Did I gain anything by changing how I am presenting the Stochastics study? I will let you decide that one on your own. However, it is clear that the Stochastic signals we transferred or emulated in the histograms called the "XYZ" and "RSI Trends" allow independent control of some of the attributes we observed in the Stochastics study. So what is the mystery indicator called the "XYZ Trend"? Why it is the third window in Figure 13-1 that we all thought looked downright useless. It is the spread of two averages on price that define the histogram. Then a 9- and 45-period moving average of this histogram was added. Not so useless after all.

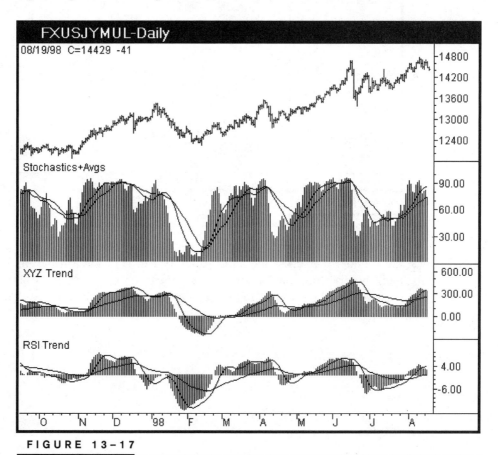

FIGURE 13-17

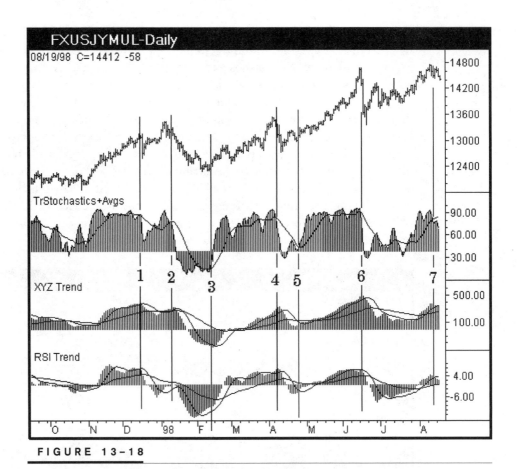

FIGURE 13-18

Once you think you have an idea with merit, you must rigorously examine it under a microscope and ruthlessly test it in a real-time market environment before you consider it to be a tool to be used in actual battle. How we prepare an indicator for final battle will be the subject for discussion in the final chapter.

CHAPTER 14

The Derivative Oscillator

In the last chapter we saw how to generate ideas that might evolve into a custom indicator formula. The first step, which only identifies new indicators with merit within a limited data sample, must then be rigorously tested with a large data base so that it becomes statically proven to be viable. Not all indicators will be intended for all markets, nor will they be used constantly. The Derivative Oscillator is a custom formula that was developed to resolve trading problems associated with complex market corrections or to provide very clean signals to help reenter a market that has a *very* strong trend. Both problems would seem to contradict one another, but in fact the same oscillator can be used as a guide in both market environments.

Traditional momentum oscillators—such as Momentum, RSI, Stochastics, and MACD—form numerous signals when a correction becomes very prolonged and drags out over a period of time. The momentum formulas themselves become less effective in very large triangles when data becomes choppy and congested. On the other hand, in very strong markets another problem occurs. These formulas may appear to become locked in a certain position and offer little information when we emotionally need them most, which is particularly true in intraday trading. I needed a visual aid that could be used with equity indices at these difficult junctures that would compliment and strengthen the signals of the other indicators you have seen applied throughout this book.

The Derivative Oscillator is the first custom formula that I developed in an effort to resolve a specific market problem. *It is not used all the time.* This was also true of the volatility bands we discussed in the beginning of Part 3. These are specific solutions for isolated problems. The formulas and periods defined are optimized for Global equity indices. Different periods would be required to use these formulas in other financial markets.

The Derivative Oscillator formula is a triple smoothed derivative of the RSI plotted as a histogram. The idea for this indicator was born from a similar evolution that we explored together in the last chapter. However, through rigorous testing, the idea evolved even further. This chapter will help you see how a new indicator is further developed from one with possible merit to one that is ready to be introduced to real battle.

In Figure 13-16 the RSI Trend oscillator formed one significant signal right on the zero line at point 2. This signal position at the zero line became extremely valuable when it was explored further. It was also observed that the Derivative Oscillator formula forms *precise* equality relationships between the crest highs and trough lows. This mathematical equality between oscillator peak highs and lows adds clarity to the identification of high-risk pivot levels without the usual lag time. At some oscillator positions I do not have to wait for the oscillator to actually roll over or upward to trigger a signal. Displacement from the zero line alone is sufficient.

Figure 14-1 is a Daily chart of the S&P 500 futures market. The oscillator directly below price is the Derivative Oscillator. The oscillator on the bottom is the industry's standard Momentum Indicator. The amplitude is the differential between a crest high and an oscillator's trough low. The equality relationship

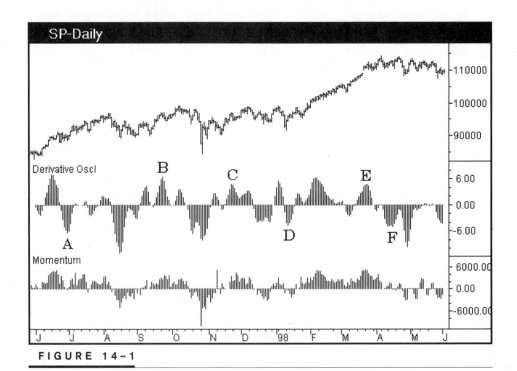

FIGURE 14-1

between crest highs and lows is always measured from the midpoint or zero line to the maximum displacement where the oscillator forms a top or bottom. In this chart, oscillator displacements A and B are equal from the zero line. Equality also occurs between points (C and D) and (E and F), then with closer examination even points (D and E) share equality displacements from zero. More information will be offered on this specific characteristic later in this chapter.

The Derivative Oscillator compared to the Momentum Indicator is clearly less noisy and offers cleaner signals. That is what I was striving for. After a volatile period in the market when fatigue is a major factor, having a few indicators that offer very clean patterns to lean on for a critical decision can be invaluable. The Derivative Oscillator cannot be used alone. This indicator is a warning that we should go look for other reasons that the market could pivot from nearby levels.

The Derivative Oscillator is not intended for bar charts under 30 minutes. The indicator's purpose is to warn us when a more extensive pattern should be expected. In these situations the fewer the signals generated by the indicator, the better. The core of this chapter was actually the first one written when I began this massive project. A revision to a journal article that I wrote years earlier seemed less intimidating than to begin with a title that read "Chapter 1." That was a scary proposition to me three months ago. Figure 14-1 recorded the market position when the book was first started in early June 1998. A fifth wave rally was favored from this correction. The next three months certainly gave us a thorough test of every method we use. I don't know about you, but I'm exhausted!

The S&P 500 has had some interesting turns and sharp moves since we tracked it live from the market highs in July in the Elliott Wave chapter. It is now Saturday, August 22, 1998. The Elliott chapter was worth the time we spent to make a day-to-day diary, but my August 15 deadline to deliver this book to McGraw-Hill has been stretched to a limit. (It takes as long to shuttle a book through production, it seems, as it does to write a book.) Even with a pressing deadline problem, I cannot resist showing you the Derivative Oscillator in the September S&P 500 as it held up so well during these tough times.

In Figure 14-2 is the 60-minute chart for the September S&P 500 on Friday, August 21. The DJIA had an interesting day freefalling nearly 300 points and then rebounding into the close to finish down -77. The S&P experienced a 45-point drop and sharp rebound closing at -7.70. Just another quiet day on Wall Street! You know you are becoming an old dog when you view such a move as, "Same old thing, different day. Here we go again," calmly swinging at whatever develops on the screen. The key reversal, however, was not a surprise as Figure 14-2 shows. The oscillator low at F was recorded at a similar extreme in this time horizon. This exact signal has been isolated and back-tested so that there is little doubt of its interpretation when the markets turn into emotional chaos. Each signal must be isolated and tested in this

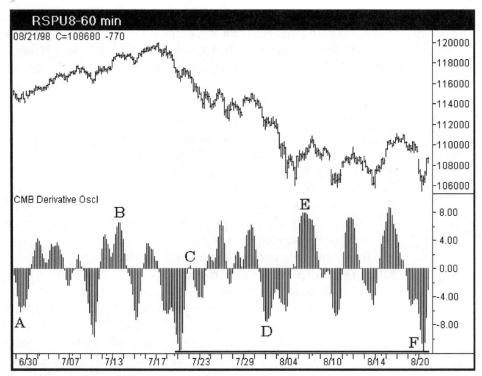

FIGURE 14-2

manner with a database that offers statistical validation. We will avoid the boring drudgery of describing columns of test results. The process was described once in the RSI chapter, and that is likely sufficient to explain the process. However, know that every signal that will be defined in this chapter requires independent testing and is an essential step in a new indicator's development.

Point C in Figure 14-2 shows you that a failure at the zero line again leads to a strong move. Also notice that the oscillator rocketed upward into the pivot at C from the prior low. Prices did not match the acceleration of the indicator—a clear warning that we discussed for all momentum oscillators about the direction of the larger trend. Equality peak displacements from the zero line form between pivots A and B, and again at D and E.

The extreme low at F indicated a sharp rebound would develop, but it is not the bottom for this decline. The suspected zigzag pattern down that was suggested in Chapter 10 remains on course. The oscillator peak preceeding point F was likely the end of wave B up. Now wave C down is beginning to unfold. These pivots need further explanation as do other signals not marked in this chart.

The charts that follow are all clearly from the first of June when the book was started. In an effort to reduce the stress of my editor and his production support staff, I will not revise each chart as the content showing how the Derivative Oscillator was developed is unaffected.

The Derivative Oscillator formula is a triple smoothed RSI. The formula incorporates two exponential moving averages and a simple moving average:

Step 1: An exponential average of a 14-period RSI is calculated.

Step 2: The result in step 1 is used to produce a new exponential moving average using a shorter period than that used in step 1.

Step 3: A simple moving average is then obtained from the result in step 2.

Step 4: The difference between the results obtained in steps 2 and 3 is calculated. The result is then charted as a histogram.

Omega *TradeStation* and Omega *SuperCharts* both use the symbol XAverage to denote an exponential moving average. A custom formula can be created for *TradeStation* in the following manner:

Input: LENGTH(14),PERIOD(9), PERIOD2(45);
    Plot1((XAverage(XAverage((RSI(Close,14)),5),3))-(Average
    (XAverage(XAverage((RSI(Close,14)),5),3),9)),"Plot")

The format to use in *SuperCharts* or when you want to change the periods within the indicator follows:

(XAverage(XAverage((RSI(Close,LENGTH)),PERIOD),PERIOD2))-
(Average (XAverage(XAverage((RSI(Close,LENGTH)),PERIOD),
PERIOD2),PERIOD3))

All equity markets should use a 14-period RSI for reasons discussed in prior chapters. The first and second exponential moving averages are 5 and 3, respectively, for Period and Period2. The simple moving average uses a 9-period in the Period3 location of the formula. I have used both a 9 and 45 simple average in this formula depending on the market. That is also what was used for the formulas with which we were experimenting in the prior chapter.

This indicator was designed for use with equity indices. The following have all been tested and applied in real-time for over six years now: the German Dax, London FTSE, American S&P and DJIA, Hang Seng, and Japanese Nikkei Indices. The formula can be used with cash currency or currency future markets. You may find that alternate periods for these markets will be desired. In the currency formula, a 45-period simple average, rather than 9, is useful. However, *never use this formula with bonds from any country.* Bonds have an entirely different character than other financial markets.

A profitability evaluation of the Derivative Oscillator as it applies to the DJIA was detailed in depth when this indicator was first introduced in a quarterly technical journal of the Market Technicians Association.[1] This evaluation will be excluded in this discussion in order to focus more fully on the application of the indicator and the specific signals that were tested. This chapter adds new information not offered in the original journal article.

OSCILLATOR EQUALITY DISPLACEMENT

The oscillator characteristic of equality displacement from the zero line between cycle bottoms and tops has been demonstrated in Figures 14-1 and 14-2. The equality displacement is attributed to the dominant market cycles and can be useful in filtering cycle noise that may add confusion when price data alone is evaluated.

DIVERGENCE

Figure 14-3 is the German Dax Index in a daily time horizon. It illustrates how divergence between price and the Derivative Oscillator will develop. The two sell signals marked on the chart show that the oscillator peaks do not confirm the new price highs. The four buy signals introduce you to the importance of each major change in direction in this oscillator. The chart also demonstrates that some markets will develop diverging tops while a single turn upward from a significant oscillator low is all that will occur for a resuming uptrend. Observing the character for a specific market is extremely important for all technical studies as we have seen. The German Dax chart has numerous signals not marked on the chart to provide you with just a foundation of the more obvious attributes in this oscillator.

BUY AND SELL SIGNAL CHARACTER

Let's move on to Figure 14-4 displaying the S&P 500 futures contract in a daily bar chart on the left and the weekly time horizon on the right. The chart deliberately omits some signals on the far left so that you may go back and study some of the unmarked signals after all the marked pivots have been defined. There are eight buy signals and eight sell signals marked in this daily chart. They are all numbered 1 through 8. The weekly chart has three oscillator lows marked with

---

1 Connie Brown "The Derivative Oscillator: A New Approach for an Old Problem." *Market Technicians Association Journal* (Winter 1993–Spring 1994, Issue 42), pp. 45–63. Market Technicians Association, One World Trade Center, Suite 4447, New York, New York 10048. Their Web site address is: http://www.mta-usa.org/.

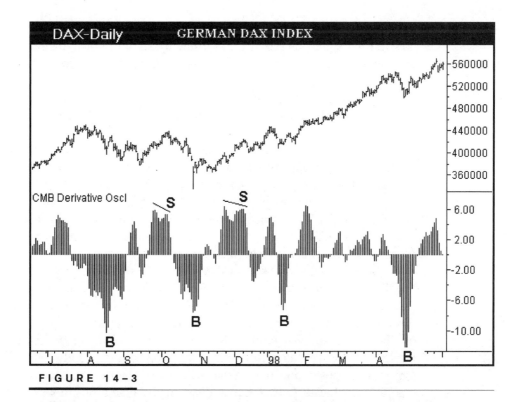

FIGURE 14-3

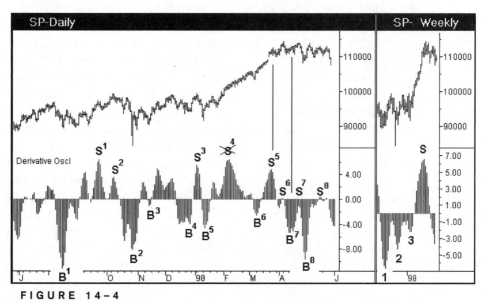

FIGURE 14-4

numbers. These three weekly lows will demonstrate an earlier discussion about how to filter signals in one period of time by an indicator in the next longer time horizon for the market. In Figure 14-4 one of the sell signals in the daily time horizon will be filtered by the weekly signals. How to interpret this chart follows:

B1. An extreme momentum low in the daily chart that is accompanied by an extreme low in the weekly chart is viewed as a strong signal. The S&P frequently produces clean spike bottoms without the need of a more complex pattern. While this example introduces using two time periods, other cross-chart comparisons such as hour and daily, weekly and monthly, are equally useful. Just allow the longer time horizon to have greater weight when comparing the shorter-horizon signals.

B2. Another major spike down at B2 is demonstrated. If you missed that B2 is higher than B1 while prices are lower showing bullish divergence, the weekly chart should offer a much stronger visual representation that a major signal is forming in the weekly time horizon for the second time.

B3. The oscillator has formed an extremely shallow drop just below the zero line that leads to another roll upward. This is subtle, but it is an extremely important signal. The buy signals at B1 and B2 are displaying pivots at higher levels. The third pivot at B3 barely crosses the zero line before a change in direction occurs. This oscillator does not change direction often so each roll up or down will offer new information for the trader. Strong market moves will frequently follow such a pattern in the opposite direction of the shallow oscillator pivot. However, also notice that this signal leads to two bearish diverging oscillator tops (not labeled) between signals B3 and B4. There is a warning for the longer-horizon trader that the market tried to break out, but was unable to do so with this most recent attempt.

B4. This shows a double bottom where the two lows in the formation define a support level. An oscillator double bottom or peak is usually an area of strong support or resistance that will restrain the market at some future time.

B5. This is a spike down that coincides with the third roll upward in the monthly chart. This is the market's third and last warning that it is trying to muster a major advance. In the weekly chart the oscillator lows form what some would view as a trend line. In this indicator always view trend lines in a horizontal position. Angled trend lines are rare.

B6. This is a simple change in direction when the oscillator rolls upward after a decline that breaks the zero line. So far, all six buy signals have been defined after the oscillator has crossed down through the zero line and rolled back upward. A change in direction is significant at any time, and if you go back to see the Market reaction whenever the oscillator rolls up, it will emphasize that the character of the resulting move in the market will vary if the change in direction occurs before it crossed the midline. Study the roll that occurs between B5 and S4 to see a clear example in a bull market.

B7. This buy signal leads to a strong move in the oscillator, but price does not keep up. The lack of momentum in price when the indicator is strong indicates a trend reversal approaching.

B8. The last buy signal marked on this chart is an oscillator extreme. If the oscillator extreme occurs on a support area for the indicator and prices are trading at a major price objective calculated by the RSI, Gann, and/or Fibonacci, do not wait for the oscillator to roll upward for a confirmation.

The sell signals in the daily chart were derived from the following:

S1. The oscillator is rolling down from a high that had not been challenged before. When this oscillator moves into a historic high or low displacement from the zero line, you can always expect that the market will consolidate in the short term but that new highs will be made allowing the oscillator to diverge or test its former range. With new oscillator lows, a new price low will occur as the oscillator forms bullish divergence near the prior range it used to view as an extreme. Between the S1 and S2 peaks is a change in direction just above the zero line. This is another warning that this particular market has sufficient strength to develop a new price high, though the oscillator will not be able to attain the form high at S1. In addition, the oscillator rolls down toward the zero line from S1 rapidly without prices experiencing much of a move down. Any time an oscillator moves rapidly without prices following, ... it means that you are on the wrong side of the market and the former trend will run the unobservant trader over without additional warning. (This has certainly been illustrated several times throughout this book.)

S2. This should be straightforward now as it is just basic bearish divergence offering a clean sell signal.

S3. This is an oscillator top near a former peak's displacement that leads to a decline. This is also the start of using the entire screen to locate the horizontal resistance or support levels.

S4. This signal should be read twice. This is an oscillator rollover that occurs after the oscillator has made a new extreme high. The signal alone could lead to a sideways market for several days. However, when viewed with the three buy signals in the weekly chart that shows the Derivative Oscillator has not even attained a displacement equal to the displacement at point 1, be forewarned that this market has a long was to go upward before a major decline could develop. The oscillator actually rolls down as the market just slowly grinds ahead. This is an excellent example of how an oscillator will move against prices. Once the oscillator rolls upward again, the strength of the rally will also increase.

S5. This peak is a sell signal that does not lead to much of a move in price. The oscillator will attempt to roll back up with prices, making new highs.

S6. The rollover occurs only after the oscillator realizes the zero line. The market is preparing for a more significant top. (In hindsight, this is quite a statement. The market from near the last pivot in this chart rolled upward once again as the market developed the fifth wave up. The horizontal trend line that should be drawn across from peak S4 in this chart marks the final momentum high that occurs for wave 5 up. Most of wave 5 develops as the oscillator is heading south. We now understand why.)

S7. This is the first time a buy signal, B7, moves the oscillator upward rapidly without prices following. The market should experience a significant decline when the oscillator next rolls over. The rollover develops *under* the zero line for the first time in 1998. A significant drop could then follow. It does unfold sharply, but as a percentage correction, it is shallow and could warn that this was only the first leg down in a more complex corrective pattern.

S8. The last signal is similar to S6 in that the signal develops just above the midpoint or zero line. (You might want to go back to signal C in Figure 14-2.)

CHARACTER OF HORIZONTAL SUPPORT AND RESISTANCE LEVELS

Figure 14-5 demonstrates more clearly the character of horizontal support and resistance levels in this indicator. The chart is the weekly DMK/$ spot market. Every oscillator pivot or signal is now labeled. The first general observation to

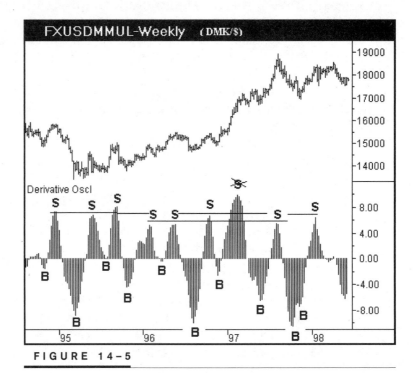

FIGURE 14-5

make is that the sell signals occur at two levels of horizontal resistance. All the Derivative Oscillator characteristics described earlier are present in this chart as well. The single sell signal that is crossed out in early 1997 occurs when an oscillator high rolls over after peaking well above the prior resistance zone. This establishes a new range for the oscillator. The characters between market bottoms and tops are different for this market.

Over a period of four years the oscillator in this chart does not offer an incorrect signal, provided that you are aware that one signal should be filtered. (The last upward pivot in this chart at the end of May 1998 was also a correct signal as are two others that follow it. The track record is still intact looking back on these earlier comments in late August 1998.)

USING MULTIPLE TIME HORIZONS TO FILTER PREMATURE SIGNALS

The monthly DMK/$ chart is offered in Figure 14-6. The one signal that was filtered in the weekly chart occurs when the monthly chart shows the Derivative

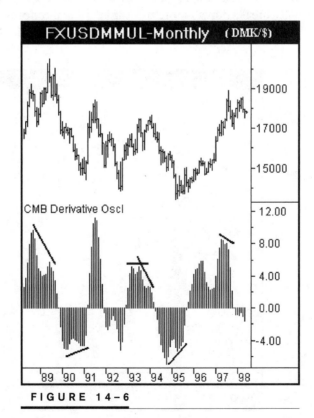

FIGURE 14-6

Oscillator was still in an uptrend after strong buy signals. This is similar to what was displayed between the daily and weekly S&P example. When you filter a signal, the permission must come from the longer time horizon chart. The monthly DMK/$ chart displays a character different from others previously demonstrated. Most pivots form divergence before the trend reversal is in force. It only helps the timing, but every pivot in the Derivative Oscillator proved to be of value over this charted period covering 10 years in Figure 14-6 . You will not find this formula of much value if it is applied to cross rates. The character of currency cross rates is better suited to the Composite Index.

DESCENDING DIVERGENCE PEAKS OR RISING DIVERGENCE PIVOTS WITH PRICE

In Figure 14-7 the weekly Nikkei chart is displayed. This market has numerous signals marked that were defined in prior charts. However, take a closer look at the three sell signals with accompanying numbers 1 through 3. The progression of lower oscillator peaks as the market forms new highs is important. The market usually breaks down before the market is able to form a fourth oscillator peak. Or a last peak will occur as a failure at the zero line. In equity markets a progression

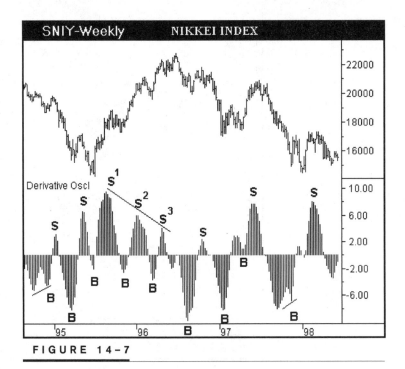

FIGURE 14-7

of three oscillator peaks or lows all approaching a displacement that is approaching the midline is common prior to a major market move in a reversed trend. In hindsight, the very last oscillator low in Figure 14-7 travels upwards, but prices do not follow. Same warning we have discussed in prior charts. The trend remains down and the market formed another low.

NEW INDICATOR SIGNAL COMPARISON WITH COMMON FORMULAS

New indicators like the Derivative Oscillator should be compared to the performance of common indicators. The weekly Nikkei chart in Figure 14-8 displays the Derivative Oscillator with the MACD. The chart has vertical lines bisecting the studies and prices to help clarify the location of the MACD signals. The signals from the Derivative Oscillator are not marked. At the first MACD signal, the oscillator shows divergence with price. It lags rather significantly, but it is clearly an accurate buy signal. The Derivative Oscillator developed a signal three weeks earlier. Then the MACD rolls up sharply and pulls back just enough to touch the slower line. This signal is not marked on the MACD, but it is recognized as the correct interpretation and use of this study. The timing is correct and occurs about the same time as a signal

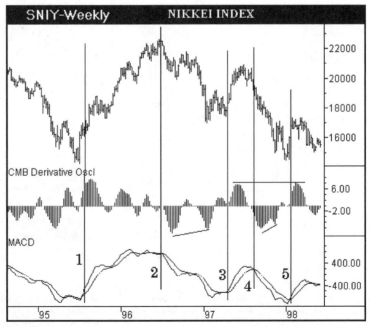

FIGURE 14-8

forming in the Derivative Oscillator. Move along to the crossover at signal 2 on the MACD. If you incorrectly interpreted the MACD, you would have sold well before the signal marked in this chart. When correctly used, the MACD is squarely aligned with the market top and dead right. The Derivative Oscillator is also correct. But if you had sold early from the Derivative Oscillator, it would have warned the trader to step aside prior to another new price high and is therefore a cleaner signal for risk management purposes. Either study performs well at signal 2 as it is a question of personal preference. We'll move on to signal 3 in the MACD. Signal 3 is correct, but relative to the Derivative oscillator, it is extremely late. The Derivative Oscillator displays bullish divergence marked on the Derivative Oscillator. The second diverging trough corresponds to the actual market low in the Derivative study, but the MACD is unable to provide any signal or warning. Signal 4 is another top, and the Derivative Oscillator had good timing. However, the MACD study at signal 4 is displaying a lag that is very common for this formula. The final signal at 5 in the MACD is a buy signal. It was late and offered no prior warning of the trend change.

The Derivative Oscillator had to perform well in both a sideways market and a strong trending market for the problems it was trying to support: sideways

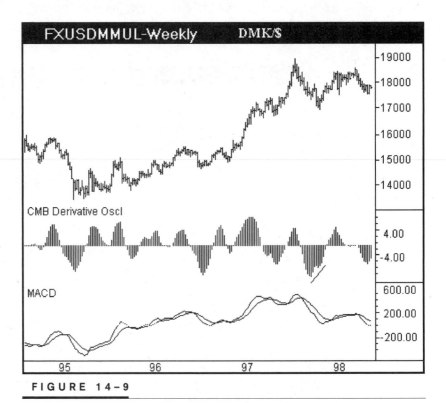

FIGURE 14–9

and fast markets. Earlier discussions in this book showed that oscillators are not just tools for sideways markets; however, some formulas are extremely difficult to interpret when the market is in a strong trend. The MACD demonstrates this difficulty in Figure 14-9 when the weekly DMK/$ chart shows the dollar strengthening. The MACD has correct signals, but they are extremely difficult to read.

Moving on to the Stochastics study in Figure 14-10, the weekly DMK/$ is used to show that Stochastics is a much cleaner signal generator than is the MACD formula over this same time period. The Derivative Oscillator in this chart is actually a compliment to the Stochastics Oscillator as it offers inter-pretation clues that are sometimes difficult to see within Stochastics. By con-necting the peaks and troughs that form horizontal levels of support and resis-tance, the plot for the Derivative Oscillator actually has a similar appearance at first to the Stochastics study. At signal 1 in the Stochastics study, it is unclear whether a buy signal is present. In conjunction with the Derivative Oscillator, a trend change is indicated and a buy signal would seem the correct interpretation

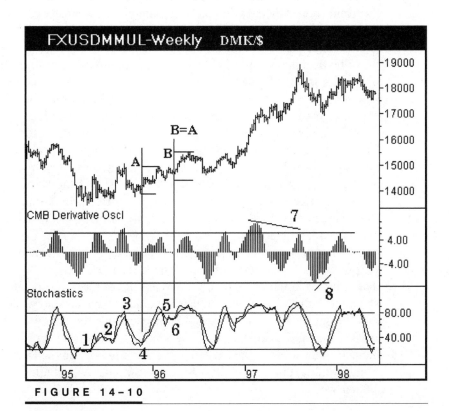

FIGURE 14-10

for the Stochastics position on the graph. At signal 2 the Stochastics study rolls over and crosses back up again giving a confusing pattern. The Derivative Oscillator also declines, but it failed to cross the midline or zero line as it rolls back up. As discussed in prior examples, when the Derivative Oscillator fails to cross the zero line, it is a distinct signal, which in this case is to be long on the dollar.

At signal 3 both oscillators provide sell signals. If you use Stochastics in a manner that requires three diverging signals prior to obtaining permission to sell, you would have a problem. But taken alone as an isolated signal, it is correct. At signal 4 both indicators are correctly positioned. The fact that the Derivative Oscillator had reversed and is rising more sharply than the Stochastics study would have been helpful. Signal 5 begins an interesting example only seen in the Stochastics study. Point 5 is George Lane's Stochastics "pop." The Stochastics indicator fell sharply to signal 4 and then rebounded immediately back to the top of its scale. This is what separates the professional trader from the retail segment: Buy the market when the Stochastics indicator has produced a pop and then rolls down to the 70 to 75 level. You mean go against the rule that one should sell when the Stochastics indicator rolls down and crosses the 80 grid line? Absolutely. (I hope this point is now clear as it is likely overstated in every other chapter.) The Stochastics pop will give you a mathematical price projection for the next market rally.

The distance the market traveled during the oscillator climb from signal 4 to signal 5 is only 50 percent of the market's move. A 50 percent move is very common, but you should also determine the calculations for a 62 percent projection as well. (We went through this in the price projection chapter too. This example makes a good summarized review.) As the Stochastics indicator declines to 75 and rolls back up, use that price low to project an equality and 1.618 relationship from the first part of the move that is marked on the price chart as A. A conservative measurement is taken if the trader incorrectly uses the wrong price low from which to make the price projection. It still will work. The distance traveled between B and A are equal. So too will the proportions taken from lessor points.

Conversely, the same price projection can be made when Stochastics rolls sharply back down to the bottom of the screen and rolls up to 20 to 25. Sell the market in this situation as only 50 percent of the move has occurred. The traders who believe the Stochastics indicator should always be sold when it crosses back down through 80 or that they should buy each time the 20 level is crossed will not survive. Signal 7, marked on the Derivative Oscillator, offers bearish divergence that helps interpret the Stochastics indicator. Signal 8 on the Derivative Oscillator is much more distinctive than Stochastics. The two studies complement one another well.

We conclude this comparative study with Figure 14-11, which charts the Rate of Change indicator with the daily Swiss Franc futures contract. This is a momentum study that is an oscillator plotted as a histogram like the Derivative Oscillator. Signal 1 on the Rate of Change study offers divergence that significantly lags the market. Signal 2 shows a similar signal as in the Derivative Oscillator. The bullish divergence at signal 3 on the Derivative Oscillator is clearly more useful than what develops in the Rate of Change indicator. The divergence displayed at signal 4 is more a question of personal preference. Both indicators show a value, and their buy signals are correct. The area in the Rate of Change indicator that is marked as signal 5 is just plain confusing. This is especially true when the Derivative Oscillator forms a sharp peak that is equal in height to the peak that formed in November 1997. A former peak extreme should always be used to project a horizontal line of resistance or support for indicator lows in the Derivative Oscillator. Signal 6 shows a clean peak with divergence in the Derivative Oscillator. The double top at signal 7 in the Derivative Oscillator is matched with a confusing pattern along signal 8 in the Rate of Change indicator.

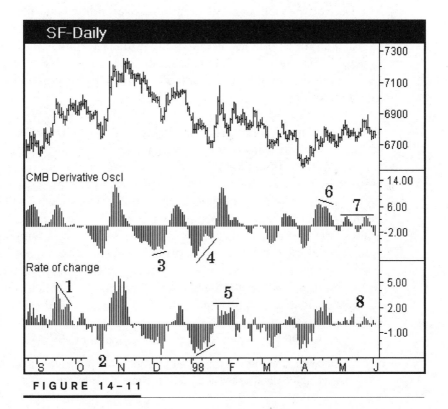

FIGURE 14-11

ADDITIONAL TESTING OF SIGNALS DEFINED IN PRIOR DEVELOPMENT WORK

The second most common study used in the industry next to Stochastics is the Relative Strength Indicator. In the RSI chapter we discussed how the amplitude was isolated and tested. I expect that, after you examine the traits just outlined in the preceding development sections of this chapter, you will have another characteristic to test. Don't leave any stone unturned in your new formula. If something new appears in other steps, it too should be given attention.

REAL-TIME EVALUATION PERIOD

All the signals highlighted for you had to be individually tested and statistically verified as was done in the RSI chapter when the amplitude of the signal was identified as being important. After rigorous back-testing and evaluating the performance of the indicator as a whole, it is still not ready for trading in real-time conditions. It must then be watched and monitored in a real-time environment. The Derivative Oscillator was monitored over a three-year period before it was used for trading. The Composite Index, which is an indicator used with all markets and all time horizons, is one of my primary formulas. It required five years to develop. The process is long and should not be rushed. Real capital should not be exposed to an experimental formula, no matter how promising the test results may first appear.

We have covered a lot of ground together as this was written over the last three months. I look forward to your comments and hope that this work will be useful and thought provoking. It takes time to incorporate new ideas into your own system. Be patient. Many ideas will evolve into something quite different. That is how much of what is offered in this book came about. The key to all these methods and techniques is spending the time required to test and examine them without mercy. Work with your formulas and techniques with a relentless passion into the small hours of the morning until they become intimately a part of you. It is only through this process that our trading methods will become part of our intuition. Allow the methods to flow and be applied effortlessly as the markets challenge us. This comes only after hours of endless work. Good trading to us both!

I leave with you a Zen Story to offer a final thought:

A rich man, fond of felines, asked a famous Zen ink painter to draw him a cat. The master agreed and asked the man to come back in three months. When the man returned, he was put off, again and again, until a year had passed. Finally, at the man's request, the master drew out a brush, and, with grace and ease, in a single fluid motion, drew a picture of a cat—the most marvelous image the man had ever seen.

He was astonished; then he grew angry. "That drawing took you only thirty seconds." Why did you make me wait a year?" he demanded. Without a word, the master opened up a cabinet, and out fell thousands of drawings—of cats.

—A Zen Story

Appendixes

Real-Time Application: Japanese Yen

S&P/BOND MARKET REPORT FROM
AERODYNAMIC INVESTMENTS, INC.

It is extremely important that Global Equity Indices not be viewed as isolated markets that respect only their own internal factors. Figure A–1 is a report that illustrates how the key puzzle piece in the global equity picture was the Japanese Yen. Intervention shortly followed that drove the Dollar against the Yen toward 133, triggering a ballistic rally in equities around the world. As with most currency interventions, the reaction was temporary, but the net short-term effect to all financial markets was extremely important for traders. Balancing the indicators across the entire financial complex is similar to playing three-dimensional chess. It can be done, but it takes tremendous effort and concentration to see when the key signals are aligned as occurred on June 15, 1998.

The text in the report will most likely be very small once it has been reproduced as an illustration in the book. You may find the text that follows easier to read:

JUNE 15, 1998

SEPT S&P—

Tonight all eyes are focused on the DJIA and S&P as we test the critical Gann support cluster at 1082.70–0.90. But the key to the next significant move is not going to come from US equity markets. We need to shift our attention to the Yen/$ which has realized the target and is accompanied by the Composite Index realizing prior historic highs in this oscillator. A decline is now very possible towards 138.60 and possibly to a Gann objective at 133. The impact of such a Yen/$ move would set the stage for a major rally in the Asian markets. The US markets have been declining in response to the Asian markets so in effect an Asian rally would take the heat off of Global Equity Indices. For months we have been watching the Hang Seng (top right) form the fourth wave up with expectations that only one of the Asian indices would then make a new low while the other did not. A five wave decline is now complete in the Hang Seng having made new lows at a Fibonacci 0.618 relationship relative to the third wave and is now attempting to turn upwards. The Nikkei did not make a new low which fits perfectly the view that the more significant Asian market turns in the past 10 years have been identified by divergences between Nikkei and Hang Seng price closes themselves. These signals were evaluated last February. Now we have the divergence in place and the monthly cycle low in the Nikkei has bottomed.

AERODYNAMIC INVESTMENTS INC

http://www.aeroinvest.com Support@aeroinvest.com Invest@aeroinvest.com

analyst: Connie Brown, CTA, Chartered Market Technician CBspz@ibm.net

June 15, 1998

SEPT S&P Close: 1085.30
Resistance: 1088.30, 1091.90, (1194.40), (1100.70) 1106.20, 1108.30, (1113.60), 1115.10, 1117.20, (1121.80), (1125.30-.50)
Support: (1082.70-.90), 1078.60, (1073.50-70), (1065.10-1066), 1060.40, (1052.30), 1046.80, (1042.60), 1037.10

SEPT BONDS Close: 123/30   (11:43 PM)
Resistance: 124/09, 123/24, (124/02-07), 124/30, 125/27, 126/25, 127/10, 128/00, 128/23
Support: (123/19), (123/08) 122/26, 122/05, 121/23, (121/05-09), (120/23-29), 120/06, 119/12

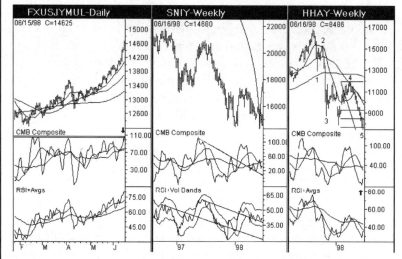

SEPT S&P-
Tonight all eyes are focused on the DJIA and S&P as we test the critical Gann support cluster at 1082.70-.90. But the key to the next significant move is not going to come from US equity markets. We need to shift our attention to the Yen/$ which has realized the target and is accompanied by the Composite Index realizing prior historic highs in this oscillator. A decline is now very possible towards 138.60 and possibly to a Gann objective at 133. The impact of such a Yen/$ move would set the stage for a major rally in the Asian markets. The US markets have been declining in response to the Asian markets so in effect an Asian rally would take the heat off of Global Equity Indices. For months we have been watching the Hang Seng (top right) form the fourth wave up with expectations that only one of the Asian indices would then make a new low while the other did not. A five wave decline is now complete in the Hang Seng having made new lows at a Fibonacci .618 relationship relative to the third wave and is now attempting to turn upwards. The Nikkei did not make a new low which fits perfectly the view that the more significant Asian market turns in the past 10 years have been identified by divergences between Nikkei and Hang Seng price closes themselves. These signals were evaluated last February. Now we have the divergence in place and the monthly cycle low in the Nikkei has bottomed. It is still visible in the weekly chart above. (middle chart) It appears the stage is now set for a major pivot in all markets... but the trigger must come from Yen/$.

The principle S&P levels are defined in the Fibonacci/Gann tables above. We will return to viewing S&P and Bond charts in tomorrow's update along with the normal shorter horizon market objectives. The S&P has realized a major target and the double zigzag decline could be satisfied suggesting new highs will now follow. We are now flat watching Yen/$ to define our next direction.

FIGURE A-1

It is still visible in the weekly chart above. (middle chart) It appears the stage is now set for a major pivot in all markets...but the trigger must come from Yen/$.

The principal S&P levels are defined in the Fibonacci/Gann tables above. We will return to viewing S&P and Bond charts in tomorrow's update along with the normal shorter horizon market objectives. The S&P has realized a major target, and the double zigzag decline could be satisfied suggesting new highs will now follow. We are now flat watching the Yen/$ to define our next direction.

Real-Time Application: Asian and European Equity Indices

S&P/BOND MARKET REPORT FROM AERODYNAMIC INVESTMENTS, INC.

Figure B–1 is an overlay of the Weekly Hang Seng, Nikkei, German Dax, and S&P 500 indices. This chart is monitored for global intermarket relationships. The Hang Seng and Nikkei markets display divergences between these indices at key junctures. It was a relationship watched for a period of time. Omega Research's *TradeStation 4.0* is unable to create overlays such as the one illustrated in this report for February 6, 1998. They force every additional market to be relative to the original *y*-axis, which incorrectly limits the trader from developing more meaningful overlays. This limitation can be overcome by creating individual charts of equal size in *TradeStation* and then making a screen capture of each. The single overlay chart can then be completed using any graphics package. The text within this report is duplicated below:

FEBRUARY 6, 1998

MAR S&P—

The chart at left is an overlay of the Weekly Nikkei, Hang Seng, German Dax, and S&P 500 indices. There is an extremely important relationship between the two Asian indices. Their own prices diverge when key market pivots develop. More importantly there is no divergence present between the Hang Seng and Nikkei data at current lows. The long anticipated cycle in the Nikkei monthly chart has not bottomed. We can expect one Asian Index to make a new low, but the other may not.

Our market has ignored a cycle low that also marked the dominant low at 953.90. Recent chop might be a stall for this cycle to pass. It is clear the pattern from the 953.90 low is extending, but the exact position within the rally is difficult to see. Ignoring Asia could mean our markets will march upwards in a third wave. The key Gann levels have been revised above,…but give me a day to form a stronger view on the short horizon.

AERODYNAMIC INVESTMENTS INC

http://www.aeroinvest.com Support@aeroinvest.com Invest@aeroinvest.com

analyst: Connie Brown, CTA, Chartered Market Technician CBspz@ibm.net

February 6, 1998

MAR S&P Close: 1018.60   +9.10
Resistance: 1012.50, (1014.60), (1022.40), 100026.60, 1030, 1028.70, 1030, (1037.30), (1040)
Support: (1015.40), 1010.0, 1007.70, (1002.10), 993.60, (985.50), (978.00)

MAR BONDS Close: 120/23   +/03
Resistance: 120/28, 122/16-22, (123/03), 123/25, 124/15, (**125/02-10**), 125/ 27, 126/18, 127/10, (127/25), (**131/29**)
Support: (120/06), (119/14), (**118/30**), (118/05-09), (117/20)

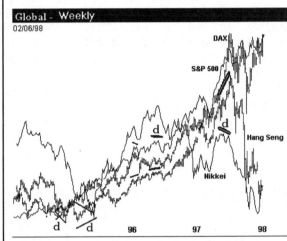

MAR S&P- The chart at left is an overlay of the Weekly Nikkei, Hang Seng, German Dax and S&P 500 Indices. There is an extremely important relationship between the two Asian indices. Their own prices diverge when key market pivots develop. More importantly there is no divergence present between the Hang Seng and Nikkei data at current lows. The long anticipated cycle in the Nikkei monthly chart has not bottomed. We can expect one Asian Index to make a new low but the other may not.

Our market has ignored a cycle low that also marked the dominant low at 953.90. Recent chop might be a stall for this cycle to pass. It is clear the pattern from the 953.90 low is extending but the exact position within the rally is difficult to see. Ignoring Asia could mean our markets will march upwards in a third wave. The key Gann levels have been revised above... but give me a day to form a stronger view on the short horizon.

FIGURE B-1

The report for April 2 shows the Expanded Flat in the Hang Seng that was discussed in Chapter 10 when the Elliott Wave Principle was covered. It offers you the chance to see the real-time view of the indicators in relationship to the chart pattern. The cycle low in the monthly Nikkei chart was viewed with great interest. The text within this report is duplicated below:

APRIL 2, 1998

JUNE S&P—

For a very long time this report has been providing warnings that the Asian markets had not bottomed. There have been overlay charts showing the Nikkei and Hang Seng divergence between these two markets that called several major market pivots. It was also pointed out that divergence was not present off of the last lows, though rallies had been favored. Last opinion was that the Hang Seng would produce wave *c* of 4 up to end a large Expanded Flat. This pattern is now viewed complete and ends wave 4 up within a very large wave *C* decline unfolding from the high. The long forewarned monthly cycle in the Nikkei is in full force right now as well. History is repeating itself that American traders seem to assume this will have no impact to North American markets. We must anticipate that S&P will eventually react to the Asian markets. The target remains (1140.30–1141.60). I am unable to define a downside target at this time,...but 1096 offers a conservative estimate.

AERODYNAMIC INVESTMENTS INC

http://www.aeroinvest.com Support@aeroinvest.com Invest@aeroinvest.com

analyst: Connie Brown, CTA, Chartered Market Technician CBspz@ibm.net

April 2, 1998

JUNE S&P Close: 1134.70   **+3.70**
Resistance: (1131.30-70), (1135.20-1139.30), (**1140.30-1141.60**), 1144.40, (1153.60-1154.60), 1159.80, 1164.80, 1177.80
Support: 1128.90, 1123.70, 1120.60, (1114.60), 1105.40, (**1095.40-1096.70**), 1092.60, (1089.20), (**1087.80**), (1081.50)

JUNE BONDS Close: 122/14   **+1/00**
Resistance: (122/16-19), (122/26), (123/16-19), (123/25-28), 124/06, (124/16-21), (124/31-125/08)
Support: (122/08), (121/16), 121/02, (120/05), 119/11, 118/26, 118/07, (117/16)

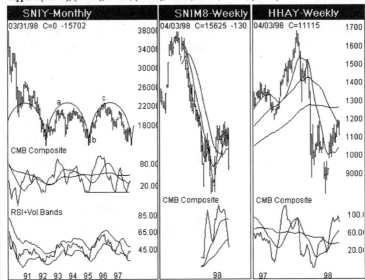

JUNE S&P- For a very long time this report has been providing warnings that the Asian markets had not bottomed. There have been overlay charts showing the Nikkei and Hang Seng divergence between these two markets that called several major market pivots. It was also pointed out that divergence was not present off of the last lows, though rallies had been favored. Last opinion was that the Hang Seng would produce wave c of 4 up to end a large

Expanded Flat. This pattern is now viewed complete and ends wave 4 up within a very large wave C decline unfolding from the high. The long forewarned monthly cycle in the Nikkei is in full force right now as well. History is repeating itself that American traders seem to assume this will have no impact to North American markets. We must anticipate that S&P will eventually react to the Asian markets. The target remains (**1140.30-1141.60**). I am unable to define a downside target at this time... but 1096 offers a conservative estimate.

FIGURE B-2

Figure B–3 will help to illustrate how European markets can be used to clarify the market position within North American Stock Indices. All three Indices in London, Germany, and the United States were aligned for a correction. The text within this report follows:

APRIL 22, 1998

JUNE S&P—

The 1141.50 level is an extremely high risk pivot. The charts above show monthly views from left to right of the DJIA, London FTSE, and German DAX. The concern is where the two "extreme oscillators" are positioned for all three markets. However, note that the Derivative Oscillator is conflicting other evidence as it is rolling upwards still. What does it mean? Likely a fourth wave is developing within an extension that needs a couple more months. But right now these markets are all vulnerable to a sharp sell-off in the shorter time horizons. Not sure how the June S&P will react to 1141.50...but know it is critical and the recent correction may be incomplete.

AERODYNAMIC INVESTMENTS INC

http://www.aeroinvest.com Support@aeroinvest.com Invest@aeroinvest.com

analyst: Connie Brown, CTA, Chartered Market Technician CBspz@ibm.net

S&P

April 22, 1998

JUNE S&P Close: 1135.40   +6.40
Resistance: 1136.50, 1140.30, (**1141.50**), (1143.90), 1148.60f, 1153.00, 1159.80, 1164.80, 1177.80
Support: 1131.80, (1130.00-.30), (1125.30), 1120.30, 1114.30, 1105.10, (1100.20-1101.70),(1096.40), (1093.20), (1087.00-.30)

JUNE BONDS Close: 120/06   -/14
Resistance: 120/14, (120/28-121/02), (121/13), 122/07, (122/16-19), (122/26), (123/16-19), (123/25-28), (**124/06-10**), (124/21),
Support: (120/01-05), 119/22, (119/00), (118/20-26), 118/07, (117/16), 117/04, (116/23)

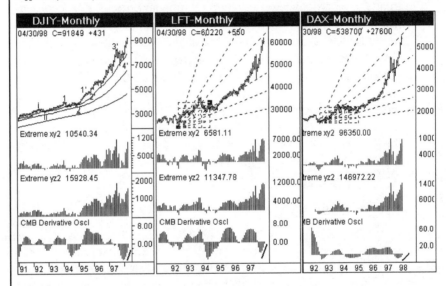

JUNE S&P-
The 1141.50 level is an extremely high risk pivot. The charts above show monthly views from left to right of the DJIA, London FTSE, and German DAX. The concern is where the two "extreme oscillators" are positioned for all three markets. However, note that the Derivative Oscillator is conflicting other evidence as it is rolling upwards still. What does it mean? Likely a fourth wave is developing within an extension that needs a couple more months. But right now these markets are all vulnerable to a sharp sell-off in the shorter time horizons. Not sure how the June S&P will react to 1141.50... but know it is critical and the recent correction may be incomplete.

FIGURE B-3

Real-Time Application: S&P/Bond Market

EXCERPTS FROM S&P/BOND MARKET REPORTS FROM AERODYNAMIC INVESTMENTS, INC.

In the Elliott Wave chapter a rare pattern called a *Leading Diagonal Triangle* was discussed that is permitted to develop only in wave positions 1 or A. An excerpt from the report for December 5, 1998 is displayed in Figure C–1. The wedge became a valuable warning that the bullish contracting triangle, favored since August 1997 in the S&P 500 Index, might be an incorrect interpretation. What made this particular wedge interpretation so difficult to accept was the fact that it followed a triangle interpretation that had been working so well for several months. The wedge idea was soon abandoned in later reports. *However, new market evidence should never be discounted.* The wedge idea had to be reassessed and adopted when it became the critical factor in the April–June 1998 correction. It was this leading wedge pattern that held the key to recognizing that the April–June decline was only a fourth wave decline in a developing five wave advance unfolding from the October 1997 low. It also helped to explain why technical indicators in May started to favor a strong rally ahead for European and American Stock Indices. The text within this report follows:

DECEMBER 5, 1997

DEC S&P—

The rally from 946.50 to today's 988.90 high is a complete five wave move. It has been repeated for over a week that MAJOR targets are…980.10, 988.20, and 1010–1014. This second target has marked a wedge from the 946.50 low. A pullback from this area to 933 would not be a surprise as the 988 target is viewed formidable. The wedge is actually a problem to our longer-horizon view. The decline may have ended in October, a better fit when compared to the German DAX. A correction now may lead to a second wave down. Wedges can occur in wave one positions, and this bears watching. Just know the triangle pattern we had tracked for months could be wrong. This would change the upside potential for wave 5 up. It would exceed 1176.

REPEAT: "There are 8348 days from the October 4, 1974, low to the recent August 7 high. On an intraday basis the DJIA high is 8340. Exceed this area and Gann will favor a 1000 point advance in the DJIA."

AERODYNAMIC INVESTMENTS INC

http://www.aeroinvest.com Support@aeroinvest.com Invest@aeroinvest.com

analyst: **Connie Brown, CTA, Chartered Market Technician** CBspz@ibm.net

December 5, 1997

DEC S&P Close: 986.60   +9.70
Resistance: 987.20, **(988.20),** (990.40), 992.70, **(1010-14)**
Support: 985.40, (980.60), 977.80, 972.40, 968.50, (964.10), (956.10), 952.60-80, 949.20, 946.80, 944.70, 943.00, (938.60-.90),
934.90, 931.10-932, (927.10), **(922.50-.80)**

MAR BONDS Close: 118/23   -/14
Resistance: (118/25), 119/03-10, (120/03-10), 121/01, 121/15, 122/07, (122/27)
Support: 119/09, 118/17, 118/05, (117/13), (116/30-117/06), 116/11, 115/31, 116/13, 115/11, 114/20

RSPZ7-120 min
12/05/97 C=98660 +970 Mov Avg 3 lines

DEC S&P - The rally from 946.50 to today's 988.90 high is a complete five wave move. It has been repeated for over a week that MAJOR targets are... 980.10, 988.20, and 1010-1014. This second target has marked a wedge from the 946.50 low. A pullback from this area to 933 would not be a surprise as the 988 target is viewed formidable. The wedge is actually a problem to our longer horizon view. The decline may have ended in October, a better fit when compared to the German DAX. A correction now may lead to a second wave down. Wedges can occur in wave one positions and this bears watching. Just know the triangle pattern we had tracked for months could be wrong. This would change the upside potential for wave 5 up. It would exceed 1176.

REPEAT: "There are 8348 days from the Oct 4, 1974 low to the recent August 7 high. On an intraday basis the DJIA high is 8340. Exceed this area and Gann will favor a 1000 point advance in the DJIA."

FIGURE C-1

In Figure C–2 the report for June 23, 1998, shows how reverse-engineering an indicator was used to identify a price objective. In this report the reverse-engineering technique offered confirmation for a target at 1176 in the September S&P 500 futures market that had been identified earlier by Fibonacci techniques:

JUNE 23, 1998

SEPT S&P—

The long-horizon objectives offered earlier this year remain unchanged....1153.40 (realized), 1176–1180.40, and then 1199 or 1207.40. The first long-horizon target range at 1176–1180 will be realized. The method at the left you have seen applied several times. We currently have a buy signal in a momentum extreme indicator. Reverse engineering allows us to see that when this indicator returns to the trend line, 1176 will be realized. The "fat bar" is a projection. In the short horizon it is believed 1135 should not be broken without challenging the view that today's decline was wave c down.

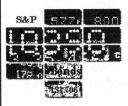

AERODYNAMIC INVESTMENTS INC

http://www.aeroinvest.com Support@aeroinvest.com Invest@aeroinvest.com

analyst: Connie Brown, CTA, Chartered Market Technician CBspz@ibm.net

June 23, 1998

SEPT S&P Close: 1142.40   -1.10 (8:04 PM)
Resistance: 1130.70, 1132.40-1133.20, (1134.40), 1140.30-1141.50, 1143.30, 1149.00
Support: 1125.20-1126, 1121.80, 1112.40, 1109.40, (1103.50),(1099.70-1100.80), 1096.70, (1094.40),1091.90, 1088.30, 1082.70, 1078.60, (1073.50-70), (1065.10-1066),

SEPT BONDS Close: 123/16   +/09
Resistance: 123/08, (**123/17-19**), 124/09,(124/17-21), 124/31, (125/16-18), 126/25, 127/10, 128/00, 128/23
Support: 122/28, 122/05, 121/23, (121/05-09), (120/23-29), 120/06, 119/12

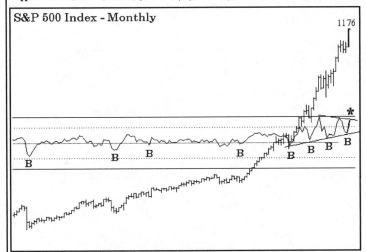

S&P 500 Index - Monthly

1176

SEPT S&P-
The long horizon objectives offered earlier this year remain unchanged.... 1153.40(realized), 1176-1180.40, and then 1199 or 1207.40. The long horizon target range at 1176-1180 will be realized. The method at left you have seen applied several times. We currently have a buy signal in a momentum extreme indicator. Reverse engineering allows us to see that when this indicator returns to the trendline 1176 will be realized. The "fat bar" is a projection. In the short horizon 1135 should not be broken without challenging the view that today's decline was wave c down.

FIGURE C-2

Figure C–3 shows a report summarizing all the technical evidence that was building against the DJIA and S&P on July 17 and into the Sunday Globex trading session on July 19. The middle chart showing the AMEX Computer Technology Index should look familiar to you as the same chart was used for Figure 6–6 when the Fibonacci chapter was written. This report shows an update to the chart in Figure 6–6. Most charts developed for this book were used in the evening reports for clients.

In hindsight we now know that July 20 marked a significant top for these markets. The technical evidence was overwhelming and appeared very conclusive at the time. You will see that the bearish report offered no alternative view for clients as none could be seen in the charts displayed in Figure C–3:

JULY 17, 1998

SEPT S&P—

This is the Gann time window. Also a Gann price objective for the DJIA at 9339, new highs developed on declining volume. Divergence is in the DJIA and Computer technology sector that warns of a pending correction. The cycle low approaching rapidly in the S&P (above left chart) is a sell signal. A five wave rally in place in S&P and computer technology and DJIA. Need more…the momentum extreme indicator displays a sell signal in the weekly charts with volatility bands "maxed" out. Anybody want to be long? Not on your life, but I can't see what is keeping the market up except that our very long term horizon target at 1199 or 1207 has not been realized. Have to believe this market is on borrowed time.

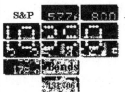

AERODYNAMIC INVESTMENTS INC

http://www.aeroinvest.com Support@aeroinvest.com Invest@aeroinvest.com

analyst: Connie Brown, CTA, Chartered Market Technician CBspz@ibm.net

July 17, 1998

SEPT S&P Current: 1193.10 (Sunday 11:48 PM)
Resistance: 1194.10, (1197-1197.60), (1199.40-.70), 1203.60, (1207), 1213
Support: 1189.50, (1184.30), 1181.00, 1177.90, (1171.20), 1161.40, (1152.30)

SEPT BONDS Close: 122/01
Resistance: (123/03), 123/24, 124/05-09, 124/17, (124/22-25), 124/31, (125/16-18), 126/02-08, 126/25, 127/10, 128/00
Support: 122/05, 121/23, (121/05-09), (120/23-29), 120/06, 119/12

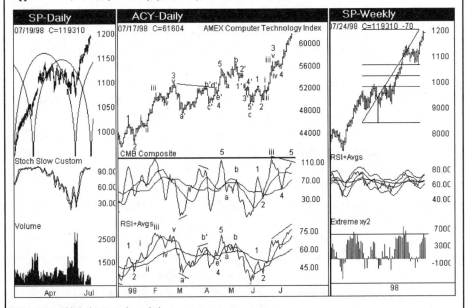

SEPT S&P- This is the Gann time window.
Also a Gann price objective for the DJIA at 9339, new highs developed on declining volume. Divergence is in the
DJIA and Computer technology sector that warns of a pending correction. The cycle low approaching rapidly in the
S&P(above left chart) is a sell signal. A five wave rally is in place in S&P and computer technology and DJIA.
Need more.... the momentum extreme indicator displays a sell signal in the weekly charts with volatility bands
"maxed" out. Anybody want to be long? Not in your life but I can't see what is keeping the market up except that
our very long term horizon target at 1199 or 1207 has not been realized. Have to believe this market is on borrowed time.

FIGURE C-3

Figure C-4 shows the evening report for July 23. The report layout sometimes puts bonds on the top of the page rather than the bottom, so the entire report
is duplicated in this figure because the removal of the bond section would have
changed the look of the original report. This report is included in this appendix
because it shows that the DJIA 8490 target was actually given to clients earlier
than first introduced in Chapter 10 when the real-time walkthrough was unfolding
within this chapter. The DJIA chart in this report was used the following day as an
example in the book for Figure 10–9. However, the report displayed a 120-minute
time horizon rather than 60 minutes as the cycles were discussed July 23 and not
discussed in the book. In hindsight this additional information that the report adds
could be of interest.

The report for July 23, 1998, allows an extremely important point to be
brought to your attention that was entirely overlooked in the book itself. When
Fibonacci *support or resistance clusters are identified, support objectives will not
become resistance and vice versa.* This is extremely important. View each as an
independent scale. Each scale defined as support or resistance has no relationship
to the close, so older support levels can still be valid after the market has passed
these levels. The resistance tables will look wrong to you. However, they are valid
because the market was expected to drop once again below 1149.60, which would
mean this resistance scale would be required possibly in the next day's trading session, even though the current market level was 1173.50 when the report was written. Therefore, the old levels were not removed from this report table and *resistance
is correctly defined below* the current market. Only new calculations will challenge
the old scale defining support or resistance. This is similar to viewing the close as
the current temperature being read from a thermometer. What is an error is that this
report did not add new support levels below the current market at 1173.50. The support table starts at 1145, which shows the late hours contributed to the omissions.

The report for July 23 would be very confusing if this had not been explained
because the levels for the S&P resistance table begin under the market. The 1182.20
level is not far above the actual market level that was traded at 12:19 A.M. in the
Globex session. In fact, the 1182.20 level marked a full Gann 360 degrees up from
the current low, and it was believed that it could not be broken. This is actually too
opinionated, and additional levels should have been added if I had been wrong.
Fortunately, the actual high was 1174.70, which occurred a few hours later.

Looking back over this report, the bond section shows that I was clearly
obsessed with 123/10. I never remember the reasons for any level in hindsight as
I am too concerned with calculations for the next move. But this bond level was
clearly overstated as the market later popped to 123/14 and then failed. The
September S&P is duplicated below to make for easier reading:

AERODYNAMIC INVESTMENTS INC

http://www.aeroinvest.com Support@aeroinvest.com Invest@aeroinvest.com

analyst: Connie Brown, CTA, Chartered Market Technician CBspz@ibm.net

July 23, 1998

SEPT S&P Current: 1173.50 (12:19 AM)
Resistance: 1149.60, 1154.20, 1157.40, 1163.50, 1172.80, 1182.20
Support: (1145), 1137.20, (1135.20), 1131.60, 1125.20, 1122.50, 1120.00, 1115.80, 1110.70, (1089.70-1090.70), 1086, 1079.30, 1076.70

SEPT BONDS Close: 123/08
Resistance: (123/10), (123/23), 124/05, 124/17, (124/21), 124/31, (125/16-18), 126/02, 126/23, 127/10, 128/00
Support: 122/05, 121/23, (121/05-09), (120/23-29), 120/06, 119/12

SEPT BONDS-

With the cycle low behind us now the odds are increasing that 123/10 will be exceeded... as long as 123/00 is not broken. The next target will be 123/23 if 123/10 is penetrated.

While it is favored that 123/10 will be exceeded, a failure will lead to nearby 123/00 and then if broken to 122/22.

SEPT S&P- *"Bigger picture... at minimum the advance from 1071 to the high is a completed five wave rally. The minimum objective is 1143.60-1145. For the DJIA the target is 9000. These are minimum objectives because there is a very strong leaning to the view that the rally from the 844 low is a completed five wave advance. That means the ideal target will be 1065.20-1067.80."*

The statement above is from prior reports and the minimum objective has been realized. Ultimately we can expect to see 1065. In the DJIA the 9000 objective was realized and we should now look to 8607 and then if broken 8490. If 1065 were broken in the S&P futures 980.40 would be considered. I believe the high is in place for 1998 excluding a b wave rally.

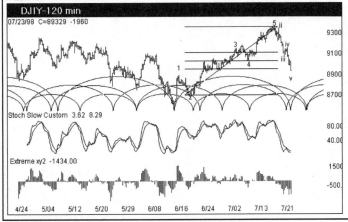

FIGURE C-4

JULY 23, 1998

SEPT S&P—

"Bigger picture...at minimum the advance from 1071 to the high is a completed five wave rally. The minimum objective is 1143.60–1145. For the DJIA the target is 9000. These are minimum objectives because there is a very strong leaning to the view that the rally from the 844 low is a completed five wave advance. That means the ideal target will be 1065.20–1067.80."

The statement above is from prior reports and the minimum objective has been realized. Ultimately we can expect to see 1065. In the DJIA the 9000 objective was realized, and we should now look to 8607 and then if broken 8490. If 1065 were broken in the S&P futures, 980.40 would be considered. I believe the high is in place for 1998 excluding a b wave rally.

Formulas

This appendix is a convenient reference for the formula figures contained within the book. There will be two noticeably absent from this list: the Derivative Oscillator formula (because it is better left in the context of its own development description in Chapter 14) and the Composite Index. (Please refer to Chapter 12.)

Stochastics and Moving Averages

```
Indicator: Stochastics+Avgs
Input: Length(X),PERIOD(Y),PERIOD2(Z);
plot1(FastK(Length),"FastK");
plot2(FastD(Length),"FastD");
plot3(Average(FastD(Length),PERIOD),"Plot3");
plot4(Average(FastD(Length),PERIOD2),"Plot4");


Indicator: RSI+Avgs
Input: LENGTH(14),PERIOD(Y),PERIOD2(Z);
Plot1(RSI(Close,LENGTH),"Plot1");
Plot2(Average((RSI(Close,LENGTH)),PERIOD),"Plot2");
Plot3(XAverage((RSI(Close,LENGTH)),PERIOD2),"Plot3");
```

FIGURE D-1

RSI Wave Study

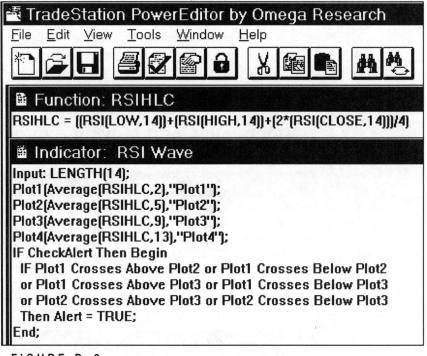

TradeStation PowerEditor by Omega Research

File   Edit   View   Tools   Window   Help

Function: RSIHLC

RSIHLC = ((RSI(LOW,14))+(RSI(HIGH,14))+(2*(RSI(CLOSE,14)))/4)

Indicator: RSI Wave

```
Input: LENGTH(14);
Plot1(Average(RSIHLC,2),"Plot1");
Plot2(Average(RSIHLC,5),"Plot2");
Plot3(Average(RSIHLC,9),"Plot3");
Plot4(Average(RSIHLC,13),"Plot4");
IF CheckAlert Then Begin
  IF Plot1 Crosses Above Plot2 or Plot1 Crosses Below Plot2
  or Plot1 Crosses Above Plot3 or Plot1 Crosses Below Plot3
  or Plot2 Crosses Above Plot3 or Plot2 Crosses Below Plot3
  Then Alert = TRUE;
End;
```

FIGURE D-2

Formula for Calculating RSI Negative Reversals

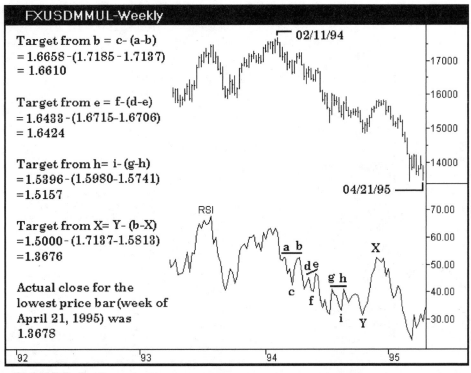

FXUSDMMUL-Weekly

Target from b = c- (a-b)
= 1.6658 - (1.7185 - 1.7137)
= 1.6610

Target from e = f- (d-e)
= 1.6433 - (1.6715 - 1.6706)
= 1.6424

Target from h= i- (g-h)
= 1.5396 - (1.5980 - 1.5741)
= 1.5157

Target from X= Y- (b-X)
= 1.5000 - (1.7137 - 1.5813)
= 1.3676

Actual close for the
lowest price bar (week of
April 21, 1995) was
1.3678

FIGURE   D-3

Formula for Calculating RSI Positive Reversals

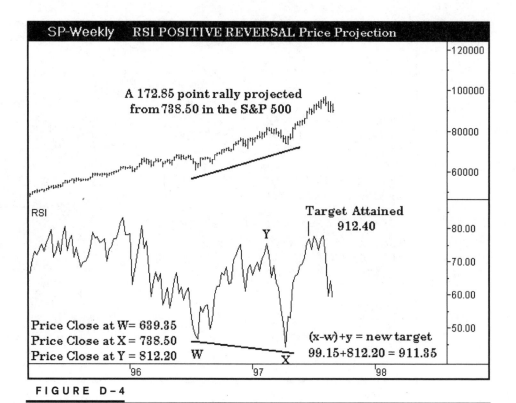

SP-Weekly   RSI POSITIVE REVERSAL Price Projection

A 172.85 point rally projected
from 738.50 in the S&P 500

Target Attained
912.40

RSI

Price Close at W= 639.35
Price Close at X = 738.50
Price Close at Y = 812.20

(x-w)+y = new target
99.15+812.20 = 911.35

FIGURE D-4

Volatility Bands for Indicators

```
Indicator:  RSI+Vol Bands
Input: Coefdwn(2.1),Coefup(2.3);
Plot1((Average((RSI(Close,14)),6))+(Coefup*(Average(TrueRangeCustom((RSI(Close,14)),(
RSI(Close,14)),(RSI(Close,14)))),15))),"Plot1");
Plot2((Average((RSI(Close,14)),6))-(Coefdwn*(Average(TrueRangeCustom((RSI(Close,14)),
(RSI(Close,14)),(RSI(Close,14)))),15))),"Plot2");
Plot3((RSI(Close,14)),"Plot3");
IF CheckAlert Then Begin
 IF Plot1 Crosses Above Plot2 or Plot1 Crosses Below Plot2
 or Plot1 Crosses Above Plot3 or Plot1 Crosses Below Plot3
 or Plot2 Crosses Above Plot3 or Plot2 Crosses Below Plot3
 Then Alert = TRUE;
End;
```

FIGURE   D-5

Derivative Oscillator: Please see Chapter 14.

Composite Index: Refer to Web address
http://www.aeroinvest.com.

Aerodynamic Fund, Ltd.

Aerodynamic Fund, Ltd., is not an investment pool offered to the general public. This is a registered institutional investment pool for "Qualified Eligible Clients" who must meet stringent requirements. The Fund is not offered to citizens of the United States of America. (Citizens of the United States should check http://www.aeroinvest.com for new information about Aerodynamic Fund, L.P., our domestic pool.) The minimum subscription is *US* $250,000. The information that follows is to answer general questions only. This information is by no means complete, and individuals wishing full disclosure and offering documentation should contact Aerodynamic Investments Inc. at the e-mail address invest@aeroinvest.com. *Requests will be forwarded to the offering agent for follow-up and will not be handled by Aerodynamic Investments, Inc.*

RECOGNITION UNDER THE BVI MUTUAL FUNDS ACT SHOULD NOT BE TAKEN TO IMPLY THAT THE FUND HAS BEEN APPROVED BY ANY REGULATORY AUTHORITY IN ANY COUNTRY SUCH AS THE U.S.A., THE UNITED KINGDOM OR ANY OTHER JURISDICTION OTHER THAN THE B.V.I. AND IT IS INTENDED THAT ANY POTENTIAL SHAREHOLDERS OF THE FUND, PARTICIPATE ON THE BASIS THAT THEY CAN AFFORD TO LOSE ALL OR A SUBSTANTIAL PORTION OF THEIR INVESTMENT.

DIRECTORY

Registered Office

Aerodynamic Fund, Ltd.
Citco Building
Wickham Cay
PO Box 662
Road Town
Tortola, British Virgin Islands

Principal Office

Aerodynamic Fund, Ltd.
Kaya Flamboyan, 9
Curacao, Netherlands Antilles

Investment Manager

Aerodynamic Investments, Inc.
Pawley's Island, SC 29585
USA
Constance M. Brown

Registrar and Transfer Agent

International Management
Services, Ltd.
Grand Cayman, Cayman Islands
British West Indies

Auditors

Goldstein Golub Kessler &
Company P.C.
New York, NY 10036
USA

United States Counsel

O'Rourke, O'Hanlan & Zimmermann,
LLP
Stamford, CT 06901
USA

Advisor on British Virgin Islands Law

Harney, Westwood & Riegels
Tortola, British Virgin Islands

Written inquiries relating to the Fund should be addressed to Aerodynamic Fund, Ltd., at the address of its principal office set forth above.

INDEX

About the Author

Constance Brown, a Chartered Market Technician and CPO, is president of Aerodynamic Investments, Inc. She is also the investment manager of Aerodynamic Fund, Ltd. investment pools for institutions.

Ms. Brown was nominated by the industry in 1997 for the Market Technician Association's Best-of-the-Best Award in the category of Momentum and Relative Strength for her originality and contribution to enhancing the performance of oscillators.

Prior to founding her own firm, Ms. Brown's analysis for the S&P was transmitted electronically in real-time during the trading day to an audience of institutional global traders monitoring her through Telerate, Bloomberg, Reuters, and DTN. The audience tracing her projections became a notable market influence. Brokers on the floors of both the Chicago Mercantile Exchange (Chicago MERC) and the New York Monetary Exchange (NYMEX) installed services to track her S&P intraday price projections.

Ms. Brown learned techniques to develop mental toughness as an internationally ranked swimmer, preparing for the Montreal Olympic Games in 1976. She then became a student of the Martial Arts and continues to be an active participant in Tae Kwon Do competitions. Her book, *Aerodynamic Trading*, applied techniques of acclaimed international coaches to the competitive pressures of a professional trading desk. The book's philosophy of streamlining our inner weaknesses to excel in high-stakes environments gave birth to the Aerodynamic Investments, Inc., and Aerodynamic Funds.